The Elements of CAL

The Elements of CAL

David Godfrey
and
Sharon Sterling

RESTON PUBLISHING COMPANY, INC.
A Prentice-Hall Company
Reston, Virginia

Copyright © Press Porcépic 1982
All rights reserved.

No part of this book may be reproduced or transmitted in any form by any means, electronic or mechanical, including photocopying, recording or any information storage, retrieval and transmission systems now known or to be invented, without permission in writing from the copyright holder, except by a reviewer who may quote brief passages in a review.

This edition of *The Elements of CAL* is produced by Reston Publishing Company, Inc., 11480 Sunset Hills Road, Reston, Virginia 22090, A Prentice-Hall Company.

It is not for sale in Canada.

ISBN 0-8359-1700-2

10 9 8 7 6 5 4 3 2 1

Printed in Canada

For Jonathan and Peter

walking always now on the West Coast trails.

Acknowledgement
Philosophical debates over the content of this book have gone on for what seems like endless years, and will certainly continue. Although none of them will agree with all of the result, we would be remiss not to acknowledge the major contributions made to the field and to our summary of it here by many learners of all ages and by the following authors and seekers: G. Beer, J. Brahan, C. Brewster, P. Buttedahl, B. Buxton, E. Chang, B. Godfrey, Marguerite Godfrey, A. Hébert, B. Henneker, S. Hunka, G. Kearsley, R. Kellison, S. Lower, R. Maclean, W. Muir, W. Olivier, B. Orchard, H. Porter, L. Sandals, D. Stenton, M. Umbriaco, M. Westrom.

Contents

1. Introduction 1
Computers and/or Teaching *1*   Computers and Learning *2*
Cal Terminology *4*   IMPS *4*

2. IMPS 7
Why IMPS? *7*   Premises of IMPS *9*   IMPS Defined *10*
Implementing IMPS *15*

3. The Definitional Layer 17
Introduction *17*   Goals Versus Objectives *18*   Goals and Strategies *23*
Disciplines and Strategies *26*   The Student as Teacher *26*
One Man Bands *27*   From Objectives to Rules *27*

4. Local Structures 31
The Local Structure *31*   The Basic Terms *32*
Adaptive Versus Prestructured *33*   The Five Basic Teaching Strategies *33*
Games *53*   Creating a Game *55*   Reinforcement Patterns *56*
General Guidelines *57*

5. Presentation 59
Basic Input and Output *60*   Screen Layout *61*   Graphics *65*
Input and Output Variations *68*   Putting It All Together *75*

6. Tracking 77
Introduction *77*   The Roles of Tracking *78*
The Grading and Descriptive Models *80*

7. Mapping 83
Introduction *83*   Segments *83*   Mapping and Languages *84*
Designing the Maps *85*   Mapping and Tracking *86*
Mapping and Course Design *87*   Mapping and Course Portability *87*

8. Student Support Structures 89
Types of Support Structures *90*   Accessing the Support Structures *93*

9. Author Support Structures 95
Introduction *95*   Facilitative Software *96*
Systems, Languages and Tools *102*

10. Site Implementation 103
Introduction *103*   Psychological Factors *104*
Design Versus Implementation *105*   Hardware Factors *105*
Language Factors *108*   Languages and CAL *111*   Standard Concepts *113*
Translators *119*   Database Management Systems *119*
Structured Programming *120*   Software Engineering *120*
Abstract Data Types *120*   Prolog and AI*121*
Some Implementation Guidelines *121*   Summary *122*

11. Network Implementations 125
Introduction *125*   Hardware Factors *126*
The CAL Architect in Network Implementations *128*
IMPS From the Architect's View *132*   Cost-Benefit Factors *135*   Summary *137*

12. Curriculum Four 139
Curriculum Four *139*   WORDS *140*   FRACTIONS *153*
The Curriculum *165*   Summary *167*

13. An Implementation 169
Introduction *169*   The Process *169*   The Implementation *175*
WORDS *176*   FRACTIONS *179*   Learners Guide *181*

14. Curriculum Four: CAL and FRACTIONS 183
Introduction *183*   Brief Introduction to PASCAL *183*   Course Map *190*
FRACTIONS Code, Documentation and Data *191*

15. Curriculum Four: WORDS 223
Course Map *223*   Code, Documentation and Data *225*   File Format *258*

Bibliography 261

Glossary 279

Index 281

Once upon a time Trurl the constructor built an eight-story thinking machine. When it was finished, he gave it a coat of white paint, trimmed the edges in lavender, stepped back, squinted, and then added a little curlicue on the front and, where one might imagine the forehead to be, a few pale orange polkadots. Extremely pleased with himself, he whistled an air and, as is always done on such occasions, asked it the ritual question of how much is two plus two....

From, "Trurl's Machine", in *The Cyberiad* by Stanislaw Lem.

1 Introduction

Although computers have been used in education for many years, it is only in the past three or four years that Computer Aided Learning (CAL) has become popular. This popularity has had one surprising and major benefit: a fresh look at our many preconceptions about the learning and teaching process. Computers will never replace teachers, but they will certainly help teachers and learners take advantage of the many ways learning can take place. CAL frees learners to learn, trainers to train and teachers to teach.

This book deals with the practical aspects of creating good CAL materials on a variety of machines and languages. At a more philosophical level, it deals with the nature of the insights brought to the learning process by the distance and abstraction made possible by CAL in real teaching and training situations.

Learning was not always managed within large institutions run by specialists and set aside from the mainstream of life. If this book has one underlying purpose, it is to encourage teachers, employers, parents, students and librarians to seriously reconsider their roles in the learning process and to use the available technologies to improve the whole of that process.

Computers and/or Teaching

Computers, although the opposite may appear to be the case when learning how to use one, are very simple beasts. Their only virtues for us are their patience and their quick memories. They themselves are of little help in clarifying the teaching process. However, the act of using a computer as part of a teaching process encourages a certain distance and abstraction which can be most useful for all those involved with learning.

The great danger for those new to this activity is the potential confusion between learning about computers and integrating the computer into your own teaching or learning process. *The Elements of CAL* assumes that the reader has

The Elements of CAL

already mastered at least one computer language on one brand of machine. If not, we suggest a quick reading of this book, looking mainly at the principles; next, an immersion course in the language and machine of your choice. Only then should you return to this book and its detailed examples.

The other minor danger might be termed CALitis, the delusion that Computer Aided Learning has something magical about it and ought to be applied in very large doses to all students in all situations. What portion of the teaching process can benefit from the use of computers depends on many factors, such as available equipment, available production resources, age of the learners, personality of the teachers, and the nature of the material to be learned. It takes a good deal of time and experience to be able to balance these factors in any given situation.

For the teacher or trainer, CAL is simply one more tool to add to the ones already in use: books, libraries, field trips, videotape recorders and laboratories. In Chapter Three, "Goals and Strategies", we discuss the relationship between CAL and more traditional teaching and training methods.

Computers and Learning

Many CAL experts have observed that most teachers and trainers undergo a change in attitude during their adaptation to CAL methodologies and practice. Often, this change in attitude is marked by an increasing awareness of the nature of knowledge. We all know and accept the fact that it is difficult, if not impossible, to know all there is to know about any given subject. Formalized education has often dealt with this problem by creating strict guidelines about what the learner needs to know at each stage of his or her education. The success of the student, and to some degree the teacher, is judged according to these guidelines.

Time spent creating CAL data emphasizes the imprecise nature of much of what we call *fact*. Watching many learners use courseware leads increasingly to the belief that the learner learns more, and more happily, when he or she has control over his or her own objectives and methods of learning. Assessment of a learner shifts from an external "Does she know *it*?", to an internal "Do I know enough? Can I learn more? Are my errors fixable?"

CAL introduces a certain amount of uncertainty into education. Uncertainty can be invigorating and create great enthusiasm, but it is best to deal with several real projects and actually implement them before becoming too precise about the theoretical and long-range implications of CAL.

Throughout the book, we will mention many of the theories and claims made by CAL experts and adherents, and some of the possible implications, but we trust readers will see some benefit in our careful mixture of optimism and skepticism.

1 Introduction

The underlying cause for the uncertainty, the enthusiasm and the change in attitude, we suspect, is the ability of CAL to provide a record, however limited, of what is taking place within the learning process. Ordinarily, the professional teacher is either fully present during the learning exchange, such as a lecture or oral examination, or fully distant, as when the student is reading or completing assignments. With good CAL materials, the teacher is at least partially present during many individual interchanges of the learner with the materials. That is a small change, but full of implications for our knowledge base about learning as process.

COMPUTERS AND LEARNING THEORY

In practice, those who teach are overworked and there is little time to grade oneself, to grade one's methods, to try different methods with similar students, or similar methods with different students – little time, in short, to apply analysis and creativity to the more basic assumptions and practices of one's work. It is enough to get it done. There are often gaps of frustration and disbelief between practicing teachers and the more theoretical faculties of education.

In the past, people tended to belong to certain educational tribes, tribes which had theoretical ideas about learning, ideas which could be implemented, tested and validated under different situations. Such groups, whether Skinnerists, Piagetists, or whatever, often fought violently with one another about theory, but converts from one tribe to another were few and assimilations were even rarer. Data was rare or plentiful, depending on the nature of the tribal theories. Those who were outside all tribes had their doubts about the objectivity or usefulness of the data presented in support of any theory.

The development of CAL has not changed the tribal system and members of any tribe tend to apply their habitual attitudes towards CAL. Good CAL, however, can put teachers in charge of gathering their own data about their own teaching environment. That is a major difference. We find that any given teacher's change in attitude is largely based on looking at the growing body of data which is gathered via CAL from numerous learner-materials interchanges. Both teacher and learner benefit from the repeated cycles of theory-application-result.

COMPUTERS IN THE HOME AND WORK PLACE

For those whose profession is not teaching, there may be even less time for looking at the learning process and less confidence in one's ability to teach. Although, in fact, every office and workplace has its own natural teachers and mentors, they are seldom formally recognized let alone given time and resources to demonstrate and expand their skills. In many firms, even formal training is very diversified and often haphazard.

The Elements of CAL

Good Computer Based Training (CBT) can put trainers in charge of gathering their own data about their particular teaching environment. For the parent or occasional trainer, such data may be less important, but it does serve as a general guideline and is useful when comparing one CAL package with another or with one's own efforts.

CAL Terminology

Like any new field, CAL has developed its own acronyms. Some key distinctions can be made.

Computer Managed Instruction (CMI) utilizes the computer to organize the learner's progress through a variety of instructional methods: print materials, audio and video tape materials, lectures, tests and perhaps even CAL.

Computer Aided Instruction (CAI), like CBT, represents a distinction based on attitude rather than on qualitative differences. Those who work in CAI rather than CAL tend to stress objectives and the careful measurement of results and to avoid discussions about goals. They may or may not be wary of tutorial methods and favor carefully structured courses.

Computer Based Training (CBT) is discussed in detail later. Many users of this term work for large firms or various branches of the military. As we explain later, the major difference is one of attitude. The learners in CBT environments tend to be paid employees and there is a far greater emphasis on efficient mastery of objectives and on comparisons of costs with traditional methods.

Throughout *The Elements of CAL* we use the term Computer Aided Learning (CAL) as the inclusive term for what others might term the categories of CAL, CBT and CAI. We consider CMI as one of many ways of using the computer as a tool in education.

IMPS

Our own addition to this terminology is Instructional Management and Presentation System (IMPS). IMPS represents our attempts to simplify and clarify the long process of conceiving, designing, verifying, coding, testing and maintaining good courseware. IMPS can be used to create courseware on any topic, written in any computer language, to run on any machine. IMPS also provides a framework for courseware evaluation.

IMPS AND PROGRAMMING

CAL is not a special kind of programming. In fact, the first seven layers of IMPS do not deal with programming at all. Only the last two layers deal with specific machines and languages. However, at the moment at least, those who wish to create courseware must know a good deal about at least one language or have access to a good programmer or programming staff.

1 Introduction

IMPS AND HARDWARE

We deliberately avoid the apparent battle-ground between micro and mainframe machines. Within a few years, that will be seen as a false distinction, at least in economic terms. Instead, we deal with the notion of low-range and high-range machines. At the moment, a low-range machine is an 8-bit micro with 64K memory. A high-range machine is anything between a VAX 11/780 and a CRAY 2.

For CAL in the 80's, the excitement will be caused in the mid-range, as the 16-bit and 32-bit CPU's move into the education and training marketplace; as the "average" machine begins to arrive with a megabyte of main memory; as authors learn to play with megabytes of disc space rather than counting up the kilobytes; as database machines become a standard peripheral.

IMPS AND LEARNING

Whatever the size and growth rate of the computing machinery, CAL can still be seen as the relationship between a very complex task — learning — and some programs on some machines. IMPS represents an attempt to clarify that relationship. Chapter Two presents a summary of the IMPS framework for courseware development. We trust that framework will survive at least a few more changes in the hardware mix and help your own efforts to develop courseware with some longevity.

CAL can be an exciting and challenging part of your teaching, training and learning life. Although CAL can be very complex, it need not be. It can be both simple and effective if properly designed. *The Elements of CAL* is designed to be a map for a voyage. The voyage will give you the skills to be a map-maker yourself, and help others to seek adventure on voyages you design.

2 IMPS

WHY IMPS?

Our own experience with CAL has covered a variety of machines, languages and environments. This variety has made us wary of introducing new languages, new systems or even new terminology. Hardware and software variations and incompatibilities are the greatest brake on the spread of CAL as a common tool for learning.

IMPS is certainly not a language for CAL, nor is it a theory about CAL. It is really just a synthesis of a good number of observations made independently by a number of experts. Its function is to help the spread of CAL by clearly separating the programming and non-programming aspects of CAL.

Although we divide the process of developing courseware into nine layers, the activities are not linear. In practice, there is always a good deal of movement back and forth among the layers.

IMPS is not concerned with specific machines and languages. You can use IMPS for courses in BASIC on Apples or for PLATO courses on large CDC mainframes. Nor is IMPS concerned with whether or not the specific CAL materials are destined for schools, factories, the home or for self-training. Although the resulting courseware will tend to be quite different, the IMPS methodology should work equally well in all of these environments.

We do recognize that CAL is fundamentally a complex process since it attempts to mirror learning. One can create simple and useful CAL, and our examples attempt to demonstrate this level.

On the other hand, the complexity of learning means that courseware developers will need all the help they can get from new software advances; we try to keep our discussions within the framework of the general development of software methodologies.

The Elements of CAL

Training versus Education

We do not agree, as is made clear in Chapter Three, that there are fundamental differences between CAL (Computer Aided Learning) and CBT (Computer Based Training). It is true that university and school experience with CAL is not exactly the same as experience in the working world. Nor are those differences limited to the size of the computers used. However, the differences are of approach rather than qualitative.

There are many insights to be gained by writing courseware under contract to external groups who have clear ideas about what they want done, and when, and for how much and about the precise meaning of mastery. At the moment, such groups tend to be organized as corporations and to be more interested in "training" than in "education" *per se*. IMPS has been influenced by both kinds of groups.

Teachers and/or Trainers

For the professional trainer or teacher, it is often difficult to separate one's ego from the course.

Few people really like to be evaluated and this attitude often passes over to courseware preparation and evaluation. Both trainers and teachers tend to utilize the power inherent in an expert/novice relationship in order to stifle dissent and criticism.

In training environments, the trainer is more likely to be forced to have a direct relationship with a "subject matter expert" and that subject expert, in turn, is likely to be very directly involved in the activity that training is directed towards. Subject expertise is thus very current.

In the educational environment, the teacher is expected to be trainer and subject expert combined. Once validated as expert in training and subject matter, however, the teacher is not necessarily subjected to daily evaluation of either kind of expertise. For example, some universities have been known to teach students about relational databases without letting the students have the opportunity to use one.

When preparing courseware under contract, one not only lacks the power to stifle criticism, but one knows the practical, money-saving benefits gained by encouraging comments as fully and as early as possible. The courseware users are often extremely knowledgeable about much of the course content. It is always easier and less expensive to edit a course *before* it is designed and coded than after.

What is difficult in these circumstances is to let the subject experts see enough of the CAL process so that they can predict their criticisms of a planned implementation.

It was this observation, our own questioning of the tenets of "easy" authoring systems, and our concern about the over-emphasis on languages, programming and systems development by CAL experts, that led us to formalize IMPS.

PREMISES OF IMPS

The two fundamental premises of IMPS are that:

- Course design and data gathering should be separated from implementation.
- Within implementations, course data should probably be separated from course coding.

These may be seen as two sides of the same coin if you wish.

Keeping the design and implementation stages well separated means that courses can be transferred usefully in the pre-implementation state. Since that stage often represents 80% of the total work-load, this may well be the cheapest way to achieve portability of courseware. Keeping the course data separate from the course coding or control structures also simplifies design, portability and adaptation. In larger courses, it is imperative that editorial changes or the addition of modular blocks of data can be made quickly and easily by non-programmers.

IMPS and Hardware

Within our IMPS framework, at least at the moment, the many differences between low-range and high-range hardware tend to create a distinction in the importance of the mapping, tracking and support layers and in the nature of the implementation (site or network).

This distinction, however, is likely to blur in the future, just as the once clear line between micro and mainframe is rapidly blurring with the introduction of low-cost, powerful, multi-user, multi-tasking minis. The effects of hardware on CAL are discussed in chapters Ten and Eleven.

No matter what level of hardware you are using at the moment, the underlying process of courseware development will remain the same. Indeed, the probabilities are that you will be moving up in capacity within the next few years no matter what hardware you have currently selected.

The Elements of CAL

IMPS and Databases

One further factor, the growth of reasonably priced database management systems, is discussed in chapters Nine and Ten. Such application packages can make standard courseware development much more efficient and can provide a useful tool for making IMPS work on large amounts of courseware under development by large teams.

IMPS DEFINED

The remainder of this chapter provides a summary of the IMPS framework. Each layer is then further defined and illustrated in a separate chapter of *The Elements of CAL*. The final chapters provide some example courseware as developed using the IMPS framework.

2.1 Schema of IMPS

ONE	Definitional Layer
TWO	Local Structures
THREE	Presentation
FOUR	Tracking
FIVE	Mapping
SIX	Student Support Structures
SEVEN	Author Support Structures
EIGHT	Site Implementation
NINE	Network Implementation

1. The Definitional Layer

In this layer, the author must outline the course goals, define the learning objectives and provide rules. Objectives are not goals, for goals ordinarily take one to a broader level than CAL can handle alone. Objectives are defined in terms of sets of related rules.

A course comprises a set of related objectives and a curriculum is a set of courses (related or unrelated).

Here is a simple example. The goal is to increase awareness of laws governing safety. The curriculum contains two courses: Driving a Car and Operating a Motorboat. Driving a car contains several objectives, including:

Simple Traffic Lights, Complex Traffic Lights, Stop Signs. In the Simple Traffic Lights objective, there are four rules:

- Red means stop.
- Amber means caution.
- Green means go.
- Only one light may be on at a time.

If the learner can master these four rules, he or she will have reached the objective: to understand how a simple traffic light works.

2. The Local Structure Layer

Given a clearly defined rule, or set of rules, and an objective, one can then deal with the local structure. Drill, Tests, and Simulations are all examples of types of local structures.

In practice, of course, a given local structure is likely to be useful for more than one objective. A course may consist of only nine rules presented via four different structures or of three hundred rules all presented in the same structure or in many other varieties of organization. But the structural principle can be kept separate from the organizational practice.

The rules, examples and questions are used in local structures in a variety of ways. Most of Chapter Four is given over to describing the major variations. A good deal of this book, as is true with most books or articles about CAL, focuses on the ideas presented in this IMPS layer. Local structures are important – they help distinguish CAL as a methodology, and can influence your selection of hardware and software. Nonetheless, the concepts presented in Chapter Four represent only a single layer. Once mastered, they fit easily into the larger schema.

3. The Presentation Layer

One way of ensuring that you do not code before you design, and do not cripple your courseware from eventual expansion once hardware of certain kinds becomes cheaper, is to deal with the presentation level as abstractly as you deal with all other levels.

In practice, of course, if you are working with a PET, an Apple, a Telidon terminal, or PLATO, it will seem simplest to ignore this layer since you know fairly well what you can and cannot do in terms of graphics, color, words per screen, input variations, etc. The presentation layer then may simply work out as a set of screen layouts which are handy for various kinds of local structures and some general guidelines about color and graphic limitations.

The Elements of CAL

Nonetheless, at the design stage, it is useful to think of ideal ways of presenting the desired objectives. Minimum requirements might also need to be considered. We should remember that whatever decisions are made here, all data and design specifications for a given course at the first seven levels ought to be portable since paper is a very portable medium: no implementation is deemed to have taken place.

If your objectives are unlikely to be explained and mastered without color and three dimensions, then say so. If your rules can only be properly demonstrated with simulations and if those simulations or certain sets of examples require presentation by videodisc, then say so. If color diagrams are better but not necessary, then make that distinction.

Site implementations may or may not have the required hardware; network implementations may wish to get the course running using some variety of terminals and or hosts.

If the presentation cannot be written down in fairly full detail before the implementation stage begins, then perhaps the design layer is not really complete and certainly you are likely to have problems with your implementation.

Much of what follows in the next four levels assumes a mid- to high-range machine. There is nothing wrong with deciding at this point that you have absorbed enough theory and want to get on with the job. If so, after reading Chapter Five, you may insert a personal "GOTO Chapter Ten" if you wish.

4. The Tracking Layer

In this layer, the various learner, instructor, author, registrar and architect requirements for analytic data are described. These might include: objectives mastered, percentage of segment or course completed; average response time, average session length; summary of student comments.

Again, if minimum requirements have been established, these should be clearly indicated. Tracking layer specifications may be quite general for a standard lesson or course description and then defined in greater detail for specific implementations where comparative analysis is to be undertaken. Some larger sites may have certain tracking minimums not necessarily met by those who first developed a course.

5. The Mapping Layer

This layer deals with all of the "pathway" questions of a specific course. Lectures and lesson plans allow only a single way through the material. The degree of choice which CAL permits can be confusing if not mapped in advance. With low-range machines, this layer may appear unnecessary since the mapping may simply consist of directing the student through a simple sequence or, at most, through a series of diskettes. However, as the sets of objectives and component materials grow, it soon becomes apparent that there can be many pathways through the same sets of objectives. At the same time, different student requirements, instructional methods and the preferences of different instructors may create distinct variations.

The mapping layer, therefore, may consist of a single formal pathway through the course, or a description of the recommended and possible pathways, or a set of descriptions reflecting variations of the course approved by certain instructors or classes of students.

This layer helps formalize the question of course adaptability. A large percentage of course adaptations can be made merely by making changes at the mapping level. A good deal of courseware which is rejected or rewritten from scratch could be adapted fairly easily if its description and code provided straightforward methods for amending the map.

Again, as with the tracking layer, an initial course description may have a fairly general specification which then becomes far more detailed within given implementations.

6. Student Support Structures Layer

Support structures are those aspects of a course which do not directly lead to the achievement of an objective. Common types of support structure are: reference, such as a glossary, a dictionary, statistical charts; and a "help" feature to provide assistance with the mechanics or structure of the course, as well as comment facilities to allow the learner to leave messages for the teacher or other learners. A structure which is a support structure in one course may be an important local structure in another course.

Support structures are not of secondary importance in a course and their potential availability is one major example of the benefits of high-range machines. Our example shows a number of student support structures which are defined at this layer but not implemented in the given Apple II implementation.

Good support structures should be accessed frequently by all learners. Those "doing well" in the course may use support structures for enrichment. Those "having problems" will find assistance in the support structures.

7. Author Support Structures Layer

This layer deals with the tools required to maintain and alter the implemented course. For the most part, once these tools have been created, they can be used repeatedly in many different courses. In general, more powerful tools are needed in network implementations. Essential tools include: registration procedures, editing procedures, mail facilities and report generation.

The Elements of CAL

It is a characteristic of low-range machine implementations of courseware that the author support structures and tools are nearly or even exactly equivalent to the tools available to the programmer. Course data, for example, is edited by editing the program. Report generation, if available, takes place only within the program.

8. The Site Implementation Layer

Layers eight and nine both deal with the implementation process, the specific ways in which you turn all this design and data into a course or a version of a course.

One function of the eighth layer is to emphasize local control over the lesson, course or curriculum. The distinction between layers eight and nine may logically be considered to be quite arbitrary and history may see more and more network implementations. But in social terms, the distinction between site and network implementations is important. If control over the course rests locally, then you have a site implementation.

At this layer, at least one machine, one language and one package of code must be involved, together with one designated author. Descriptions within this layer may include additional machines, languages and code. For example, a conceptual model for a large course on Language Arts and/or Calculus may exist. All seven of the first levels may have been well defined and the data prepared and stored. A local site may accept those first seven layers and implement part of the course on a PET or an Apple. Let us say the PET implementation is in BASIC and the Apple is in PASCAL. The site implementation layer would then have two parts and would describe both implementations in terms of the original model. Included in this layer would be the two sets of system documentation covering the PET and Apple implementations in detail.

9. The Network Implementation Layer

Many different layers of networking may be described within this level.

At a very simple level, two schools may agree to swap diskettes on a regular basis so that given courses can be updated. At a slightly more complex level, courseware for specific machines may be stored centrally and downloaded. Ideally, a given site could search a central database not only for conceptual models covering desired learning objectives but also for code and documentation covering implementations of those objectives that matched their own hardware and software facilities. The network might be either a production service network that provides design strategies, data and model courseware to sites; or an analysis service network that provides analysis services for tracking data; or a physical network, providing on line courseware from a host or group of host machines.

IMPLEMENTING IMPS

IMPS may be used in three ways. As a general design tool for small, straightforward courses, one needs little more record keeping than a page or two on each relevant layer.

On larger courses, IMPS provides a handy way for ordering print and computer-stored data. Much of what appears in the first three layers becomes part of the documentation for other users of the course. Some of it becomes direct data for use within the course.

When courseware is developed by teams, the layers provide a functional way of dividing the tasks while keeping the whole project coherent. Good ideas which did not work out at the implementation layer can be stored away awaiting the development of better languages and machines. Variations in implementation for different learners or different environments need only be documented separately within those layers where the differences are important.

Finally, IMPS is only a concept, a way of describing reality. It is expressly forbidden for anyone to write a software development language called IMPS.

3 The Definitional Layer

ONE	Definitional Layer
TWO	Local Structures
THREE	Presentation
FOUR	Tracking
FIVE	Mapping
SIX	Student Support Structures
SEVEN	Author Support Structures
EIGHT	Site Implementation
NINE	Network Implementation

INTRODUCTION

In designing IMPS, we attempted to generalize the process of courseware creation based upon our observation of many educational and training projects. Although some of the projects we observed were well-organized and very productive, the current pattern of development in many tends to be chaotic or, at best, idiosyncratically organized.

The structure of IMPS is an attempt to conceptualize the inevitable stages of development through which each project *must* pass, so that each stage or layer can be throughly understood.

The first layer to be described, defining objectives and rules, is the most important; all other layers depend upon it.

We have divided this chapter into three sections. To a certain extent, only the third portion of the chapter describes the precise nature of the definitional layer; the first and second portions deal with the surrounding factors which often make it difficult for the definitional layer to be perceived as the starting point or to be accomplished in a clean and natural fashion.

17

The Elements of CAL

GOALS VERSUS OBJECTIVES

One of the first major difficulties beginning authors find with the techniques of CAL stems from a confusion between goals and objectives. Although they believe they have made the distinction between the more general concepts implicit in goals and the specific objectives which will lead to that goal, they may in fact have failed to make this distinction properly.

Creating the program for the computer reveals this confusion quickly because the computer does not really understand goals. Computers insist on taking things one at a time and in dealing with each element in a fairly straightforward fashion.

If your goals are ambitious and somewhat hazy, as they often should be, then do not rush into CAL. To date, our own experience leads us to say that CAL is only really useful (and courseware is only quickly created and tested) when the author can specify the set of objectives of the course in advance and then define those objectives in terms of a clear list of specific rules.

What CAL is Not

CAL is best seen as *one* of a number of teaching methods useful in helping an author and a group of learners reach their goals. In schematic form, that statement might appear as follows:

3.1 CAL in Context

Personal Methods	Media Methods	Computer as Tool	Delivery Methods
lecture	books	word processing	printouts
tutoring	video tapes	analog data collection	file transfer
seminars	films	accounting	databases
			networks

1. PERSONAL METHODS

Personal methods include lectures, discussions, guided field trips, tutorials, notes and grading, plus joint planning of the teaching process and mastery

3 The Definitional Layer

targets with the learners. In the majority of learning situations, personal methods employed by the instructor are the most effective and, in many cases, the more personal the more effective.

We like to point out, with reasonable irony, that the dedicated individual teacher, especially on a one to one basis, is a remarkable scanning, processing, and output device. The student can find none better. CAL must model itself on some set of the functions that teachers and trainers use.

2. MEDIA

Books, films, videotapes, and flashcards will, of course, continue to play a major role in learning. In many cases, the learner's copy (whatever the media) is a duplicate of some collection of facts, opinions and entertainment which cost a great deal to put together. Don't reduplicate what is already inexpensive.

You should avoid spending time transferring pages of books to a television screen and calling that CAL. You should also avoid attempting to imitate complex maps or film presentations of complex machinery in the eight colors and limited visual space ordinarily available on CAL delivery devices.

3. THE COMPUTER AS TOOL

At the moment, the best use of low-range computer power in educational situations is to let the learners use these machines as tools to do the things such machines do reasonably well: word-processing, data sampling, computation, and demonstrating the nature of computer languages and operating systems.

CAL implies that the computer takes on some limited portion of those complex processes by which information is passed from one individual to another in a structured manner. Use of the computer as tool, in those terms, is not CAL. That is not to say that the student does not learn a good deal from having a computer as tool, but only that the role of the computer is different; no tracking, for example, is taking place. The computer is being used as a tool and the goal is to facilitate the student's mastery of that physical tool.

One very interesting development in the coming decade will be the close integration of the two models: CAL and computers as tools for students. Built-in CAL courses for new machines and languages are one example of this. In another example a student might collect all the spelling errors from a month's worth of word-processing files using a computer-based spelling checker and submit these to an analysis package. The analysis package would then put together a custom designed CAL spelling course to remedy the kinds of spelling errors found within the files. Or, students may write their own drill and practice modules.

The Elements of CAL

4. THE COMPUTER AS DELIVERY MECHANISM

The computer can be considered as one more useful medium without involving it in CAL. Computers are a handy place to store lecture notes and grades. And they are fairly quickly becoming useful tools for the production and storage of low-cost print and graphic materials. Even more significant, the arrival of low-cost, powerful database machines will mark a major change in education. More computer power may be used for this purpose than for CAL or for general computer tools.

Again, integration will create useful questions in the coming decade. If the instructor stores a set of lecture notes, when and how should the students receive them? If the instructor stores corrected student essays for a year or two, should future students have access to them? Should students be encouraged, or forbidden, to build databases of essays on specific subjects?

CAL can claim neither the full domain of teaching nor the full domain of use of the computer within education and training. The rest of this book, however, does concentrate on the role and nature of computers when used very directly within the learning process.

What are Objectives?

Let us take an example of a teaching situation where you are looking at various methods you might use to transfer information and skills. Suppose that you really want your students to "understand Shakespeare". That is a goal. And you may make a good start with some of the students, especially those that share the goal. But often teachers move from goals to methods (and especially to those methods that worked for them during their student days) without paying too much attention to objectives.

CAL, in fact, is probably not too useful for such a goal because it really is difficult to specify objectives when the goal is to "understand Shakespeare" or "appreciate modern jazz" or understand what it means to "be a good citizen of the world" or appreciate the "wonders of modern science".

However, even when the goal is to start the student towards an understanding of *King Lear*, one must begin somewhere. In addition to lectures, visits to England, dramatizations, movies, and visits from local actors, there might be some basic vocabulary, history, background, action sequences, character analysis, or details of settings that you feel are crucial to the understanding of this play.

The student's need to understand such facts can be seen as the basis for defining objectives. At the moment, CAL can only begin with the definition of objectives.

3 The Definitional Layer

The Building Blocks

The three building blocks of CAL are simplicity itself:

- *rule*
- *example*
- *question*.

THE RULE

A rule is any single, testable element of the objective. We use rule for the general term just so we do not have to keep saying: a rule is a rule, a definition, a statement or a practice procedure.

This single element may be a rule in the ordinary sense: e.g., all sentences begin with a capital letter; or, matter cannot be created or destroyed.

It may also be a definition. Assuming that the objective is to teach some basic electronics terminology, the elements might be definitions of *erg, volt* and *watt*.

To allow for the more general case, the elements within the objective could be statements: e.g. "King Lear had three daughters"; "*The Elements of Cal* is full of dubious assertions"; "the sun comes up in the east."

It is true that if statements are testable, they can usually be restated as rules or definitions or as part of some larger rule or definition. Even if some statements are not easily testable, however, they can be part of a CAL structure, especially the inquiry structure.

In some cases it is legitimately difficult to define a rule. This problem may arise when one is testing mastery of specific physical skills. One of the most commonly successful uses of CAL is to improve basic musical skills associated with "ear training". If the objective is to develop relative pitch discrimination, for example, you can devise a set of practice procedures with related tests in order to help the individual attain mastery. The rule, however, remains a testable fact: the defined interval of a major second is exemplified by the difference between G and A, or C and D.

THE EXAMPLE

An example is a single expression of any rule. It may include within it expressions of other rules in addition to the rule for which it is designated.

If the rule is complex and relies on the learner's comprehension of component rules, then the example may itself need to be quite complex.

Some rules can dynamically generate their examples on the computer and some can not. This distinction has some important implications for the nature of the local structures and the general design of the course.

The Elements of CAL

THE QUESTION

A question may be defined as any single query or test situation posed by the computer to the learner, which depends on the learner's mastery of a rule or set of rules in order to provide a correct answer.

Again, some rules, with a little manipulation, can generate their own questions fairly quickly using simple algorithms; some can not. Our two sample courses, one verbal and one mathematical, illustrate this point.

RULES AND OBJECTIVES

An objective comprises one or more rules. Obviously the objective of understanding the diction of *King Lear* is far more complex than the objective of understanding the rules of addition and subtraction. Nonetheless, as defined, both objectives consist of a number of what we call rules.

The same rules may be part of more than one objective. Some disciplines also tend to be more rule-oriented than others. Whatever the discipline, however, the general observation holds: CAL works well in presenting a set of rules, even when the set of rules is fairly complex and interactive. However, if your goals cannot be broken down into objectives and sets of rules, then be prepared for some fairly difficult and frustrating work.

RULES, OBJECTIVES, GOALS

A traditional course consists of goals and objectives. However, ordinarily not all of the goal may be present as objectives. Grading on student progress towards the goals must be subjective. Grading on student mastery of the objectives can be measured in terms of student mastery of the component rules, whether CAL is used or not.

IMPS, Goals and Objectives

The structure of IMPS is based on these basic observations. It recognizes that few teachers articulate their objectives as well as they articulate their goals and that few trainers articulate their objectives as well as they articulate their individual rules. It is easy to find examples of curriculum guidelines which are precise about objectives and rules and other examples which treat their goals as objectives, sketch in their objectives, and ignore rules and definitions altogether. Much student confusion is caused by hazy distinctions among goals, objectives and rules.

Although much of the time spent in preparing CAL is spent in the refinement of objectives and rules, too often that time is spent *after* the author has begun programming. IMPS insists that you create your objectives, rules, examples and tests *first*. If you can not, then you have probably chosen the wrong method for attaining this portion of your goals. Rather than CAL, you

3 The Definitional Layer

should consider lectures, books, films, field trips, or databases, in order to meet your established goals.

GOALS AND STRATEGIES

When we were attempting to disentangle the various chaotic strands of courseware development methods, it became clear to us that a distinction between goals and objectives was not sufficient to explain all the confusion. We have grouped a number of the complicating factors under the heading of strategies. These represent approaches to CAL, based on economics, the nature of the discipline being studied, or the nature of a learning theory. What all these factors have in common is that they attempt to redefine the CAL process to better fit their own approach. IMPS attempts to provide a model which is broad enough to make this need for redefinition unnecessary.

1. Implicit Mathematical Strategies

Many of the early users of computers were mathematicians or engineers. Their solutions to problems tended to be linear and left-brained. By contrast, good teachers tend, at a certain level, to function like artists: holistically, and with a good deal of right-brain pattern seeking which includes looking for patterns in the content, in the students and in the relationships between students and methods and content.

It is not surprising that a high percentage of all courseware, and of excellent courseware too, is in the field of mathematics or in technical areas such as digital logic and engine maintenance. It does not necessarily follow, however, that all good CAL will follow these patterns. The humanities, for example, may require a far more extensive use of database methodologies than mathematics ever will.

Even large CAL sites assume that programming is difficult and insist that the CAL facilities should be designed to allow anyone to program quickly. This is probably a serious fallacy and the major contributor to ineffective CAL. Programming is still a difficult art, and complex CAL is difficult to program. However, there is a distinction between the complexity of any course and the length of the course. IMPS encourages the creation of courseware with a length and a degree of complexity only as great as required by the necessities of the objectives. Complex courseware may require the assistance of skilled programmers at the implementation level. But keep in mind the distinction between the complexity demanded by the needs of the course, and the complexity of the subject itself. When teaching different subjects using the CAL mode, the degree of difficulty may vary greatly. However, some components of a course in any subject may be taught using quite straightforward CAL methods.

If your content is not in the least mathematical, then it will often seem that the computer is working against you when it comes to implementation time. We

The Elements of CAL

trust that our two contrasting examples in Chapter Twelve will help make it clear that CAL courseware need not be limited to mathematical content despite the strong historical ties between math and the machinery.

2. The CBT Strategies

Linked to this historical pattern of a bias towards the mathematical has been the steady growth of Computer Based Training (CBT). There is often something mechanical about effective CBT. On the other hand, when one speaks of effective use of computers for learning, one is clearly obliged to take examples from the CBT area. Although a good deal of the early CAL work took place in universities, colleges and faculty of educations, that work often seemed to fade out or come to a dead end when given individuals left the scene or when certain pieces of equipment became obsolete. At the moment, many experienced practitioners of CAL have switched to CBT, or to examining the role of the computer as tool, or to moving through the development cycle again using low-range machines.

CBT has two advantages to speed its development: money and status. The former may be obvious, but the latter might seem a contradiction. Trainers tend to have less status than educators just as critics often lack the degree of fame of artists. But educators who engaged (or indulged) in CAL were usually treated with some suspicion by other educators. Educators are often rewarded for publishing, not for teaching, and ten years spent developing good CAL materials might produce no "visible" effects.

By contrast, trainers are rewarded for training. A CAL expert, who might be considered somewhat eccentric within his or her own university, often found the money and status available with a move to a corporation's training division to be an irresistible combination.

The fundamental difference between the two types of institution is not in the methods used but in a major external function: cost-accounting. CBT experts tend to have *precise* methods for examining the costs of what they are doing and defining the benefits.

Let us take a hypothetical example. Training in Digital Logic II comes in at $3,900 per trainee for direct costs. We have 356 trainees in that course per year and the average wages and travel cost while taking the ten day course is $2,200. How much do we save per year if we cut training time by an average of two days? CBT experts would always have an answer.

By contrast, educational experts tend to have *general* methods for defining the costs of what their organization is doing and to accept common assumptions about the social benefits of the institution's activities. For example, our university has an annual budget of $110,000,000 and does a great deal of good for students, the nation and the economy of this city. It makes important research contributions in medicine and engineering.

3 The Definitional Layer

There is little doubt in our own minds that most major development work in CAL during the 80's will take place under the guise of CBT and with a strong emphasis on cost-effectiveness. Very slowly, but very surely, these ideas will cross over to the institutional level.

CBT AND THE TEAM APPROACH

CBT people distrust the "goals" that remain elusively beyond the range of the CAL people and CAL people distrust the ability of the CBT practitioners to purchase hardware and software that lies elusively beyond the range of their own budgets. In fact, little is different in what the two groups do, but a good deal is different in how they tend to do it and to speak about it.

Although the distinction between CAL and CBT, we assert, is mainly one of status and approach and not fundamental, one strategic factor has been very useful to us in defining IMPS. The CBT clans tend, with good reason, to favor the team-of-specialists approach. Such teams might be comprised of a team manager, an instructional design expert, an editor or artist, and one or more subject matter experts.

In theory, this looks like a good idea, but in fact it often turns out to be expensive. The programmers want to start programming and the artists want to start creating and the subject experts tend to distrust the instructional design experts (probably because they suspect that these were the ones who invented the term *subject matter expert*). Nobody really wants to create a lot of printed files of rules, examples and tests and organize these according to objectives. Indeed, many systems do not encourage such activity.

The principles of cost-effectiveness often encourage both haste and a reluctance to experiment. However, a good deal can be learned from the complex teams and the general approach ought to be experienced by everyone serious about CAL.

The problem teachers experience when working as groups is that they do not really share the same goals. Often, the greater the number of participants in the creation of an examination, the greater the degree of blandness possessed by the exam. What happens, in this instance, is that conflicting goals are eliminated and the poor student is left, as is all too often the case, with the lowest common and the least offensive denominator.

If groups of teachers cannot agree on their common objectives and on how to define the sets of related rules, then the students are probably going to suffer unnecessary ambiguity. IMPS encourage teachers to deal with these questions before programming begins. If minor differences remain, then the ambiguity can be provided for in the course structure. If major differences remain, then you are perhaps dealing with goals rather than objectives. Dealing with goals may quite properly encourage ambiguities.

CAL has an interesting role to play in bringing certain questions of consistency to the forefront. At the moment, it is often only the students who see the patterns of inconsistency present in different versions of what might seem to be the same set of rules or definitions. It is often laziness hiding under the banner of "a personal" approach to the subject.

The complex teams used by CBT may often lead to expensive CAL or to unnecessary refinement and internal battles. They may ignore some of the higher questions of education. Nonetheless, they do make possible a great deal of clarification of the courseware development process. IMPS owes a good deal to the methodologies implicit in such team creation of courseware.

DISCIPLINES AND STRATEGIES

It is interesting to rank the academic disciplines by how amenable they are to being communicated via the medium of CAL. The scientific nature of biology and anthropology, for example, make it simpler to specify objectives in an educational environment. The traditional and Boolean logic taught in philosophy courses offer interesting challenges to the CAL author. On the other hand, some aspects of physics, chemistry and biology are perhaps too "philosophical" to be easily broken down into a set of objectives for presentation to learners.

At the moment, there is very little exchange between disciplines. Yet because CAL authors tend to be more gregarious than many of their colleagues, there have been some interesting examples of the kind of cross-disciplinary research and development that CAL demands.

THE STUDENT AS TEACHER

One of the major advantages of CAL, in theory, is that the student is not forgotten. It is a good rule of thumb to allow all vexatious questions of technique or strategy to be answered by reference to an ideal and invisible learner. Will it work for the learner?

The real test of this philosophy, however, comes when you are able to present the students with the early layers of IMPS. At any point, it is possible to present the student with the design strategy, the techniques, the evaluation criteria, and the data of a planned course. This is a difficult activity only because it is so uncommon, but we recommend it.

If you have lofty goals as a teacher, it is almost a *sine qua non* that the learner does not share them, yet! If you only have objectives, however, why not let each learner share in those from the beginning? CAL is more explicit than other forms of teaching. Its target is 100% mastery.

If showing the students how you are trying to get there is possible and useful, why not do it? Sometimes you might want to do it before they begin the course, sometimes during, and sometimes after. At times you may want to sequence the explanations as mastery is gained. But we have found that the very act of explaining the method has two excellent results. It leads to greater participation by the learner since there is nothing mysterious about the process and it tends to raise questions of a fairly high order about teaching methodologies, learning practices, and the many ways in which your course could be improved.

ONE MAN BANDS

One of the reasons many teachers have an ambiguous attitude towards CAL is the common occurrence of the one man band. The one man CAL band has tended to be male, slightly fanatic, always frazzled, and driven into being a perpetual fund-raiser. There are reasons for this. CAL is not yet an established discipline and is not supported at many institutions. In addition, good CAL requires a broad range of skills and a deep interest in how learners learn and how they do not learn. Unfortunately, such skills and interest are not as common in institutions as many would like to believe.

It is interesting to note that microcomputer CAL has not followed the same pattern. Although the CAL hacker is not an unfamiliar sight, the low cost of the machines and the obvious fascination of the technology has attracted what must be described as more "normal" teachers into CAL. Any province or state is likely to have several hundreds if not thousands of teachers who at least profess an interest in the field. Indeed, the growth of the field has turned some of the less insular one man bands into prophets with clans of their own.

A great deal can be learned from the one man bands, however quirky they may seem at first glance. Much of what they have learned has been paid for at some cost and should not needlessly be relearned, however senseless it may appear at first sight. Indeed, the continuing research into higher levels of CAL, such as the role to be played by large databases and artificial intelligence theories, will continue to center around these early experts.

FROM OBJECTIVES TO RULES

In many instances, the move from objectives to rules is not difficult. Often the curriculum guide provides a reasonable model which can be supplemented by the lesson plans of the teachers involved. In the training field, there are many subject areas which have already been well modeled in these terms.

In such cases, there may be minor difficulties with the organization of the set of rules, with the hierarchy of the rules, or with the assumptions, i.e. those rules that you can trust most learners to have already mastered.

Wording of the rules is important and it is often useful to begin by creating a number of ways of expressing each rule so that they can be understood by

The Elements of CAL

learners with varying vocabulary levels or of different ages. This process costs nothing in that the variations are often required, but it also tends to point out hidden combinations, rules which are themselves small sets of rules. Even when the skill level of the students means that these rules can be presented as they are, it is good to consider whether or not such hidden combinations might present a problem even for a small percentage of the target learners.

If all goes well, then discussion and approval of the set of rules with variations by all the instructors involved in the process completes the first task in this layer. One can then go on to discuss the basic examples and questions suitable for the target learners.

Implicitly or not, your goals and objectives have been described in terms of target learners. The greatest success in defining objectives, phrasing rules, selecting examples, and designing local structures will occur when the target learners are most exactly described. If the target learners are quite unknown, several revisions, based on information gained in tracking and comment, may be required. The author is learning about the learners.

Often, however, even when the intended learners are well known, creating the set of rules is the most difficult portion of the whole process. This is especially true of subjects in the humanities or of training courses that deal with real world activities such as management, counselling or planning.

Our two example courses demonstrate the major difference between courses in the sciences and courses in the humanities. The rules for fractions are well-known and not subject to much debate. Our example course from the language arts area, however, is deliberately restricted because we are well aware of the many pitfalls in such fields.

Once, trapped in the known complexities of adopting Chomsky's theories of generative grammar to the actual teaching of grammar, we decided, for a change of pace, to whip off a course on something simple and certain, say the rules of punctuation. There were indeed lots of rules and definitions, hundreds of books, in fact, but not only did the books often fail to agree, the rules themselves were full of those words that one quickly comes to recognize as dangerous when attempting to implement CAL: *if, unless, usually, in many cases, except when, provided that*. Eventually, we examined over 100 books looking for a good and consistent set of rules for punctuation. Completeness was much more of a problem than consistency, but consistency was a major problem.

Eventually, we ended up working out our own set of rules based on the various functions served by punctuation. That set of rules was turned into a book which is now in its third printing.[†]

[†]*Softwords Complete Guide to Punctuation*, (Victoria, B.C.: Press Porcépic, 1981).

3 The Definitional Layer

It was many months before we got back to Chomsky and there made a different kind of discovery. There are a number of areas where one might say that pseudo-science has taken over. Lévi-Strauss's work on patterns of myth may be a good example. Chomsky's work is another. Our hope and expectation had been that his patterns of generative grammar could be used in reverse to create a simulation model for language that would function as algorithms do in mathematical areas and obviate the need for large banks of examples as data for learning about language construction rules. In fact, without hopeless limitation of the semantics, Chomsky's patterns were no more useful than the more traditional descriptive terms. Neither would allow us to generate meaningful, and only meaningful, sentences.

Ultimately, all that work became useful for designing a course about compilers, but at the time it certainly appeared to be a complete waste.

The Rule of Four Cases

In analyzing subject matter, you will find four possible sets of circumstances under which you must build your set of rules. The simplest case is when the existing rules do work. Certainly when you are beginning to experiment with CAL it is best to start with these cases.

The next simplest case is when the existing rules are incomplete or inaccurate, but a proper set can be found within a reasonable time. Often the best CAL arises out of these situations because the courseware serves a double function, it clarifies as well as instructs.

The most dangerous case is where the existing rules are incomplete or inaccurate and some promising solution appears to remedy the problems. Often you cannot really test the new theory until a certain amount of your courseware development is done. If the remedy fails, then you have wasted some time. The only consolation is that these experiences, if unusual, often make good topics for papers or presentations.

Finally, in the many cases where no well-known set of rules exists, you may end up by admitting that there is usually a very good reason: the subject is too complex or too abstract for rules. This may mean the area is outside the domain of CAL altogether.

Alternatively, it may be useful to show a pattern. Computers can be used as rapid seekers and presenters of patterns. Often the set of patterns in a given subject area is far larger than any text or any group of lectures and demonstrations can illustrate.

The Elements of CAL

From Rules to Examples and Questions

Once, however, you have established the set of rules, then the other two tasks, building examples and questions, are relatively straightforward. When the examples cannot be generated, they will have to be churned out. This is an important task and often best left to the learners themselves. They can quickly weed out the more useless examples and suggest additions that may seem a little strange to you but often work most effectively because of their language, style or irony.

The establishing of related questions often serves as a handy check on the form and validity of your rules and objectives. IMPS is not a lock-step process. The relationship between local structures and questions is a strong one. It is often helpful to establish the local structures and consider presentation methods before preparing the questions in detailed form.

You need to think not only of what it is about the rule, definition, question or skill that can be tested, but about how the set of rules relate to one another. What are the patterns that the learners might see in this set of rules? What is to go into the learner's short term memory and what into long term? How can your questions and local structures help them learn and retain what they learn? You are far more likely to amend the questions in any course over the long term than the rules and examples.

Most CAL methodologies are in agreement on the need for good rules and examples. It is when, where and how to ask questions, and how to deal with responses, that tends to separate one school from another and to create the intense debates. Chapter Four provides a formal view of the primary structures linking rules, examples and tests.

4 Local Structures

ONE	Definitional Layer
TWO	**Local Structures**
THREE	Presentation
FOUR	Tracking
FIVE	Mapping
SIX	Student Support Structures
SEVEN	Author Support Structures
EIGHT	Site Implementation
NINE	Network Implementation

Your basic task in designing the local structure is to determine the best way to help the learner meet each objective.

A knowledge of theories on how people learn might help, but common sense will get you through most decisions. If you are not an educator by profession, do not worry. You know how to learn: you have been doing it all your life. Respect your own opinion. It is comforting to know that research into teaching and CAL has not yet shown that one teaching strategy is superior to another. This means that, with a little experience, anyone can create effective CAL. If you are an educator, you will already have preferences for one strategy over another. Using CAL does not mean you have to change the way you teach, but it might give you a new perspective on the things you have been doing all along.

THE LOCAL STRUCTURE

Each local structure should be designed as the best way to teach a single objective. The objective, as explained in Chapter Three, is comprised of one or more rules, and the examples and questions which go with each rule. These building blocks become key components of the teaching strategy.

The Elements of CAL

The five teaching strategies which are described in this chapter differ from each other in: 1) the choice of building blocks to be used (you might have questions only in one local structure, rules and examples only in another); and 2) the way the building blocks are connected (how much learner control, for example). As explained in detail below, the differences between strategies are often a matter of degree — which building block is emphasized — and of subtle assumptions about the nature of the rule being taught.

Many of your courses will use the same local structure for each objective. If your goal is to teach the basic rules of punctuation, each objective might consist of one rule of punctuation and dozens of questions and examples. Once you have created the best local structure to teach a given rule, you may want to use the same local structure for a number of related rules. More complex courses may have objectives which differ enough to warrant the development of several different local structures.

THE BASIC TERMS

Prompt, interaction, response, feedback, motivation, adaptive, sequence, pre-structured, keyword, reinforcement: the language of CAL. These terms all relate to a few key concepts of teaching and CAL.

No matter how complicated the connections between the rules, examples and questions may look, the local structure consists of *interaction* between the learner and the computer. This interaction is always based on a *question*, asked either by the computer or by the learner. Sometimes the computer will ask a question by just sitting there, waiting for the learner to do something before it will act. Sometimes the learner's question is also silent. For example, the learner may key in an answer to a test question posed by the computer. This doesn't look like a question, but in fact the learner has said "Here is my answer: do you think it is right?"

The question posed by the computer, but not based on a rule, is called a *prompt*. The learner's reply to a question or a prompt is called the *response*. The computer's answer to a learner's response is called *feedback*. Feedback is usually based on looking through the response for a *keyword*. The keyword, or keywords, is the set of characters you feel will indicate that the learner knows the answer to the question asked or has chosen a viable option. The identification of appropriate keywords is an important part of CAL and takes practice. The continuous process of question-response-feedback is called the *sequence*.

Every learner response must have feedback. *Reinforcement*, however is used to encourage or *motivate* the learner to continue toward the objective. Reinforcement will not occur in answer to every learner response, but will occur according to a pre-defined pattern.

4 Local Structures

ADAPTIVE VERSUS PRE-STRUCTURED

The type of feedback received by the learner determines whether the teaching strategy is adaptive or pre-structured. In a *pre-structured* teaching strategy, the computer has only a few ways of handling learner response. The sequence of events designed to move the learner toward the objective will be the same for everyone. In an *adaptive* teaching strategy, the computer can handle a wide variety of responses from the learner and use those responses to determine the best way for him or her to reach the objective. With an adaptive strategy, the course is tailored to the needs of each student in each session. It is important to remember that adaptive and pre-structured are opposite ends of a continuum. Although totally pre-structured courses do exist, totally adaptive courses have not yet been developed. All courses created to date fall somewhere between the extremes, with many aiming to come as close as possible to the adaptive teaching strategy.

Why, increasingly, is adaptive CAL the goal? Each person learns differently, at a different speed; learning appears to take place best when the instructor responds to the learner's needs. A good teacher can identify problem areas and give extra help where needed, can identify areas of special interest and give bonus projects, and can tailor his or her vocabulary to the student's level. Adaptive courseware also has the potential for this responsiveness, to a greater or lesser degree.

However, pre-structured CAL can also be effective. In the classroom, pre-structured CAL can be used to relieve the teacher of routine testing and drills, while at the same time make these exercises more interesting for the student.

The different teaching strategies should not be graded as "adaptive" or "not adaptive". Within each strategy there is ample allowance for variation; it is only important to indicate that a particular strategy requires a lot of adaptability to function well, whereas another strategy can do quite well, or suit specific needs, on a pre-structured basis.

THE FIVE BASIC TEACHING STRATEGIES

Drill
Test
Inquiry
Simulation
Tutorial

33

The Elements of CAL

Drill

BASIC DESCRIPTION

A drill teaching strategy consists of any combination of rule, example and question. The response to the question is identified as either right or wrong, and some attempt is made to indicate the probable source of error and remedy the misconception. There is no complicated interactive diagnosis of the source of the learner's error.

THE SEQUENCE

Here is a standard pattern for a drill local structure sequence: the question is presented, the learner responds, the response is checked against the anticipated correct response. Whether the response was correct or incorrect, the learner is given feedback and presented with another question. This sequence can be represented by the *state diagram* in Figure 4.1.

Each incorrect response is checked to determine the category of error (Figure 4.2). If the learner has keyed in an unanticipated response, a drill can only assume error, display the correct response and continue. Anticipated incorrect responses must be checked to determine appropriate action. You will have to

---

4.1 Drill: A Basic Pattern

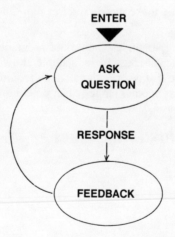

4 Local Structures

determine at which point remediation should be offered and whether the remediation will be computer or learner controlled. The result may be: ignore the error and continue the sequence; repeat the question; try another prompt; accept error as incorrect, but continue questioning; accept error as incorrect and move to some form of remediation or a support structure. After any of these actions, the sequence continues to the next question.

The drill basic pattern can be varied in a number of ways. You might decide to allow the learner to select how many questions he or she would like to be asked. It is usually a good idea to let the learner stop the sequence at any point. You may decide to limit the number of entries into a particular sequence. The sequence might end under computer control after four correct responses, or four incorrect responses, for example.

A record of responses can be used to allow a drill sequence to adapt to the learner's strengths. For example, if the objective contains a total of fifty questions, ten on each of five rules, the drill sequence could stop asking the questions

4.2 Some Response-Feedback Variations

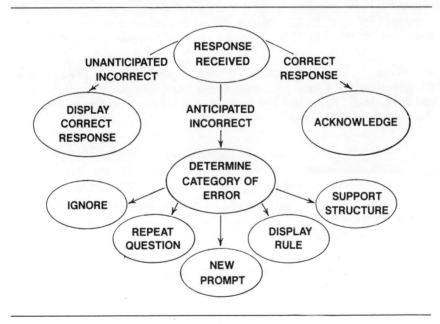

The Elements of CAL

on a particular fact once the learner had recorded seven correct responses. In this way, the sequence would eventually concentrate on the areas of weakness.

Another method is to record the learner's state of knowledge for each rule. Each rule, for each learner, will have a 0-10 rating, where $0=$ "totally unknown" and $10=$ "totally mastered". This weighting system allows you to take into account a variety of learning experiences that the simple recording of right and wrong responses does not cover. The weight can be used to select the level of difficulty of questions, number of questions, relationship of examples to questions, and any of the other variables in a drill structure for each learner and thus create an adaptive course. You determine the conditions for incrementing the student's knowledge. For example, you may decide to start all learners at 0. Simply reading the rule once may increment the learner's knowledge to 1, or you may decide that the student must answer 4 questions correctly before the weight can be increased to 1. You may use a diagnostic test to determine the initial weight for each rule, or you may ask the student to guess at his or her knowledge.

RULES AND EXAMPLES

Drill can be used to allow the learner to practice applying rules learned elsewhere in the course or off-line. When this is the case, the rules and examples will probably be presented to the learner as feedback to correct or incorrect responses. For example: "Sorry. You forgot that period is used to end a sentence." or "That's right. Here's another example of how you could do that..."

Drill sequences can begin by presenting a rule or rules and examples, then questioning the learner on the material seen. Figure 4.3 shows an example of this type of drill. The basic pattern for the questions, however, remains the same and the rules and examples can still be used as feedback. The learner may be given more than one question on the same rule or example.

THE QUESTION

Drill questions must point to one correct answer. The student should be able to respond correctly with a single character or word, or a short phrase.

Questions for drill can be stored as data or generated algorithmically. Math questions are easiest to generate, followed by some types of science questions. It is possible, with careful attention to grammar and syntax, to generate other types of questions.

Drill questions can take the form of an example, or a statement of the rule with parts missing, or a question specifically written to match the rule.

4.3 One Form of Drill with Rule or Example

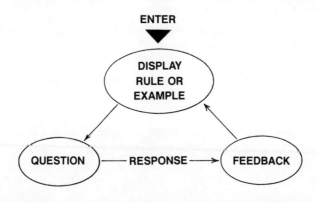

FEEDBACK

In drill, feedback must indicate whether the response is correct or incorrect, and may offer remediation. Most experts feel you should always tell the learner the correct answer when the response is incorrect. In this case, the feedback to an incorrect response might include a statement of the rule. You can experiment with leaving this out.

Remember that reinforcement is not the same as feedback and do not be too generous with your praise. In this type of local structure in particular, the constant appearance of "Hey, that's terrific!" will start to sound false.

An optional type of feedback is to let the learner see his or her score, during the sequence, at the end, both during and on completion, or whenever requested.

DRILL: GOOD FOR

- Helps learners memorize simple facts.
- Excellent for large groups with limited access to terminals because a lot of material can be covered in a short time.
- Easily within the capabilities of all languages.
- Lets inexperienced learners follow the mechanics of the course.

The Elements of CAL

- Works well with pre-structured courses because it clearly reinforces the main mapping decisions.

DRILL: LOOK OUT

- Limited feedback means the learner may become frustrated by not being able to identify the reason he or she keeps getting certain questions "wrong."
- The learner may become bored with the question types and feedback. In drill questions, it is particularly important to have a bank of expressions to call on for feedback.
- Not the best choice if you are trying to explain complex ideas or want to encourage the learner to think in imaginative ways.

Test

BASIC DESCRIPTION

The question is the only building block used by a test strategy, although responses are evaluated according to a rule or rules. The results may or may not be recorded.

Of course, drill also asks questions and evaluates responses. The difference is that in test no attempt is made to give assistance or emphasis to areas of weakness.

A test may contain questions based on rules that are taught in different objectives in the course.

THE SEQUENCE

A test consists of a pre-determined number of questions which are asked of the learner. Whether the response is correct or incorrect within the boundaries set by the author, the learner moves from one question to the next until the sequence is finished. Figure 4.4 shows the basic pattern. Test questions may be generated according to an algorithm or stored as data. You may decide to have the questions appear in the same order for each access by each learner, or you may decide to vary the order of presentation. For two tests to be absolutely equal, they must contain the same questions on the same rules, in the same order. Of course, a satisfactory similarity can be achieved if the questions for two tests are generated according to the same pattern.

QUESTIONS

Why test? To see if the learner knows the rules. What does "knows" mean? It can mean any or all of the following. Has the learner memorized the rules? Can the learner make considered personal decisions based on the rules?

4 Local Structures

4.4 Test: A Basic Pattern

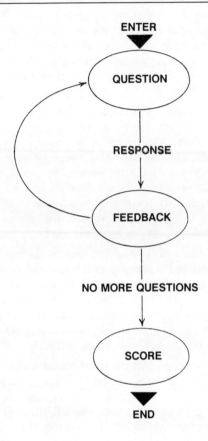

The response-feedback variations in Figure 4.2 do not apply in a test local structure.

Can the learner apply the rules to solve simple factual problems? Can the learner use the rule to create something new?

You cannot cover all of the above facets with the same type of question. An important part of a test local structure is deciding which types of questions you will use. The following question types are defined according to the kind of response expected of the learner. These question types are also used in the other teaching strategies.

The Elements of CAL

True or False questions appear to be the simplest question types to create. The learner is presented with a statement, often an altered form of the rule or example, and asked to indicate whether it is true or false. To make T/F questions into a useful test, rather than a guessing game, is difficult. To provide the learner with some variety, consider this type in combination with other types of questions. Because it is easy for any learner to master the mechanics of T/F questions, also consider this strategy for learners new to CAL or those who are unable to use the full facilities of the keyboard. T/F questions are only useful for inexact testing of factual knowledge.

Multiple Choice questions are familiar to almost all learners. The question and a choice of responses are displayed. The learner is asked to select the one response which is correct. Variations include asking the learner to select the incorrect response and allowing several answers, or none, to be correct. It is important that *distractors,* or incorrect answers be factually and grammatically possible. Multiple Choice questions are often under-used, since they are considered to be an option only for simple tests of fact. However, because the learner does not have to type in the response, the subject matter can be quite complicated, with subtle differences between right and wrong answers.

Matching is a variation of multiple choice. In matching, the learner is presented with two lists and is asked to match elements of one list with another. Screen size limits make sophisticated matching questions difficult to construct, but graphics and cursor-positioning input can solve some of the problems. Matching is useful to test fact memorization, such as dates for historical events, and can also test understanding of simple cause and effect. Pattern matching is useful for increasing cognitive skills in younger learners.

Short Answer questions include questions to which the learner responds with one or two words, and variations on this pattern, such as fill-in-the-blank. Because the learner is not presented with the options, the author must spend some time considering all the variations which the learner might key in which will be considered correct. Which, if any incorrect spellings will be accepted? Make sure the question is bullet-proofed for errors: if the correct answer is "whales", the response "not whales" may also record as correct if the sequence simply looks for the keyword "whales". Due to the complex response checking which is required, short answer questions are often limited to tests of simple facts.

Essay type questions begin by asking the learner a question which requires a lengthy response, or by suggesting a topic or topics to become a focus for an essay. You may want to try creating a computer-marked essay question by searching the response for a series of keywords, but any attempts to date have been unsuccessful. There are certainly too many variables to make this an effective means of testing. If you want to ask essay questions, and essay answers are

4 Local Structures

the only way of testing understanding of subjective concepts, store the learner's response for later manual grading. Make sure you have enough memory to store long answers.

All of the above types of test questions can be used singly, or in combination, to create test local structures. If you record all learner responses, your tests will improve with age. By watching for patterns in response, you can get a clear idea of weak points both in the test questions and in local structures within the course.

It may appear that computer testing is limited. Actually, the restrictions reflect the fact that only a limited range of learning is truly testable.

FEEDBACK

In a test local structure, the feedback must let the learner know that his or her response has been received. You may want to acknowledge the response as correct or incorrect, but do not give any remedial assistance during the test.

A test sequence should finish with some type of "score". This may range from a simple "Your score: 5 correct in 10 questions." to a detailed analysis of the learner's problems and suggestions for future objectives. You may also want to provide the learner with information about scores during the test. Other information, such as time elapsed, is optional. CAL can be made extremely competitive if time and scores are announced, but most authors avoid this option.

TESTS: GOOD FOR

- Placement tests can be used to position a new learner in the course.
- Tests can determine which objective the learner should move to during a learning session.
- Tests can be used to diagnose sources of continuing errors.
- A good test can tell you if your course is working the way you hoped it would when you defined goals and objectives. It is a test of both the learner and the author.

TESTS: LOOK OUT

- Computer-generated questions add a variable which must be considered in comparative testing.
- A learner may be profiting from the course in ways which cannot be measured by the test structures. Do not allow tests intended to determine if objectives have been met to become road-blocks to an otherwise enthusiastic learner.

The Elements of CAL

- Cheating at a computer terminal can be quite easy unless the learner is closely observed. If this is of concern to you, some control can be exerted by limiting the time allowed to answer each question.

Inquiry

BASIC DEFINITION

Inquiry-based CAL is close to the border of information retrieval. The learner indicates which rules he or she wants to see, and is shown only those requested. Inquiry may include examples, but does not include questions based on the rules. Because the basis of this strategy is to allow the learner to select data as he or she wishes, the objective must define the rules which can be accessed by the learner. In many cases, this will be the entire database.

THE SEQUENCE

The basic pattern is as follows: the learner requests data, the data is displayed, the learner requests more data or ends the sequence (Figure 4.5).

An inquiry local structure can allow the learner to select from choices offered on the screen, or key in the name or location of the information he or she is looking for. A slightly more adaptive pattern would present the learner with an initial menu and refine the topic down to a single accessible rule.

RULES AND EXAMPLES

Consider having the key points on a topic displayed initially, then offering the learner more information if desired. Or, display the rule and offer the learner the option of seeing an example.

THE QUESTION

In inquiry structures, the computer questions are in the form of menus, or prompts, directing the learner to key in the identifying keyword for the item of information he or she wants. The question-based-on-rule building block is not used in this strategy.

The learner must know which keywords will be accepted. Once the database is of any length, this can become difficult. An on-line or hardcopy subject, alphabetical or numeric index can help.

FEEDBACK

In inquiry, feedback is limited to helping the learner with the mechanics of the structure and prompting to help the learner identify more closely what he or she is looking for. See Figure 4.6 for some possibilities.

4.5 Inquiry: A Basic Pattern

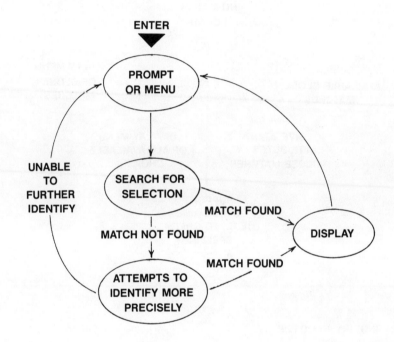

The Elements of CAL

4.6 Some Inquiry Identification Variations

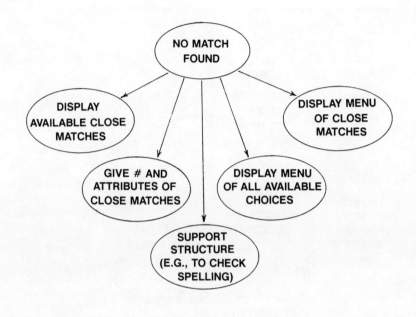

INQUIRY: GOOD FOR

- Use this method for increasing awareness on topics — in the same way one looks things up in a dictionary or encyclopedia.

- The only method to use for support structures such as glossaries.

- Gives the learner a great deal of freedom. By browsing through the available information, the learner will learn what he or she is ready to learn and may discover areas of interest otherwise unknown.

- Good for large groups — each "lookup" can take a matter of seconds.

- Easy to program in any language — if the database is small.

- Combines well with other local structures to make a combined CAL-Information System. Also combines well with non-computer exercises.

4 Local Structures

INQUIRY: LOOK OUT

- Because learning is indirect with the inquiry browsing structure, it may be difficult to test results.
- Requires the course author to have some basic understanding of database management. If there is a lot of data and a poor database structure, look-ups can take too long to be useful.
- Do not leave the learner tangled in a series of menus. It is very frustrating to have to move up and down several menus in order to find one small rule.
- It can be difficult to show the learner what material is available.

Simulation

BASIC DESCRIPTION

The main feature of a simulation strategy is a *scenario* which is displayed on the screen. The scenario is constructed according to a set of rules and examples and is usually designed to represent "real life". The rule and example are combined in ways that force the learner to guess, make assumptions or think in intuitive ways in order to respond to the question. The learner's responses alter the scenario.

A simulation may also invite the learner to take control and create the scenario by feeding in the key features *(parameters)*. The scenario which is created will be built according to the rules defined for the objective.

THE SEQUENCE

A simulation is a process, based on one or more rules, which presents itself in a dynamic form. In order to accommodate all the possible combinations of cause and effect, the sequence requires a complex branching structure which will vary to meet the needs of the local structure.

The sequence in a simulation local structure must focus the learner's attention on one scenario at a time, however. Figure 4.7 shows the simplest form of the basic pattern.

RULES AND EXAMPLES

In simulations, the rule and example building blocks are used to create a model on which to base the simulations. The effectiveness of the simulations will depend on the fidelity of the model. Simulations may work with the rules "known" to the learner, or using the simulation can be a process of discovering the rules.

The Elements of CAL

4.7 Simulation: A Basic Pattern

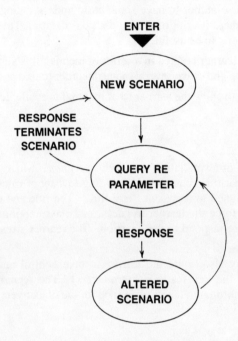

QUESTION

In most simulations, questions take the form of instructions to the learner, or choices of action. Any response provided by the learner which will work within the rules of the model are correct. A learner will have an indication of error if the alteration to the scenario is not what he or she anticipated.

Some simulations may ask questions of the learner, based on the scenario. The questions should challenge the learner to look at all aspects of the situation presented and should not point to one correct answer.

4 Local Structures

FEEDBACK

Because a response to a simulation is neither right nor wrong, the main feedback to the learner is the change in the scenario which results from his or her response.

SIMULATIONS: GOOD FOR

- Simulations encourage *inductive* learning. This means the learner is not asked to memorize facts, but is led to form his or her own opinions about the underlying rules which are governing the simulation. This is the best strategy if you want CAL to approach moral or social issues.
- Simulations can be used to help the learner envision complex processes which are not easily described in terms of single rules or sets of rules.
- Simulations are particularly useful in the sciences where they can allow the student to "perform experiments" which would be too dangerous or costly in a real laboratory.
- The basic sequence of simulation makes it ideal for instructing in any rules which are primarily cause and effect.
- Usually very popular with students and an excellent structure for students to create or help design.

SIMULATIONS: LOOK OUT

- Not the best choice for groups because each sequence is time-consuming. You can get around this by dividing the large group into small groups and asking each group to decide on a common response.
- It can be difficult to create an algorithm to drive simulations of subjects which are not primarily mathematical. In this case, the course requires extensive data to function.
- In order to create the model you must be able to define the system exactly. This often seems simple, but turns out to be very difficult for many subjects. If you select objectives properly, the difficulties are reduced.
- Due to the adaptability and flexibility of a simulation strategy, such a local structure requires extensive tracking support if you want to record the learner's progress and evaluate the strategy and structure.

The Elements of CAL

Tutorial

BASIC DESCRIPTION

Tutorial CAL is the most difficult teaching strategy to define because its most important aspect is that it be highly adaptive. It combines all three building blocks, rules, examples and questions, in any way needed to get the job done. Tutorial CAL differs from the other strategies in that in the event of continued learner error the learner goes into an interactive diagnostic sequence designed to determine the source of error.

Tutorial CAL may also allow the learner to ask the computer questions about the material presented. Allowing such questions results in a tutorial structure that is highly adaptive and consequently very difficult to construct.

THE SEQUENCE

Tutorial CAL requires a complex branching system to handle the variety of feedback to student responses which is the key feature of this teaching strategy. It is difficult to define a basic pattern, but Figure 4.8 suggests a useful beginning point.

Tutorial handles anticipated incorrect responses in ways similar to those described under drill (ie, determines category of error and acts accordingly, see Figure 4.2). It is in handling unanticipated incorrect responses that tutorial CAL uses a different approach: a series of questions to diagnose the source of learner errors. Figure 4.9 suggests only some of the possibilities.

You will have to decide how many incorrect attempts to answer will be allowed for each question. At what point will the sequence offer remediation? Who will control the remediation?

Remember to ask the learner for information you need to determine what to do in case of several incorrect responses. Do not be afraid to use straightforward questions such as, ''Are you tired? Do you want to quit? Was the question too hard? Was the data easy to understand? Do you want another question or more information?''

You may also want to consider the ''state of knowledge'' record described under drill as a means of controlling all or part of the tutorial sequence.

RULES AND EXAMPLES

The diagnostic sequence must have, built into it, methods for handling anticipated problems which concern the rules covered by the objective. The adaptive nature of tutorial CAL allows you to instruct the learner in complicated

4 Local Structures

concepts which may not be easily explained in one or two sentences. If your computer's memory will allow, consider storing the same information at different reading levels. Offer the learner a selection of question types and numerous examples to help clarify complicated questions.

4.8 Tutorial: A Basic Pattern

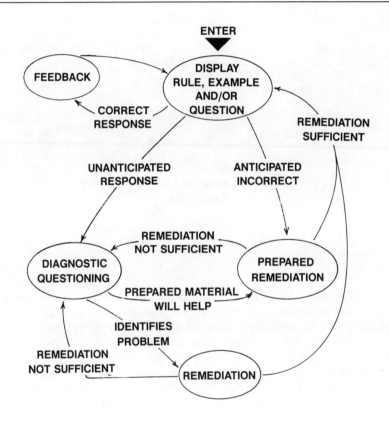

The Elements of CAL

4.9 Some Types of Remediation

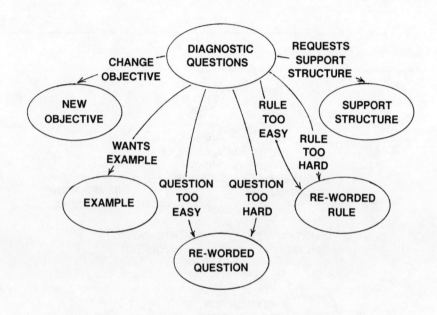

It is very likely that a diagnostic sequence in a tutorial local structure will identify a learner weakness which involves a rule that is not part of the learner's current objective, or a rule that is not available in the course. You may decide to move the learner to a different objective automatically, or simply suggest the learner leave the current objective and try the other. Whatever you do, make sure the learner understands that he or she has been moved or all your careful work of defining objectives has been wasted. See Chapter Eight, "Support Structures," for the kinds of things that should be handled by other structures (such as, problems with the mechanics of the course).

Tutorial CAL may present the learner with rules and examples worked into a scenario similar to that described in the section on simulation. A response to a tutorial question based on a scenario will not be used to alter the scenario, but may lead to more complex questioning.

4 Local Structures

THE QUESTION

In tutorial CAL the question may allow for more than one correct answer. You can "weight" these answers to determine feedback. This means that when you indicate the anticipated responses, you give each response a weight from, for example, 1-5. Four of your anticipated responses may have a weight of 1. If the learner responds with one of the four, you assume he or she is developing an understanding of the key concepts in question. Two of the possibly correct responses are weighted 2. One of these responses may indicate that the learner understands the main facts, but is missing the broader application. And so on, to meet the needs of your tutorial session. This weighting system can also be used to indicate "degree of correctness" if all anticipated responses are not equally correct. In this case, of course, each anticipated response would have a unique weight.

It should be possible to answer the question with a few words or numbers. A tutorial sequence may contain more than one question based on the same displayed rule or example. An effective use of this is to move from asking questions about the facts to slightly more complex questions testing comprehension of concepts.

If you are allowing the learner to ask questions of the computer, make sure he or she knows the range of flexibility allowed. You might consider identifying keywords to the learner, such as "who" "how" "when", etc. This will make your job easier when it comes to feedback, but will also restrict the adaptability of the sequence.

FEEDBACK

The responses in a tutorial sequence require processing at a sophisticated level. This is what allows a tutorial structure to tutor the learner.

You will have to indicate a wide variety of anticipated wrongs. The anticipated wrong should indicate the type of mistake the learner is making and then offer help with that aspect of the objective.

Tutorial CAL attempts to adapt to each learner through the variety of feedback provided. Feedback in a tutorial sequence could include any or all of the following (see Figure 4.9):

re-display data,
offer immediate remediation,
offer access to a support structure,
suggest learner leave this objective and try another,
ask the same question in a different way,
ask a different question,
suggest the learner take a break,
guess at what the learner meant.

The Elements of CAL

The learner redirection may be very much within the learner's control, or entirely computer-controlled.

If the learner is allowed to ask direct questions, the feedback must be able to identify what the learner wants if he or she does not respond to the prompt with a keyword. The only way to do this is to revert to the computer asking questions of the learner.

TUTORIAL: GOOD FOR

- Individual use of the computer for a long period of time.
- With friendly prompts, tutorial CAL can create a very secure environment for an inexperienced learner.
- Complex pre-structured mapping decisions are neither required nor desirable.
- Great for several learners working at different levels with different objectives based on the same rules.
- A good strategy for teaching concepts, but the more difficult the concepts, the more difficult the sequence is to develop.
- Allowing the student to ask questions opens the sequence up to its greatest adaptability.

TUTORIAL: LOOK OUT

- Requires a sophisticated recognition of responses which are misspelled, oddly worded or otherwise conceptually correct while literally incorrect.
- Requires a great deal of computer memory to store all the alternate data.
- Ties the computer to one person for a long period of time.
- Results very much depend on the ability of the subject expert and designer to predict anticipated wrongs.
- Probably requires a sophisticated CAL language and a good database management facility to be really effective and practicable.
- It is difficult to predict results and may be hard to get direct comparisons of student progress without complex tracking systems.
- Be careful to provide good mapping information or the learner will never understand the goal of the course, or the objectives.
- Don't begin allowing the student to ask questions unless you have extensive feedback to make it worthwhile.

4 Local Structures

GAMES
Basic Definition

You might want to consider games as another strategy. We do not do that because each of the five strategies can, with greater or lesser success, become a game. A game has:

- an identifiable beginning,
- at least two players, of which one may be the computer,
- something denoting the end of a game (i.e. a goal),
- rules to outline the way the game is played (perhaps with a hierarchy of rules or patterns such that the game can be played at varied levels of skill).

Most importantly, however, the learner must think the game is fun. This may be an insurmountable contradiction. If you are at all obvious about the *objectives* of the game, the players will rightly suspect that it is not a game and they will not participate with the same degree of enthusiasm.

Games are based on rules, skill and luck. The skill and luck may be incorporated into CAL, but the *rules* of a game are usually based on some incomplete or fantasy scenario. The game world may be limited, as in Monopoly, an abstraction of battle, as in Go or chess, or quite convoluted and imaginative, as in Dungeons and Dragons. Players may move through a hierarchy of understanding and mastery. Nonetheless, one would seldom mistake the game board for the real world. Even the very young are extremely clever at distinguishing between a game world rule and a real world rule. It would be most interesting to do some research where computer games were "taught" and made part of the world that adults impose on children. If so, would even PAC-MAN lose his appeal?

The human desire to play games will remain mysterious. CAL authors will probably feel an irresistible urge to move into the territory of games in order to encourage learning, but one suspects, and hopes, that the territory of games may at the same time utilize the technologies to escape beyond these advancing dragons. For the sake of believers in games, we outline the probable strategy of the encroachers.

Games for Learning

Our first learning is done through play. Playing house is a simulation. Hide and Go Seek develops skills of deduction and reasoning. Games in CAL offer the opportunity for the course author to allow the learner to return to what may be the most natural and comfortable way to learn. The measurable value of games as a learning tool is a subject of disagreement among experts, but it is gaining increasing acceptance in the classroom. [Dennis]

The Elements of CAL

The key building block in a games local structure is the rule. In order to function as CAL, the rules which govern the mechanics of the game must have some relationship to the rules which the learner must master in order to reach the objective.

Mention computer games and most people think of bright graphics, mechanical explosions and speeding cars, spaceships or monsters. These "video games" are a type of game which teach skills that are content independent and do not have a direct application in the real world. Hand-eye coordination and certain aspects of deductive thinking are two of the skills a learner might develop from such games.

It is unlikely that the learner will ever have an opportunity to shoot space monsters, and should that opportunity arise, even less likely that the experience in the game represents a real world situation closely enough to be of benefit. In educational terms, the objective of such games is limited to amusement and that is why they are often banned from computers in schools. However, why not use these types of games as reinforcement or to help new learners become familiar with the terminal?

These "pure" games can be combined with questions and examples based on rules which are connected to the objective. For example, a learner may be allowed one move in a tic-tac-toe game for each math question correctly answered. In this type of a local structure, you would use a drill or tutorial teaching strategy, with the game as reinforcement.

A more sophisticated CAL game uses the rules which the learner is trying to master as the rules which govern the mechanics of the game. Scrabble to teach spelling is an example of such a game. Any drill or test local structure can be turned into this type of a game by setting up some method of competition. The key variables are the number of correct responses and time taken to respond. The learner may compete against his or her own best time, a class average, or other learners at other terminals or the same terminal.

Simulations tend to make the most interesting games of this type. Being dynamic, and having a certain portion of their rule structure hidden, they are closer in form to most pure games than any other local structure. It is always easy to add a degree of fantasy to a simulation. A learner may take on a role, for example as queen of a kingdom, then solve certain problems which befall the inhabitants. Success in the game may depend on understanding the rules of supply and demand, ecology, etc.

In the types of games so far described, the learner is aware of the rules and his or her responsibility is only to memorize them. Games which encourage inductive thinking can be created by keeping the rules hidden. Success at such a game depends on the learner's abilities to deduce the rules. This is easiest to do with a simulation local structure which allows the learner to guess at a course of

4 Local Structures

action, see results, and form opinions about the rules which might be governing the scenario. Many popular adventure-type computer games are based on just such a structure.

CREATING A GAME

Games are potentially of infinite variety. You might want to start by adapting a favorite non-computer game. Card games based on *the luck of the draw* are usually easy to adapt. Board games can present problems unless you are clever with graphics.

Consider localizing your game. Perhaps a variation of *Monopoly* using local street names, or a simulated kingdom based on the school the learner attends.

GAMES: GOOD FOR

- Games often allow more than one person access to the terminal at the same time.
- If it is fun, motivation won't be a problem.
- Games are comfortable for people with computer fears.
- Learners who do not like competing with other learners may be more willing to risk losing to a computer.
- As with simulations, games are an excellent mode to encourage student participation.

GAMES: LOOK OUT

- Some learners do not enjoy competition. The resulting stress can inhibit rather than aid learning.
- Many games emphasize battle, killing, conquest and other popular human pastimes. Try to allow your creativity to move in the direction of creation as motivation instead of destruction.
- Many games reward the player who thinks most like the designer of the game. Try to build as much flexibility as possible into your game so that innovation also receives reward.
- Games often require graphics to be effective. This means a higher investment in equipment (see Chapter Five).

The Elements of CAL

REINFORCEMENT PATTERNS

Every learner response must have feedback. Feedback lets the learner know the computer is listening and provides important information. Reinforcement, however, serves two important purposes. First, reinforcement can be designed to encourage the learner to continue behavior that indicates he or she is moving toward the objective. Reinforcement can be provided in answer to a correct response, or after a certain length of time (the assumption, perhaps false, being that time in the course is always moving the learner toward the objective).

Second, and perhaps more importantly, reinforcement can be used to clearly indicate to a learner when an objective has been reached. Learners use two types of memory: short-term and long-term. Although the goal of a course is to move a body of knowledge into the learner's long-term memory, a specific objective will rely on short-term memory for achievement. Once the objective is reached, the learner can release some information from his or her short term memory and experience a feeling of accomplishment. Providing the learner with this feeling of accomplishment when a task is completed is called *closure* and is an important aspect of course design.

A *reinforcement pattern* must be defined for each local structure. Any reinforcement pattern can be matched with any teaching strategy. For most courses, reinforcement will take the form of a textual message, such as, "Terrific, Alice, you are really starting to understand punctuation." or, "Good. You have completed Lesson Two." Try for a random selection of message forms. A little humor is important, but do not be condescending. Reinforcement can, depending on the age of the learner, take several other forms. The learner might be allowed access to X minutes of a favorite computer game for every correct response. A graphics sequence can be a treat if you do not overdo it. Showing the learner his "score" in a sequence can be encouraging if presented in a way which emphasizes the learner's accomplishments. Game strategies have their own type of reinforcement (winning).

Considerable research effort has gone into learning and reinforcement in general, and reinforcement in CAL in particular. There is evidence that reinforcement designed to encourage movement toward an objective is more effective if it is used sparingly. The first "pat on the back" for a response has the most distinct positive effect. Continuous reinforcement loses its power — the learner has nothing to aim for. This is also some evidence that retention is increased if there is a delay between response and reinforcement.

Take a look at the state diagram for the teaching strategy you have chosen. Where should reinforcement occur? After the response? After three responses? Only after correct responses? Consider the entire course map. Where should closure reinforcement occur? Perhaps after each objective. Perhaps only after a test local structure.

Reinforcement patterns based on the number of learner responses may be consistent throughout the course (reinforcement every five responses), or variable, popping up in a random fashion. Remember that the value of the reinforcement will diminish if there is no connection between good performance and reinforcement. Reinforcement based on time spent in the course can also be presented at regular intervals or in a random fashion. If this type of reinforcement is worded correctly, it can encourage learners who may not be responding correctly to stick with the course. Of course, it is also useful to combine the two types of patterns: first correct response after five minutes receives reinforcement, for example. There is some evidence to suggest that random reinforcement encourages a higher level of attention over a longer period of time.

GENERAL GUIDELINES

The following points are common to all types of teaching strategies.

Rules and Examples

In some local structures, rules and/or examples will be displayed for the learner to read. Similar guidelines apply to both rule and example.

- The rule or example must relate to the objective in a way which can be understood by the learner.
- Keep to one rule and one or two examples per screen.
- Match the vocabulary and sentence structure to the target learner.
- Keep the text short. Everything should fit on one page.
- Don't use complicated graphics unless they are a definite advantage over a verbal description.

The Questions

- The question must clearly indicate what type of response is expected from the learner (ie, single word, letter, essay, sentence).
- The anticipated correct response must be an expression of the rule.
- The question should be clearly worded and clearly separate from any other information which may be displayed with it.
- Vocabulary and sentence structure must be appropriate to the learner.
- The question must relate to the objective in a way which can be understood by the learner.

Feedback

- You must identify the correct response.
- In some cases you must also identify the incorrect responses you think the learner will key in as a response to the question.
- You must create appropriate feedback for a correct response. Be inventive. It's a good idea to have a collection of responses stored which can be randomly selected.
- If you have identified anticipated incorrect responses, you must also create appropriate feedback for these. The form this will take will depend on which local structure you are using.
- You must also have a way of dealing with totally unanticipated responses. This will vary with the teaching strategy.
- The vocabulary of feedback must be appropriate to the target learner.

The Sequence

- Each local structure may combine questions, rules and examples according to a different teaching strategy.
- You should be able to create a diagram of the local structure sequence for each objective.
- Each sequence must have an identifiable beginning and end.
- The local structure sequence must be independent of course mapping.
- The sequence must define the reinforcement pattern.

5 Presentation

ONE	Definitional Layer
TWO	Local Structures
THREE	**Presentation**
FOUR	Tracking
FIVE	Mapping
SIX	Student Support Structures
SEVEN	Author Support Structures
EIGHT	Site Implementation
NINE	Network Implementation

In this chapter we will discuss various ways of presenting the course to the learner. The goal is to give the learner all the information needed to understand the subject matter and mechanics of the course, without slowing the process down with unnecessary detail.

Presentation consists of two main parts: providing output to the learner and receiving learner input. For most courses a screen will be the main output device and a keyboard will be the input device. The presentation layer is also where you put your mapping decisions into action by telling the learner where he or she is in the course and by making sure the learner knows what options are open at each point.

Certain aspects of course presentation depend upon the hardware you have available. Do not, however, get trapped into thinking you need fancy equipment in order to do anything exciting. There are basic principles that you can and should follow no matter what equipment you are working with. After that, use your imagination and let the restrictions of your equipment encourage creativity.

The Elements of CAL

BASIC INPUT AND OUTPUT
The Keyboard

Except for young learners, the keyboard is the only input device needed for the majority of CAL courses. A keyboard contains a set of alphanumeric keys in the same configuration as a typewriter keyboard. The keyboard may also contain various special function keys which do not appear on a typewriter keyboard.

All keyboards are equipped to perform the two input actions: input text and position the cursor. In fact, the keyboard is the only device which allows the learner to input text. A keyboard is less well equipped for quick and easy cursor positioning. Various keys, including special function keys, and combinations of regular and special keys, are used to move the cursor from one part of the screen to another. Movement is left, right, up or down, only.

A keyboard may offer access to an alternate character set. This character set is accessed by hitting a special key, in the same way capital letters are accessed with the "shift" key. Examples include mathematical symbols and the Cyrillic alphabet. If your terminal is for a specific use, make sure it has the characters you need.

Small differences in design can mean great differences in comfort to the learner. A detachable keyboard is usually the best bet if several different people will be using the terminal because the height difference between screen and keyboard can be easily adjusted. Manufacturers delight in making up new variations of the keyboard. Look out for problems such as sticky keys and a poorly positioned return key.

The Screen

Although some courses may also use other methods of output, most CAL will output to a terminal with a view surface — a screen. The first used and still most common screen type is a cathode ray tube (CRT), which looks like and works like a television screen. The front of the tube is covered with a phosphor (usually green, grey or amber). Images appear when an electron beam lights the surface in a specified pattern.

For text screens, screen size is described in terms of columns and lines. This is important when working out screen design. The standard size is 80 columns by 24 lines. Variations include: 40×24, 64×16, 32×16 and 40×20.

5 Presentation

SCREEN LAYOUT

There are three kinds of information which you will display on the screen: map information; course material such as menus, rules, examples, questions; and, in more complex courses, standard prompts that indicate to the learner what he or she can do next.

A simple local structure could be presented by displaying the interaction between learner and computer on a line-for-line basis. The learner would type a line, a response would appear below it, the learner's response would appear below that and so on. The old information would stay on the screen until it was forced "over the top" by the accumulation of interaction.

This is probably the least desirable way to present a course. The screen is cluttered with information which is no longer relevant, prompts become confused with information and it is very difficult to indicate to the learner the "pathway" he or she has chosen. You should only resort to this method if your hardware restrictions leave you no choice (for example, if you are using a very old terminal or printer terminal).

Instead, think in terms of "screens" or "pages" of information. This allows you to design, and therefore control, exactly what the learner will see at any given moment and to organize the display for the best educational impact.

Begin by marking a piece of graph paper in squares which correspond to the screen size you are using.

Now designate regions of the screen for each of the types of information which will be displayed. The common term for these regions is *window*. We find the best method for many courses is to have mapping information appear in the top quarter of the screen, course material and learner-computer interaction in the middle two quarters of the screen, and available choices regarding movement through the course in the bottom quarter. These proportions are approximate only. (See Figure 5.1 for a sample worksheet for such a screen design. See the sample courses in Chapter Twelve for an application of these screen design guidelines.) The location of these windows should not change during the course. This means the material that must be displayed for any local structure should fit within the windows. Next, mark off windows inside the major windows. These will indicate the specific lines where each type of display will appear (Figure 5.2). You must be consistent. For example, always display the question in the same part of the central window. By making it easy for the learner to get the mechanics of running the course out of the way, you allow each learner to spend more time learning.

For the most part, the windows you have described are for your benefit. The learner will only be aware that certain information always appears in a specific spot. You may want to add some horizontal or vertical "lines" to help clarify the situation. One or two is a good idea, but be careful. A complicated

The Elements of CAL

screen design with tabs and lines will take longer to display and may ultimately be more confusing than a simpler design.

5.1 Design Worksheet

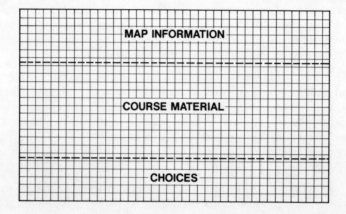

5.2 Display Windows

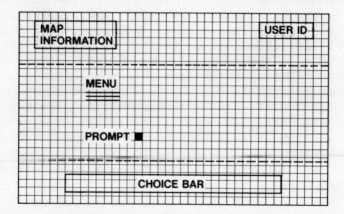

5 Presentation

A good screen layout is:
- interesting without being distracting,
- consistent from one part of the course to the next,
- immediately self-descriptive.

TESTING THE DESIGN

Now that you have a static screen layout, imagine it in action. Make a copy of the flowcharts or state diagrams you have created for each local structure, some sample rules, questions, examples, and any feedback, help messages or special prompts you think you might want to use. With all this material assembled, start moving through the course, imagining what the screen will look like at each point. Move down, backwards, into the support structures from all points — just as you will when you are debugging the first running version.

You will have to decide, character for character, exactly what will appear on the screen at each point in the course. You may want to do this by actually writing the displays on graph paper. This is a big job for even a small course. Once the initial design is checked and verified, you need only do a sample of each type of display. From this, you can determine any character or format limitations, then write the data into data structures and data files in the normal way. This step-through to do screen design may point out problems or inconsistencies in either local structures, support structures or mapping.

Start with the top of the screen. How will you indicate the learner's location in the course? Will all the routes be visible, like this:

Enter
Unit 1
Part A

Or will the label just read "Unit 1", and change to "Part A" when the learner moves down a level? You may decide to make all pathways invisible and use the top window to show time elapsed (for example, in a game). How will that be shown? Figures constantly displayed, or flashed up every minute? You will have made some of these decisions in the local structure and mapping layers. Now you must make sure the screen design will work to support your decisions.

There is scope for creativity in the central display. You can choose to clear the whole screen when a new question is asked, or just the central window. Consider whether color would help. Is there going to be a long wait while data is being read in? If so, would a graphic be useful to entertain the learner? Or will the graphic create further delay?

Determine any character limitations which will affect the creation of rules, examples or questions. Try to fit some sample rules into the screen design. Suppose you have decided, in the local structure, that the rule and question will

The Elements of CAL

remain on the screen at the same time. Now you see that there is not enough room for the lengthy rule and complex question. Will you alter the screen design? Shorten the rule? Do the limitations of your output device mean you must alter the local structure? Or should you change output devices?

The bottom window is optional. If each learner always read instructions properly and never made mistakes it would be very easy to write a fast-running course. The fact is that some learners will read the manual, practice a few times and always remember that "Q" means quit; other learners will remember Q means quit, but will not be able to figure out when they can do that without an indicator on the screen; and many learners will need to have a constant on-screen reminder. The majority of learners will begin using a course needing a great deal of information, but they will need less hand-holding once they are familiar with the course. Your job is to decide how all the information can be made available when required, but without crowding the screen.

In courses with several support structures and several pathways between local structures, we often use a continuously-displayed choice bar for the bottom section (Figure 5.3). This lets the learner know which choices are available at all times. You may allow the learner to suppress the choice bar once he or she is familiar with the course. Some courses may not offer enough variety to make a choice bar necessary.

5.3 Choice Bar

| U)p Q)uit H)elp C)omment |

Text Format Variations

Your terminal may offer choices in how you display the text within the screen layout. Remember that special effects are unwise unless the result is going to make something clearer to the learner, and do not design your course around a terminal-dependent option if you want fully portable CAL.

If they are available on your terminal, use both upper and lowercase characters for your textual displays. Slight changes in type size are a good way of clearly distinguishing between one aspect of the display and another. If possible, avoid over-large letters and long passages in capital letters.

5 Presentation

Some terminals offer variations such as *flashing,* which allows you to select parts of the display to flash on and off, and *inverse video,* where the usual screen display is reversed (green letters on a black screen will reverse to show black letters on a green screen). These options are useful for getting the learner's attention. Use them for such things as error messages, or short-term prompts. But keep in mind that it is extremely difficult to read passages of text which are displayed in other than standard formats.

If you have a color terminal, you may want to experiment with using color to highlight displays and create emphasis. Make sure the background and text colors demonstrate good contrast. Consider using color in the portion of the screen which tells the learner where he or she is: a new color for each level in the course, for example. In general, however, color text displays may easily become difficult to read unless planned carefully.

GRAPHICS

Text Versus Graphics

A *graphic* is any attempt to put an image instead of words on the screen. The image may be: a graph or chart, a meaningless design, a logo or a "realistic" picture. The graphics may be in the course as part of the instruction, to improve the readability of the screen or as reinforcement.

Graphics are very much hardware dependent, and the selection of a graphics system must be done with care. A course which depends on graphics to function will not be as portable as a course which is mainly text.

GRAPHICS HARDWARE

There is considerable difference between the capabilities of one graphics system and another. You will have to consider both how easily the graphics can be created and the quality of the display. Creation devices are described under Input Variations, this chapter.

Graphics terminals are available in a wide range of price and quality, either color or *monochrome* (shades of gray). A color terminal will offer shades of gray, and a range of other colors. Gray shades are created by varying the number of electrons hitting the surface of the screen. The other colors are created by mixing different intensities of red, blue and green, in the same way color is created on a color television. Figure 5.4 shows the standard range of colors and prices based on an intelligent terminal or a micro plus monitor. Graphics terminal screen quality is described in several ways, most importantly in terms of *resolution.* Resolution refers to the number of dots of light *(pixels)* which go to make up the images on the screen. Just as the quality of shading and fineness of line in a mosaic is improved by using smaller pieces of stone, the quality of CRT image is improved by using more dots to create each image.

5.4 Color

Colors on Screen	Quality of Display	Price range
4-8 from a choice of 4-8	coloring book	$1,500 - $5,000
8-16 from a choice of 8-256	cartoon like	$4,000 - $10,000
64 from a choice of 256-16M	color TV	over $10,000

Thus, *high resolution* provides better quality images than does *low resolution*. In fact, these terms are relative, and each manufacturer will describe a different number of pixels as high resolution. Figure 5.5 is a rough guideline to resolution and quality. Graphics are in a relatively early stage of development and some less expensive graphics creation systems are cumbersome to use. With imagination, innovative and exciting courseware can be developed.

Graphics to Teach

The idea of using images such as graphs, diagrams or pictures to help explain facts or concepts is not new. A graph, for example, can quickly show general relationships of size whereas a list of numbers may require either lengthy explanation or analysis to make the same point. Some people find it difficult to learn at all without a visual message. You can use graphics plus written explanation in a CAL course in the same way illustrations are used in a book.

5.5 Resolution

Pixels	Quality
256 × 256	acceptable
512 × 512	good color
756 × 756	excellent color and good monochrome
1024 × 1024	excellent color and monochrome

5 Presentation

There are research results which indicate that learner rate of comprehension when shown graphic material is four times faster than with print displays. [McKenzie] If the learner learns more in less time, there can be more access to the course for all learners. This may help balance the extra time required to create good graphics.

It is also important to remember that all learners exercise a different part of their internal learning mechanism to learn with images and therefore often learn not only the rules being taught, but new ways to learn.

With CAL, however, you can take graphics further than just a picture in a book – the images can move and change as the learner watches the screen. For example, graphs can be altered to show the effects of a learner's decision in a simulation situation. You could use color and shapes to show "migration" of animals across a map. With skill and a good terminal you can approach animation. The trajectory of a baseball in a physics experiment could be demonstrated in this way. It is also possible to give the learner a sense of being in a different physical space. Flight simulators used to train pilots are an expensive and sophisticated use of computer graphics to teach in this way.

Graphics for Design

You might want to add a logo to your screen layout, or interesting shaped colored windows to make the screen easier and more pleasant to read. Consider using symbols to indicate mapping decisions and available choices. Remember the points discussed under layout, however, and do not crowd the screen.

Graphics for Fun

You could also call this graphics for motivation. You might reinforce a completed test series with an amusing or attractive display. You might substitute a smiling face for "correct" as feedback to learner response.

Games are often where the most work has gone into interesting graphics. Graphics in games vary from simple dots and lines used to simulate a learner-controlled "ping-pong" game, to attempts to create physical surroundings such as a cave in an *Adventure* game. The interactive graphics used in games often require special input devices (see Input Variations, this chapter).

Guidelines for Graphics and CAL

BUILDING

Graphics can be slow to build. Take the time to design the graphic so that it builds in a meaningful way. In a graph, for example, design the display so that the X and Y axis display first, then the coordinates, then the connecting lines.

The Elements of CAL

This allows the learner to think about what's happening while it is happening, rather than "waiting to see what it will turn out to be" before considering the meaning.

PORTABILITY

Beware of designing graphics that look great on a fast system, then expecting them to look the same on a more limited system. Always program in modules which allow you to remove graphics and graphics-dependent parts of the course in the event that you want to run the course on a slower machine, or one without the right attributes.

RECYCLE

Keep a bank of often-used standard graphics displays that you can plug into the appropriate spot in any course.

LESS IS MORE

The experienced learner will get tired of waiting through the same series of graphics, no matter how wonderful they appear the first time or how clever you were to be able to create them. Make sure you never ruin the carefully planned screen layout by decorating the essential information with too many graphics, and always give the learner a chance to cut off a long display.

When you are using graphics to teach, aim for a precise single statement. Do not provide too much information at once.

PSEUDO GRAPHICS

You can experiment with limited graphics even if you do not have a graphics terminal. For example, use dashes, hyphens and l's to create a graph, with the points plotted with x's. (See Figure 5.6.)

INPUT AND OUTPUT VARIATIONS

Input Variations

Input variations are provided by various devices which allow the learner to position the cursor. Cursor positioning is very important in creating graphics and essential for any interactive graphics used for instruction in CAL. Specialized input devices can give access to CAL to learners who, for physical reasons, are unable to use a standard keyboard. Some experts also believe that very specialized input devices can create a more "natural" way for learners to communicate with the computer. An example of this is the full LOGO Turtle, or robot, which moves about under control of a simple, large-scale input device that even very young children can master. [Papert]

5 Presentation

5.6 Pseudo Graphics

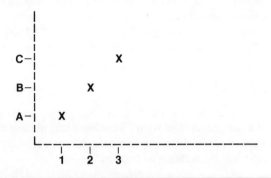

5.7 Input and Output Devices

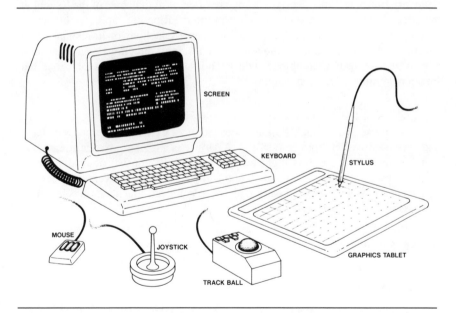

The Elements of CAL

The key factor in determining the efficiency of an input device is how accurately the learner can position the cursor. This is classed as *fine* or *coarse*. The trade-off is often money for quality. The space bar or special function keys on a keyboard are the cheapest and least efficient means of positioning the cursor (assuming your minimum purchase will include a keyboard). There are many different input devices available, ranging from $20.00 to several thousand dollars. The devices listed here are some of the standard types which you may want to experiment with. Each device is available in a wide range of quality and price.

PADDLES AND JOYSTICKS

A paddle is a small device which allows the cursor to be moved in two directions: up and down, or left and right. Thus, in order to have the full rage of movement, you require two paddles per terminal. Most micro-computers can be easily modified to accept the addition of paddles.

The learner moves the paddle, which is either hand-held or sitting on any surface, and the cursor moves in a relative way across the screen. Use of a paddle requires practice to develop the necessary hand-eye coordination.

Paddles allow coarse to fine cursor positioning, they are simple to use, relatively sturdy and inexpensive. They are often used in games of the "shoot at the target" variety. They are not useful in the creation of graphics, but can be used by learners to position the cursor for menu selection, or in response to a question. A joystick allows movement in all four directions – an important advantage. A joystick combined with keyboard is the start of a laborious but functional graphics creation system.

MOUSE AND BALL

A Mouse and a Track Ball are both attempts to make the process of hand and eye coordination more convenient. A Mouse is a match-box size square box with buttons; a Track Ball is slightly larger and usually consists of a ball in some kind of a frame. The device is rolled along any surface and movement is echoed by the cursor. When a desired pattern has been achieved, the position is recorded by pressing a button on the device.

Both of these devices are rugged and convenient to use, as long as a flat surface is available. They are currently more expensive than paddles or joysticks.

GRAPHICS TABLET

A graphics tablet consists of two parts: the tablet surface and the stylus. The tablet consists of a menu of items such as color *graphics primitives* (shapes such as circle, arc or line); and a drawing surface which corresponds to the screen. The stylus is moved across the electrostatically charged tablet. When a coordinate for a desired shape has been reached, a button on the stylus is pressed and the image is accepted.

Because a graphics tablet most closely resembles the action of free-hand drawing on paper, it is to date one of the most flexible methods of creating graphic images. It is also the most expensive. Cursor positioning with a graphics tablet can be quite coarse if the learner is inexperienced. Because of this, and because of the high cost, and relative fragility, a graphics tablet is not a good choice as a learner input device for most CAL.

LIGHT PEN AND TOUCH SCREEN

A light pen and a touch screen are both attempts to allow the learner to interact directly with the screen. A light pen is a special pen with a photo sensitive diode on the tip which can be used to pinpoint a specific area on a screen. A touch screen is a screen with a "mesh" (usually of light) across the surface. Any object (a pencil, or a finger, for example) can be used to point to a section of the screen. The point at which the mesh is interrupted is recorded. If a terminal does not already have a light pen, modification is usually complex and expensive. Commercial touch screens are expensive, but they can also be used with a keyboard in the normal fashion.

Both of these input devices are useful for CAL designed to meet the needs of learners not able to use a keyboard. Younger learners can "point" to pictures or words on the screen. Unfortunately, neither of these devices are precisely accurate, and this can create many problems for both the learner and the author. A learner may point very closely to the correct object, but not closely enough to have the response accepted. This means that a large "correct" area must surround each item and fewer items can be displayed on the screen. Because the cursor location is very coarse, this device is not a useful alternative for learners handicapped by motor-coordination problems.

KEYPAD

A *keypad* is a small set of special function keys in a hand-held device which resembles a calculator. A keypad will contain numbers 0-9 and any special function keys needed for its specific use. Keypads are often used for games, or page-turning information systems such as Telidon, where the only learner input required is a selection from a very limited number of choices.

A keypad may contain keys which allow the learner to position the cursor, but only if this ability is required in the application.

The Elements of CAL

VOICE RECOGNITION

Computers that are able to understand the spoken word exist, but such devices are in an early stage of development. Simple one-person voice recognition is available in a micro. The learner must spend time "training" the computer to recognize command words. For example, a micro capable of recognizing the words "up", "down", "left" and "right" would allow a learner to position the cursor with verbal commands only. The vocabulary is limited, however, and such a system is not useful for a micro that will be used by several different learners.

Considerable research time and money is being spent on developing voice recognition for more than one user, but such devices are still quite expensive and not practical for most CAL applications.

INPUT FOR SPECIAL EDUCATION

Physically and mentally handicapped learners have special input needs which must be considered. CAL has great potential for developing the individualized instruction which is needed for learners with these types of difficulties. However, use of a standard keyboard for input makes a good proportion of courseware inaccessible to handicapped learners.

A variety of devices to meet the special physical needs of learners or the needs of a specific course have been developed at research institutes such as the National Research Council's Medical Electronic Section (Canada). A recessed keyboard, for example, allows the learner to move across the surface of the keyboard without accidently hitting the wrong key. Head and foot operated switches, and a pneumatic control which allows the learner to input by sucking or blowing on a mouthpiece are just some of the other devices which may be of use to physically handicapped learners. Special *concept* keyboards which replace standard characters with pictures have been used in courses for mentally retarded learners. [Hallworth and Brebner]

Output Variations

PRINTERS AND PLOTTERS

Printers are by far the most useful output device after screens. Printers come in a range of quality and price. Even the poorest quality printer is useful with almost any type of CAL.

Printers are used to get *hard copy* of any of the data stored in the computer. Learners can use printers to obtain copies of examples, questions, test results, charts, graphs or pictures. The learner or the author can use the printer to generate hard-copy quizzes or tests to be answered on or off-line; or to generate

5 Presentation

copies of the data to act as text books. The author can use the printer to get copies of learner records, check the data, or get copies of learner work such as essays which must be seen by the instructor.

There are two main types of printers. A dot matrix printer creates each letter out of a series of dots. Such a printer is fast. It can print out graphics (quality varies) and readable, but not attractive text. An impact printer works the same way a typewriter works: a plastic or metal key, on a ball or daisy wheel, strikes a ribbon which prints onto the paper. Impact printers produce better quality text, but tend to be slower than a dot matrix printer and are not useful for graphics. A third type of printer squirts jets of ink directly onto the paper. Color is available in dot matrix printers and ink jet printers. *Plotters* use a pen, or group of pens (one color or several) to draw lines on the paper. Current minimum price for a reasonable text printer is $800; minimum price for a printer which prints acceptable graphics is approximately $2,500.

BELLS, WHISTLES AND BEEPS

The addition of sound to CAL suggests exciting possibilities for all learners. Language courses and CAL for the blind are the two which usually come immediately to mind. There is also evidence that both learning and retention are improved for any lesson when the learner is reinforced both visually and aurally. Of course, a machine which can talk is a definite adavantage for learners who cannot read, or cannot read well. You may want to try sound for correcting serious continuing errors, or for reinforcement. Some learners find games of the "shoot-at-the-target" variety more enjoyable with the addition of explosion-like sounds.

There are two ways of outputting sound. A series of messages or sounds can be recorded on a tape or cassette which is connected to the computer. The program simply gives the instruction to play message X as feedback to response Y. Because the messages must be accessed in a sequential fashion, response is often slow.

Sounds can also be generated electronically by writing programs to control a speaker in the terminal. Most micros have this ability, but the range is usually limited to non-verbal whistles, beeps, "explosions" or "music". Some more sophisticated devices have certain words programmed in that they can generate. Market demand for such devices is likely to rapidly lower the prices.

Sound has one serious disadvantage. As described in this chapter, under voice recognition, it is difficult to have the learner speak back, the natural response to a verbal message. For classroom use, the addition of a cassette is one more piece of equipment to coordinate, and the noise may disturb other learners not using the course.

The Elements of CAL

SLIDES & VIDEO

Computer-controlled slides or video presentations open up a quick and easy way to provide visual stimulation without spending hours creating graphics. The equipment is comparatively expensive, but perhaps worth the cost for subjects such as art history where teaching is difficult, if not impossible, without reproductions of the originals. Again, costs should continue to fall.

Courses designed to take advantage of slide presentation must work within the limits imposed by an eighty-slide carrousel. With videotape, it is difficult to identify a specific still frame. Both output devices suffer from working best in a sequential access method and can have slow response time. The addition of the presentation equipment to a terminal can result in a site which requires a mechanical genius to set up and keep running. A fairly large budget would be required to make several such work stations available at once.

Careful instructional design is necessary to coordinate the visuals with the text. The text presented on the text screen must keep reminding the learner to look at the visuals. Physical arrangements also become complicated. A straight side-by-side arrangement of screens does not work because the learner must be able to keep both screens in view, while comfortably concentrating on one. One expensive solution, the PLATO terminal, allows you to combine screen action and slides by projecting images onto the back of the screen.

VIDEODISC

Videodisc is a new technology which promises to expand the borders of CAL. Although videodisc is most distinctive because of its output possibilities, it is also a different kind of storage medium. A videodisc resembles a record. When it is played, the learner receives color pictures (either moving or still), text, and sound. Unlike videotape, access to the frames on a videodisc need not be sequential.

A videodisc player can be controlled manually. The learner can start and stop, or select a spot on the disc by referring to frame numbers. What makes videodisc exciting for CAL is that the videodisc player hooked up to a microcomputer creates a multi-media terminal without all the timing and interface problems which occur when tapes, cassettes and projectors are added to a site. In some cases only the videodisc display will be required, in other cases a terminal screen will be needed for text. Any input device can be used to interact with the course.

The current problem with videodisc is the time and expensive equipment required to create the master disc. Although copies of the disc may sell inexpensively, current estimates suggest that it costs $1,000 to $10,000 to create a

5 Presentation

minute of videodisc material. (Twenty minutes of videodisc can represent 6-12 hours of instruction.) [Kearsley, *Videodisc in Education*] As Kearsley suggests, this means videodisc is currently most suited to CAL with a wide audience and unchanging content. Because of this, several large training projects. are currently exploring the use of videodisc. [Ibid.]

PUTTING IT ALL TOGETHER

Quite a choice. By all means experiment with any gadgets which take your fancy, any screen design which might meet the needs of your course. But for any actual implementation, keep it as simple as possible. Go back to your goals. Examine your target learner and your objectives. Will fancier dispays or special devices help the learner learn? If not, leave them out.

6 Tracking

ONE	Definitional Layer
TWO	Local Structures
THREE	Presentation
FOUR	**Tracking**
FIVE	Mapping
SIX	Student Support Structures
SEVEN	Author Support Structures
EIGHT	Site Implementation
NINE	Network Implementation

INTRODUCTION

One of the major differences between mainframe and micro implementations falls under the heading of tracking: a general term for the recording of data about the learning process as it takes place.

From the learners' point of view, self-selection of material, of pathways and of learning environment is the key to CAL. For the instructors, tracking is equally important.

No matter how well prepared we are as instructors, how quickly we return tests, how perceptive we are about learning differences, we seldom are able to obtain and maintain detailed statistics about what is going on in the classroom.

CAL is different from many other computer activities in that the tracking or recording component is often more important and far more extensive than the actual teaching program. A simple course with clever algorithms (as we will see in Chapter Fourteen), can be stored on a single diskette. However, if we put one hundred students through such a course and gather all the useful data about their response time, their complaints, their queries, their wrong answers, etc., we may easily end up with another 100 diskettes full of data generated during the learning sessions.

The Elements of CAL

At the moment, on most 8-bit micros, this full level of tracking is not a practical possibility. Nonetheless, there are two good reasons for spending some time on the principles and practice of tracking.

Even with limited storage, some elements of tracking can be implemented. Also, specific variations of the course can be created to record any chosen set of factors. If you suspect, for example, that a given question is causing trouble for some students, you can implement a program variation to watch over student reactions to that portion of the course.

In addition, with the development of faster and more useful integrated circuits continuing, the sub-systems for full-scale tracking should be available at reasonable cost ($5,000) between 1983 and 1986. One particular development, the Intel 86/440, acts as a relational database machine, which in CAL terms could mean a great simplification of the tracking portions of courseware as well as of the data entry and editing processes.

When such machines are common and reasonably priced, the main difference between low-end and high-end CAL practices will disappear. In the TIC-CIT multi-user CAL system as now implemented and marketed by Hazeltine, for example, one CPU is utilized primarily for recording data while a second CPU organizes and presents the actual course.

THE ROLES OF TRACKING

One way to begin looking at tracking methods is to consider what you would do if you had two or three assistants who were designated as observers. They could not teach directly, but they could report to you (confidentially) on how you taught.

Registration

At first, you might assign them fairly menial tasks, such as registration. This is simple and straightforward on larger machines. You might have 100 students in four classes and keep track of their usage on a weekly basis. At registration time also, you could provide different entry parameters for different individuals or classes. Perhaps you might decide that some classes should follow a stricter set of pathways through the material. All large systems provide extensive registration data as a base for organizing other forms of student data.

Grading and Progress Tracking

Registration processes then merge into grading or progress reports. The simplest form of progress tracking is pass/fail. A set of objectives is defined and the mastery criteria established. With 100 students, you might want nothing more than a single milestone with exceptions passed on to the instructors.

Alternatively, the individual could be compared against groups of learners, both current and historical. But, pass/fail is a fairly wide measure and in good CAL all students eventually pass unless they drop out. Patience, after all, is the machine's chief virtue.

Ideally, you want to record the rate and nature of each learner's mastery of each single objective. Here, the free assistants become invaluable. They can time the learners' response. They can check and record wrong answers. They can keep track of "close" answers. When these figures are compared against standard results, you will be able to quickly isolate student learning problems. Tutorial or lecture help can then be applied accurately according to verified need not simply out of some habitual pattern.

Progress and Content Analysis

At a certain point in the tracking process, the boundary line between progress and content analysis is crossed.

If one student takes three times as long as usual to master a rule or group of rules, then that student clearly needs extra help with that portion of the course. Recording this problem is progress analysis.

If most students take much longer, then perhaps there is something wrong with that portion of the content and presentation. Storing similar data on many students as they face the same problem is the first step towards content analysis. Tracking may clearly indicate that you have some problems as an author, and so become a useful component of the analysis and editing cycle.

What is the solution? If the tracking layer is well-implemented, there are a number of steps you can take before making changes. Compare the different tracking records. Perhaps the problem is in the presentation or range of the examples. Perhaps it is the wrong local structure, or the wrong combination of local structures. Perhaps it is a lack of structural refinement: too many compressed steps or some missing links. Talk to the students. Have a joint discussion with learners who are benefiting from the course and those who are not. Once the problem is cleared up, then further tracking should demonstrate the success of the analysis and the remedy.

Comments

Equally useful are the comment or complaint mechanisms described in Chapter Eight. Make sure there is a real author or instructor to take care of the complaints, however. The silicon assistants are not too good at solving these complaints.

The tracking layer must ensure that comments are seen by all relevant instructors and authors. You will need a general methodology to record, organize and make available comments on individual courses, and related sets of courses.

The Elements of CAL

All of the student support structures described in Chapter Eight can be tracked, not only within individual courses but across sets of related courses or versions of courses. Which of the student support structures are accessed most often? What effect does their presence have on student acceptance of the course? What effects does it have on student accomplishment? These kinds of questions cannot be answered without collecting some numeric data as the course is being used.

Pathways

More difficult to utilize, perhaps, are statistics about pathways. On large machines whole teams of assistants could be utilized analyzing the various ways that students move through courses and how that affects their progress. This analysis could be used to identify individual learning styles. Some pathways that learners choose may indicate a preference for graphics over verbal explanations, some a desire for full mastery, some a fondness for taking risks, for getting in over their head. This is, in the long term, more useful information for both the learner and the instructor than mere tests of mastery of various subjects.

THE GRADING AND DESCRIPTIVE MODELS
Why Bother with Tracking?

As pointed out in Chapter Four, studies to date do not indicate that there is really a best structure or pattern for CAL. Using tracking to find or validate the *best* structure may be a wasted effort. However, results from the tracking layer of good courseware, if used co-operatively by learner and author, can can help a learner see that there is something very individual about how he or she prefers to learn and whether or not the preferred ways are the most effective ways.

Some feel that this step into epistemology is the most important stage in learning development. In *Mindstorms,* Seymour Papert points out that giving children the opportunity to choose between alternate styles of thinking provides them with the opportunity to serve their apprenticeships as epistemologists, that is to say they "learn to think articulately about thinking." [Papert].

It is not only children who can benefit from the opportunities to learn about learning. Until you identify how you learn, each learning task is a whole new problem, both of method and content. Being able to observe the results of the tracking layer of good CAL courseware gives learners confidence: they know how to learn, whatever their degree of mastery of the subject.

Tracking is the major tool by which courseware can be improved in both the technical and a humanistic sense. It can put a certain objective distance between the teacher and his or her ways of organizing and presenting materials Although it may be simpler to begin with what we term the grading model, the descriptive model, which insists on learner participation, is more fruitful.

6 Tracking

The Grading Model

One way to look at tracking is by considering the purposes and processes of grading. This is a well established practice with its own methods and standards. Its role is to indicate errors to the student and to provide some kind of a relative ranking. Computers can facilitate that process as long as you are dealing with clear objectives.

This approach leads you to consider the following items as part of a standard tracking report:

Student: James James
Class: Group 5.

Objective: Rules W, X, Y, Z

Rule: W

Sessions: 2
Examples viewed: 3
Test practiced: twice
Test results: mastered in 5 tries.
Test pattern: unrecognized, right, wrong, right, right.
Wrong answer =: thorny
Unrecognized =: firetree

Response times:
Examples: on screen for average of 35 seconds.
Practice time: 240 seconds.
Try 1: 32 seconds.
Try 2: 15 seconds.
Try 3: 40 seconds.
Try 4. 18 seconds.
Try 5. 12 seconds.

Time to mastery for Rule W: 427 seconds.

Comparative times for Objective:

W: 427 seconds.
X: 360 seconds
Y: 668 seconds
Z: 220 seconds.

The Elements of CAL

A Descriptive Model

In general, there is little reason to direct this information to the instructor if the learners are fully participating. The grading portion of CAL is usually done instantly and ought to be directed to the learner at appropriate moments. Some of this information may need to be collected for the author, but the author requires a somewhat different view of it.

Course Analysis

Objective: Rules W, X, Y, Z

Period: xx to yy

Total accesses: 487
Average time to mastery: 1400 seconds.
Average time by rule:

    W: 380
    X: 220
    Y: 580
    Z: 220

Detail by Rule:
For comments, see File: WXYZ.33
For common unrecognized, see File: WXYZ.34
For wrongs, see File: WXYZ.35

Obviously, these reports could be quite extensive and still somewhat mechanical. You can track the pathways by student and by class and compare those against performance results. You can track wrong and unrecognized responses by rule, by segment, by student and by class and look for patterns that might identify learner difficulties or faulty course design.

In the descriptive model, however, these possibilities should be presented to the learner and it is the learner who should decide on the tracking pattern most useful or probably useful if they are to meet their goals and objectives as quickly as possible. Remember, you are dealing with individuals. All of this raw information belongs to certain individuals. Who else has more right to see it and use it?

7 Mapping

ONE	Definitional Layer
TWO	Local Structures
THREE	Presentation
FOUR	Tracking
FIVE	**Mapping**
SIX	Student Support Structures
SEVEN	Author Support Structures
EIGHT	Site Implementation
NINE	Network Implementation

Introduction

Mapping is a term that we have developed to deal with the various ways that local structures, support structures and course segments can be organized. Such organization can be quite simple; local structures might be considered as the natural elements of the mapping layer. At the other extreme, the organization of segments, options, prerequisites, class and individual variables can become almost overwhelmingly complex.

This chapter provides an introduction to mapping rather than a systematic set of definitions and procedures, since most course authors using this book will not yet possess the hardware and experience that makes mapping one of the main development areas for professional CAL teams. Even among such teams, mapping must still be considered as more of an art than a science.

Segments

In order to arrange the local structures into a course map, it is often necessary to add another layer of organization: the *segment*. We have used the term "segment" to refer to as much of what is intermediate between local structure and course as is possible.

The Elements of CAL

A segment of a course can be a logical group of rules which may be dealt with via different structures. (See the sample course WORDS in Chapter Twelve.) Or, a segment may be the implementation of a strategy (i.e. simulation, testing, adaptive tutorial, drill) covering a number of rules which may or may not be closely related.

For example, a course in language arts may have been implemented on a fairly large machine. A segment of that course may deal with the rules related to descriptive grammar and another segment with those related to generative grammar. Each segment may contain several objectives presented via several different local structures.

Conversely, a segment of the course may be seen as language arts simulations, or as entrance tests, or graduation tests. The simulations might demonstrate and query sentence construction drawing on either descriptive or generative models. The tests might simply allow the learner to demonstrate that she has a given degree of mastery of certain rules of punctuation, grammar and logic deemed appropriate for her grade level.

One instructor may want to map the course in such a way that punctuation comes after grammar and generative grammar is handled before descriptive grammar. Another instructor may decide to let learners choose their own pathways, but to require them to master all materials designated as Grade Eight level or lower before moving on to the Grade Nine and above materials.

A third instructor may have some different pathways and in addition want some special support structures to be available even during tests. A fourth may not believe in grade levels and wish to have all references to them removed.

Within bounds, the mapping layer permits such variations to be described in advance. If this is done, the earlier definitional layers and much of the implementation coding need not be redone simply to handle such variations.

Mapping and Languages

One of the major advantages procedural languages (such as PASCAL, C, NATAL and ADA) have over languages such as BASIC is that they facilitate extensive mapping. You should be careful, however, not to let your current language of choice or available hardware unduly influence your desired mapping patterns. Extensive maps may be described at this layer, but not all mapping patterns need to be implemented immediately. If local structures are well designed and self-contained, they can be linked together in later implementations.

7 Mapping

Mapping and Hardware

As with tracking, mapping tends to mark a boundary between CAL on 8-bit micros and CAL on larger machines. The main constraint found in low-range machines is lack of main and secondary storage. As a result, mapping tends to consist of a physical map or list of where all the relevant (and current) diskettes are (or should be) located. Our example courses make little reference to mapping.

However, even a simple 20 megabyte hard disk shared among a number of micros begins to overcome the limitations of the Apple or PET in this regard. The merging of micro and mainframe CAL programming styles has already begun and will continue as the availability of low cost storage hardware adds the possibility of mapping and tracking to lower-range machines.

Designing the Maps

In order to introduce the theory of mapping, a continuum might be established by examining a very simple problem and a very complex one.

THE SIMPLE MAP

Let us assume that your personal methods include a good deal of graphic explanation of concepts via the handy technology of the blackboard or overheads. Your first computer is a PET and you produce some good drill materials on, let us say, learning French verb patterns.

You face a certain amount of frustration with the black and white screen and the limited, stick-figure graphics available. However, somewhat to your surprise, you find that a certain amount of learning does go on and you are relieved of some of the rote teaching. In fact, certain learners seem to do better with straight textual explanations and repetitive drill and practice.

Then, you move up, perhaps to a Commodore 64 (made by the same firm) and suddenly have Sprite graphics, color and a built-in music synthesizer as a substitute for your chalk and Staedler pens. In a few frenzied weeks you have tossed out the old version of the course and created a new one, with, let us say, "dynamic" parsing of verbs so that the learner can watch a given infinitive "move" through its transformations in eight living colors. Many of your rules, definitions and examples can now be cut down a good deal since the main explanation is done through these graphic enhancements.

As you expected (or hoped), many learners love the new feature. Some, however, perversely prefer the former version. Why not experiment, you say, and putting a selection module at the front, you allow learners to choose the older, "long-winded" textual explanations or the newer graphic version.

The Elements of CAL

This, at a very basic level, is mapping, the organization of segments and options within a course.

THE COMPLEX MAP

At the other extreme, let us imagine that you teach in an ideal school where CAL has been running for ten years on very flexible powerful machines and a benevolent administration has allowed you to purchase and create large amounts of compatible, portable and functional courseware. For any given set of objectives, let us say, again, those represented by mastery of irregular French verbs, you have a large variety of courseware segments and local structures representing a range of methods, presentation modes, etc.

Together with the learner, you can sit down in front of an interactive terminal and "construct" a course by linking together various segments or local structures. The learner can help create the "map" of her course, deciding where to be restrictive and where to be open, when to choose graphic modes and when textual, where to place the tests, which kinds of tests she prefers and which are to be avoided. This is mapping at a somewhat higher level.

Such systems do not, and may in fact never, exist, but the concept illustrates one polarity of mapping. The learner, the instructor, the author, and the architect all have different mapping needs and it is important that these be kept separate. In the above example, the learner makes many of the mapping decisions ordinarily made by the instructor or author.

At the same time, even within the "free-form" mapping represented by our example, the instructor may want to insist that every learner master a given core of irregular verbs or have demonstrated a mastery of regular verbs before moving on to irregular verbs. Conversely, the instructor may want to compare the results of learners who began with regular and moved to irregular with the results of those who worked in the opposite pattern.

Mapping and Tracking

In the example above, the learner may have selected courseware from a number of authors. Wherever possible, each author wants tracking records kept so that the the courseware design can be improved. In a dynamic course creation mode, however, certain tracking records might not remain valid. A systematic and "engineered" approach to courseware creation thus becomes very important. Even in our dynamic creation example, it ought to be possible to provide each author with some records of each learner's activity: ratio of rights to wrongs, time elapsed, ratio of rules to examples to tests, etc. However, records that depend on static mapping constructions within the original course may no longer be valid. If the author wants comparison results of a "selected" module versus a module our learner has not selected, then the author is going to be out of luck this time.

7 Mapping

In such an ideal situation, the role of the architect, as defined in Chapter Eleven, becomes quite important in insuring that each specific methodology fits within the general framework of CAL implemented at the given site. Activity outputs should be classified and all generated data should be properly typed so that the various authors and instructors can retain the maximum analytic data no matter how the components are mapped together by individual authors, instructors or learners.

Mapping and Course Design

In general, most situations fall between the extremes and are closer to the simpler patterns. The specification of a mapping layer for all courses may appear superfluous, but even in its simpler forms this layer of description often solves arguments by demonstrating that conflicting choices can be handled as courseware options. Many courses can be written with a "variable" map structure and then various "closed" maps can be added to the program if and when desired.

Thinking about maps helps keep the author from creating complex courses in which the learners easily get lost. If they can get lost, then the author should provide some representation of the "map" of the course on the display unit at all times, with greater "depth" available as required.

Complexity and variety are cousins. Variety keeps courseware interesting for the learner, but when the map is too complex to summarize, you probably have a good indication that your course is too large and should have some of its segments turned into courses on their own.

Mapping and Course Portability

In its simple or in its more complex forms, the mapping layer should encourage the development of courseware that is friendlier and far more personal in the eyes of the various instructors.

There are two major reasons that so much potentially useful courseware is deemed unacceptable by instructors other than the author. The first can usually be traced to certain rules or examples or phrasings that offend the instructor for one reason or another. Proper separation of data and control code, and the availability of good editing facilities to amend the data ought to greatly reduce this problem.

The second is displeasure with the way the course is mapped out. Provided that the mapping layer is properly described and the code well-documented, a version of the courseware with revised maps ought to be far quicker to implement than would a re-invention of the entire piece of courseware from scratch.

8 Student Support Structures

ONE	Definitional Layer
TWO	Local Structures
THREE	Presentation
FOUR	Tracking
FIVE	Mapping
SIX	**Student Support Structures**
SEVEN	Author Support Structures
EIGHT	Site Implementation
NINE	Network Implementation

In designing your course you will have to make decisions about rules the learner must master for each objective, the number and combination of examples likely to be required, and the types of tests which will tell you and the learner if he or she has reached the objective. The local structures reflect your decisions on teaching strategies, and the mapping has been designed to most efficiently and creatively move the learner through the course. The course may offer a selection of methods for learning the same set of rules, or the method may be totally pre-structured. Everything will be designed to meet the needs of the target learner.

Now think of the learner who is a little off target. Although still part of the target group, this learner may have problems with parts of the course material because background skills are weak. For example, the learner cannot meet the objectives in a course on adding fractions because he or she cannot add whole numbers. In a history course, the learner may understand early Ontario history quite well, but the examples occasionally contain unfamiliar words. Or, the learner may understand the course material perfectly, but have problems with the mechanics of running a CAL course (cannot find the return key, does not know how to operate a multiple choice question). Often, a CAL course will be useful in identifying and classifying learner problems. A good CAL course will anticipate the slightly off target learner and develop *support structures* to give the learner extra help when required.

The Elements of CAL

Support structures are those aspects of the course which do not directly lead to the achievement of an objective. Therefore, in a course on adding fractions, extra drill on adding fractions is a local structure. Drill on adding whole numbers could be a support structure designed to help learners with basic addition problems. In a course on addition, both addition of whole numbers and addition of fractions may be local structures. Thus, a structure which is a support structure in one course may be an important local structure in another course.

Support structures are created with the same building blocks (rule, example, question) and same basic patterns (drill, test, tutorial, inquiry, and [rarely] simulation) as local structures (see Chapter Four, "Local Structures"). In the fractions example, it is likely the piece of code that runs the whole number drill will also run the fraction drill.

TYPES OF SUPPORT STRUCTURES

The following suggestions are just that. Invent any type of support structure which meets the needs of your target and off-target learner. Keep in mind that although support structures are secondary to local structures, they must be important, often-accessed additions to the course. They require as much attention in design as other aspects of the course, particularly because a learner accessing a support structure is likely to be having problems with the course. Each of the following support structures is defined according to the need it serves in a course.

Reference

This type of a support structure allows the learner to look up extra or background information which he or she may need to understand the course. It may also be a quick reference for facts which the learner is not expected to memorize. Examples of a reference type of support structure include: a general dictionary to look up meanings of words, glossaries of terms or acronyms designed to specifically meet the needs of the course, tables such as a periodic chart or average rainfall statistics. Although you must be careful that no important rules are only available in the support structure, it may contain a summary of the course material, or important aspects of the material.

A reference support structure is based on an inquiry local structure pattern and is learner controlled. This type of support structure is very simple to construct and extremely useful for all learners. Learners having problems can get help from the reference structure, other learners can use the information in it for enrichment. You may find it useful to have several different types of reference support structures in the same course (a glossary and a periodic chart, for example).

8 Student Support Structures

Help

We reserve this expression for the part of the course which provides information to the learner about the mechanics of the course. To a certain degree, the complexity of the course will determine the complexity of the help structure. As a general rule, help should be available at every level of the course.

All CAL courses must have some sort of assistance to the lost learner. You may be limited to a simple message such as, "Sorry you don't understand me. Why don't you quit and talk to the instructor?" Spend time on your help sequence and obtain learner feedback to make it more efficient. You may decide to display a map showing current location and choices available. Often, all that is required is a careful explanation of the available choices.

Help should also provide assistance for learners who do not understand how to handle a particular type of test or drill question. In this case, help may move the learner into a diagnostic support structure, or a remedial support structure (both described below).

Comment

It's so frustrating – you just can't reason with a machine. – Angry Learner.

Learners need to feel that they are dealing with a responsive intelligence, not an unreasoning and dogmatic machine. Yet, once the author has identified "2" as the correct answer to $1+1$, the program will only accept "2" as the correct answer. In most cases, the author has designed the feedback to explain the source of error and the learner will continue wiser in the subject matter. Sometimes the learner will not feel satisfied, and insist the answer to $1+1$ would be 3, if only the computer understood the laws of X. A comment support structure allows the learner to leave a message for the author or instructor.

In addition, comment can be one of the most valuable tools in course maintenance. You may think you have explained a particular rule in concise and easy-to-understand prose. In the first week of use, however, every learner "comments" that he or she doesn't understand the rule. You have received valuable information about the course and the learner has been given an outlet for frustration.

A comment support structure is a variation of the inquiry local structure pattern. Instead of looking for a match to a learner's input, comment receives and stores the input in a way that makes it simple for the instructor to read the comments and relate the comment to a specific rule, example or question.

Make it easy for the learner to enter the comment and, if possible, allow him or her to amend comments. Give positive reinforcement and an indication of what action will be taken and when to expect the action to take place. This may be simply, "Thank you for commenting. The Maintenance Author will look into the problem." Devise some way to respond to each comment: an on-line mail message, messages when the learner enters the course, or a hard copy memo sent to the learner.

Another exciting possibility is to allow the learners to see each other's comments. For example, a passage discussing capital punishment may be followed by something like: "I disagree. What about case X. Mary S." In this way, each learner contributes directly to the course, and the computer becomes a pathway to learner-learner interaction. Of course, you may want to edit learner comments to decide which will appear in the course. In a classroom, you may want to assign groups of students to act as editors.

Diagnosis

Your course may be structured so that a designated number of wrong answers to certain questions will quickly point out the learner's area of weakness. This is likely if you have a complex drill structure, almost certain if you are using a tutorial method. Some courses will not do this, however, or the source of error is not one which can be identified by the local structures. Consider designing a support structure to diagnose student problems. The need for diagnosis may be learner controlled or determined by the learner's error pattern.

The diagnostic sequence will only be able to identify the types of problems you suspect in advance that a learner might have. For example, you might suspect a learner in grade four may have trouble adding, which would effect his or her ability to add fractions. A few sample addition questions would identify that kind of a problem. But what if the learner can add, but still can not add fractions? What next? You will probably need a tutorial type of sequence to identify any complex problems. It is easy to see that diagnosis, as a support structure, could become several times more complex than the course. Be careful. Only use it if you know what kinds of problems you are looking for. Diagnosis is, however, very useful for determining if a student's errors are based on not understanding the rules, or not understanding the mechanics of the question.

The learner must be left with specific instructions at the end of a diagnostic session. A prompt message might suggest the learner change objectives or access a support structure such as help or glossary. You may move the learner into another local structure, or a remediation sequence. Whatever you do, be careful that the learner understands what is happening, and how it all relates to the objective.

8 Student Support Structures

Remediation

Here is where the line between support structures and local structures can grow faint if you are not careful. Remediation takes the form of drill or tutorial on rules which are not part of the learner's current objective. So far so simple. But what if the rules the student needs remediation in are part of the objective of another local structure in the course? Then the student should be told to "back up" in the course and move to a different local structure. If most learners end up back-tracking, consider re-defining the pathways for your course.

Remediation sequences must be short and specific or the learner will loose sight of the objective. A remediation sequence will often be the result of a diagnostic sequence. If all of the learners need considerable remediation in your course, re-examine your definition of the target learner and reconsider your objectives.

ACCESSING THE SUPPORT STRUCTURES

Our tendency is "All structures available to all learners at all times." That is, "help", "glossary", "comment", etc, are available to all learners at any time in the course. After accesssing a support structure, the learner is returned to the point in the course from which the structure was accessed. This access to additional information encourages the learner to learn as much as he or she wants to learn, or is capable of learning. It often leads to learners discovering new areas of interest.

We find the best way to keep the learner moving toward the objective, but aware of the options which are available, is a combination of menus and choice bars (described in Chapter Five). Support structure options are displayed in the Choice Bar, while other pathway choices are displayed in a menu. Because the choices on the choice bar are consistent, they quickly become familiar to the learner.

Nevertheless, it is important to talk about the exceptions. You may decide that certain structures will only become available once a learner has mastered a certain set of rules. For example, you may want the student to learn the meanings of certain words, and demonstrate mastery by passing a test, before allowing the glossary to become available. In this way you can help insure that the glossary is an occasional support, not a permanent crutch for important core rules.

You may want to remove certain support structure options during a test. This is in keeping with the traditional methods used to curtail cheating. In individualized instruction, however, what is to stop the learner from having a hard copy of all the information at hand? Can you justify such a restriction, in terms of the goals and objectives? Consider other ways of describing learner performance, such as time to respond, number of accesses to support structures, etc. (This is covered in more detail in Chapter Seven, "Tracking".)

The Elements of CAL

Consider All the Resources

All your support structures need not be accessed via the computer. In fact, some experts suggest that the interaction of CAL and standard learning support structures such as books, conversation, and other media greatly enhances the effectiveness of the CAL. [Howe and Ross, CAL81 Symposium] You will have already identified your goal, and the aspects of it you believe can be reached using CAL. Stick to your decision and take advantage of the interplay between CAL and non-CAL learning materials.

For example, the course might provide each learner with a hard copy of a series of questions for off-line research, then a series of CAL practice drills, simulations or tests based on the researched material.

Remember the Map

Make sure the learner understands when he or she is in a support structure, what is supposed to happen while there, how to get out, and where he or she will be when the support sequence is finished. Design support structures into the course. Don't tack them on as an after-thought.

9 Author Support Structures

ONE	Definitional Layer
TWO	Local Structures
THREE	Presentation
FOUR	Tracking
FIVE	Mapping
SIX	Student Support Structures
SEVEN	**Author Support Structures**
EIGHT	Site Implementation
NINE	Network Implementation

INTRODUCTION

Authors and Instructors

Many successful courses are created by an experienced author or team and them put into action by other teachers or trainers in addition to the original creators. All involved, however, have a direct role in the maintenance and improvement of the courseware.

A distinction between author and instructor is useful for such courseware. An instructor, in this sense, is a teacher or trainer who utilizes a course as part of the teaching cycle, and may contribute directly to its improvement, but is not involved in the role of an author.

With most low-range machine courseware, the same individual often plays the role of author and instructor or simply uses a purchased piece of software without contributing to the maintenance cycle in any way. From mid-range machines on up, however, the author/instructor distinction may be made and is very necessary if one is to fully describe this layer of IMPS.

The Elements of CAL

Facilitative and Application Software

Software packages can be divided into two classes: facilitative and application. Most familiar software falls into the application category. Examples are: text editors, accounting packages, games and environment analysis packages. These software packages basically perform the same task over and over again. They are the level of software *seen* by the user.

Any given piece of CAL courseware is an application, a course for teaching music skills, for example. The creation of CAL courseware is thus similar to the creation of application packages; and productivity, in terms of software development, has often been demonstrated to be closely tied to the nature of the facilitative tools.

Facilitative tools are those software packages that provide the environment for applications to be created, to be run efficiently, to interact with other applications, and to be amended quickly and accurately. One could be philosophical and say that facilitative tools are the applications used by those who create applications.

In this chapter we describe the tools used in the creation and maintenance of courseware. We also discuss the differences in author support likely to be found when comparing low-range and high-range environments.

In general, it must be noted that CAL tools are almost exactly the same tools that one requires for development of any general application software. The existence of large-scale, CAL-specific systems, such as PLATO, may have created a false distinction in the minds of some, but it is difficult to demonstrate any major differences.

FACILITATIVE SOFTWARE

1. Languages
2. Operating Systems
3. Text Editors
4. Program Editors
5. Formatters
6. Graphics Editors
7. Debuggers
8. Mail
9. SCCS
10. Report Generators
11. PERT
12. DBMS
13. Software Development
14. System Documentation
15. IMPS Support.

1. Languages

The languages you work with are your major facilitative tool. The relationships between languages and courseware development is discussed extensively in Chapters Ten and Eleven.

At first, it may be difficult to look on a language as just a tool, especially if you have just spent six weeks gaining a reasonable degree of mastery over BASIC during your off-hours.

However, after the first stages of your learning curve are complete, say after your first four or five courses are up and running, consider the nature of your chosen language very carefully. Spending $500 and two months work to get beyond BASIC may seem like a waste. What you are unlikely to count up are the hours you spend on each of your applications – your courses. Often, the extra expenditures on buying and mastering a higher level language can be recovered within one or two application developments.

2. Operating System

The next most important facilitative tool is the operating system. What component facilities does it provide access to and how easily does it do its job? How friendly is it? How widely used is it? What is the current rate of development? How many others in your field use it? Does it make available, in a reasonably coherent fashion, all of the tools you are likely to require while creating your courseware?

Some initial answers to these questions are provided in Chapter Eleven, but each individual case is quite different and you must provide your own final answers.

In theory, one of the advantages of dedicated large systems, such as PLATO and TICCIT, is that the operating system is fine-tuned for courseware development and operation. The difficulty with this theory is that system development is the most expensive form of software development. Thus, special purpose operating systems do not *necessarily* benefit from the development momentum of general purpose operating systems such as UNIX. Their user base is too small to attract innovation and they are tied to a given machine. Rarely do they have the flexibility and special features of those general purpose operating systems which have survived in the marketplace long enough to build a large base of users on different brands of machinery.

There are, for example, dozens of text editors for CP/M and at least a dozen excellent relational data base management systems that can be purchased to run under UNIX. We doubt that many entrepreneurs will bother to develop parallel facilities and the same range of choice for PLATO or TICCIT systems.

The Elements of CAL

In some instances, the dividing line between language, operating system, and facilitative tool can be less than distinct. We discuss their relationships at the end of this chapter.

3. Text Editors

Often the most visible facilitative tool is a good full-screen text-editor. As an author, this is the tool that you will spend most time with. We feel there may be some hazy correlation between the quality of the text editor on a system and the suitability of that system for CAL. Good text-editors, like good CAL courses, are designed to make the user contented, productive, and unaware of the underlying machinery.

Luckily, almost all new systems pay careful attention to their text-editor. Avoid the few that do not.

4. Program Editors

A variation of the text editor, available on some systems, is the program editor. This handy tool "knows" the syntax of the selected language. If, for example, you type in **if** then it will add the **then else** and position the cursor so that you can input the content of the **if** command. Large numbers of the most common kinds of input errors are thus avoided.

5. Formatters

One of the ways that CAL connects with non-CAL methods of teaching is through the use of the computer as a printing tool. By separating data and control, IMPS makes it possible to format and print components of your design, data and code.

Such components could include a list of the current objectives for class discussion, a personalized individual list of mastered and open objectives for a learner-instructor session, or a set of test items for an in-class review. Other ideas have been presented in Chapter Five. The original file used to describe the presentation layer of the fractions course for the programmer was quickly incorporated into Chapter Thirteen for typesetting. In fact, this entire book was written, edited and prepared for typesetting using the formatting tools of UNIX.

A good formatting tool makes all printed materials look more professional. Any proper operating system should permit you to prepare your working materials for professional typesetting. For a good read, if you like math and typesetting, try *TEX and METAFONT: New Directions in Typesetting*. [Knuth].

If you are in a position where you must "sell" CAL to your fellow instructors, these kinds of printing facilities often demonstrate the practicality of CAL and help bridge the distance between current methods and CAL methods.

6. Graphics Editors

The creation of graphic images is a necessity for courseware in many disciplines. On low-range systems, there are usually limited facilities for graphics production and the software packages are an extension of the standard language. On larger systems, there may be a full range of tools for making graphics and the results may easily, or not so easily, be incorporated into an application written in a given language.

As is true with database developments, the advantage of portable, widely based operating systems is very important for those who need graphics facilities. The new and more powerful packages and standards coming along in the 1980's are likely to be most quickly incorporated into the most popular operating systems.

7. Debuggers

We recognize that most beginners will probably ignore almost everything we have to say about the importance of all the pre-implementation layers. They will want to start coding immediately. If this is true in your case, then interpreted languages, such as BASIC, have the advantage of showing up language errors on a line by line basis. If you type in a line which contains an error, that line will not work.

Compiled languages, on the other hand, do not demonstrate any errors until you have compiled the program. Both interpreters and compilers must inform you of of run-time errors. The tools that help you find errors are called debuggers.

The quality of debugging facilities in your system is a relatively invisible factor, but a very important one, especially during the early portions of your learning curve. At the beginning, the only way to evaluate these facilities is by seeking advice from people who know a number of languages on a number of systems. With experience, you will develop some expectations about the kind of error checking, response messages, and related tools that you consider minimal, normal and very useful.

8. Mail

On network systems, a mail function is a very important tool within courses. Learners should always be able to send messages to their instructors and to the course author. In practice, it is very useful if they can send mail to one another since this helps make the computer seem less forbidding.

When courseware is being developed on a network, a mail facility is indispensable. This applies to every layer of IMPS since a team will want to stay in constant touch during the design, implementation, and maintenance cycles.

9. SCCS

Some operating systems provide quite sophisticated tools for dealing with different versions of programs. In network implementations, with a number of co-operating authors, a SCCS (Source Code Control System) can rapidly become an indispensable tool.

You may have three functioning but distinct versions of a course. Agreed upon improvements may affect only two of those versions directly, but they have to be at least recorded in the documentation of the third so that later improvements can be made in a consistent fashion to all three versions.

10. Report Generators

Many application packages produce a great deal of output as part of their primary function. CAL is unique in that its major output comes from its reporting functions, as described in the tracking layer.

Implementations on low-range machines tend to have little or no activity at this layer. All other implementations, however, tend to generate a great deal of data about the progress of the learner in the course. If this data is to be useful, it must be easily produced and easily processed.

Whatever the language you select, it ought to be able to gather and produce runtime data in a form that can be easily accessed. Some CAL languages, such as NATAL, contain some of these facilities within the language. In most other cases, the procedures and functions will have to be created as part of a library.

11. PERT

Professional CAL development usually requires some form of critical path planning tool. The team must know about the various components of the course and where each stands in terms of an overall schedule. For most site implementations, these tools are not required. PERT-like packages are available on some micros, however, and it is always useful to compare your planned time to complete each layer against your actual time.

12. DBMS

The major change in terms of tools for authors in this decade is the growing availability of reasonably-priced database management systems (henceforth, DBMS). A DBMS is one large step up from file systems. Good ones allow you to easily store, restructure, retrieve, and massage large amounts of data without having to pay too much attention to the low-level or physical details of storage.

9 Author Support Structures

Their obvious advantages (for course content, for programming complex courseware, for storing the tracking layer data, and for giving new authors access to existing programs, segments, or local structures, and documentation) should not disguise the dangers of selecting an inadequate or over-priced version. Many packages are described as term database management systems but are really only file handlers of very limited sophistication. Others are reasonably powerful but greatly overpriced.

Our own bias is towards relational type systems. One should be able to purchase a very reliable package for less than $5,000 and those prices should tumble rapidly. But buyers beware. For a thorough introduction, see *An Introduction to Database Systems* [Date]; for a good explanation of what is relational and what is not, and the advantages of both, see [*Computerworld* Sept. 82]

13. Software Development Cycle Tools

Also of major potential importance, but a good deal more experimental, are various software development tools which attempt to cover much more of the development cycle than do programming languages. A good introduction is Wasserman's "Software Tools and the User Software Engineering Project." [Riddle, Fairley] See also Osterweil's concise introduction to development methodology and Riddle's work on design modelling in the same text.

14. System Documentation

Although not strictly a tool, documentation about the various portions of the system is extremely important. The best tool in the world is useless if you can not find out how to turn it on and off or how it hooks up to other tools. Especially in network implementations, with many extant versions of a given course, system documentation becomes very important to allow co-authors to modify their versions to fit with local conditions or hardware.

15. IMPS Support

To some extent, IMPS is a special case model of a software development methodology. In theory, it would be possible to write some tools that implemented this model. In practice, there are too many unknowns and variables (and too little money in the field) to encourage development in this direction.

At the level of site implementations, IMPS can be supported very nicely either by pen and paper or by a decent text editor. At the network level, data from the various layers can conveniently be kept in a small hierarchy of files on the system. Even for the largest of existing operations, we find a relational DBMS a more than sufficient tool for organizing the component data of a given course and its implementations.

SYSTEMS, LANGUAGES AND TOOLS

From the point of view of an author, it does not matter where the necessary facilities reside, within the language or within another facilitative package, so long as they are all accessible, easy to learn, inexpensive, robust and well-linked.

From the point of view of a purchaser, the questions are quite complex. Some languages lack facilities that others have, but may be very popular, or be the best choice for the only available piece of hardware, or be well-linked to a necessary facility such as a graphics editor. Until an author gains a good deal of experience, it is difficult to predict the role of the various tools. If you do have purchasing options, it is best to define your ideal set of tools and then compare the real world alternatives against the ideal.

From the point of view of software development in general, some facilities, such as calls to a DBMS, may be added into languages, but most will be created or expanded as part of an orderly "toolbox" for the developer. CAL will probably move in the direction of operating system consistency. That is, CAL languages will not be the crucial factor. Those operating systems that are portable, that are widely used, that have more and more available tools, will likely have CAL languages and related facilities available as part of the system.

In the longer term, it will be easier for an author to work within such a system than to work in a CAL-specific system or in a portable language running under various hardware-dependent operating systems which lack the characteristics indicated above.

Author support structures are extremely important for productivity at the design, implementation and maintenance layers. CAL-specific systems are unlikely to have the market momentum of systems which are designed to provide very similar facilities to the wider community of application developers.

10 Site Implementation

ONE	Definitional Layer
TWO	Local Structures
THREE	Presentation
FOUR	Tracking
FIVE	Mapping
SIX	Student Support Structures
SEVEN	Author Support Structures
EIGHT	**Site Implementation**
NINE	Network Implementation

INTRODUCTION

To some extent, the distinction between site implementation and network implementation is an arbitrary one. Nonetheless, there are a number of technical and psychological factors that make the distinction a very useful one.

This chapter points out those technical and psychological distinctions and then deals with the major factors affecting a simple site implementation. Chapter Eleven deals with the details of network technology, with those factors relating to network implementations, and with the major cost-benefit questions specific to the implementation layer. Chapters Twelve through Fifteen detail examples of site implementations of courses.

What is a Network Implementation?

There are technical definitions of networks and one substantial distinction not ordinarily made. A "real" network is a linked set of computers, each individual computer possibly having its own array of connected terminals. In practice, people tend to term any collection of terminals attached to one host computer a network. Since there is no other term for such a collection of slaved terminals, the semantic confusion will no doubt continue. For the purpose of these two chapters, however, we will assume that a network means a set of linked computers.

By a network implementation, we mean the final preparation of coded courseware for use by learners on a given set of linked computers in a variety of locations and the maintenance of that courseware in some consistent fashion.

What is a Site Implementation

By a site implementation, we mean the final preparation of courseware for use by learners on a given machine in a given physical location and the maintenance of that courseware locally. By definition, that machine might have a number of local or distant terminals attached to it.

At the moment, most courseware is being prepared in site fashion, although various interesting exchange and networking experiments are underway. Most sites also develop their courseware on single user machines.

PSYCHOLOGICAL FACTORS

The possibilities for site implementations on these inexpensive microcomputers is a major cause of the resurgence of CAL. Teachers and trainers tended to be very leery of CAL when it was delivered from a distant source. This wariness did not apply to books or film strips because the teacher could exert a good deal of choice over alternatives. These media forms do not threaten to replace the teacher; they do not model as large a portion of the instructional process as CAL does.

Such psychological factors are just as important, in practical terms, as the logical factors. The theoretical danger is that CAL might end up divided into two mutually destructive camps. On one side, there would be smooth, professional production of highly effective, highly expensive CAL materials — without a market. On the other would be found widely diversified, non-standard, highly localized production of "free" materials, often inadequate to their purposes, which could end up doing a good deal of damage to the image of CAL among the non-committed.

IMPS is designed as a bridging mechanism between these two possibilities, a way of helping to insure widely diversified production of low-cost professional materials. IMPS permits the exchange of courseware at the design and data level as well as the implementation level. It encourages multiple implementations. It provides a hierarchy of sophistication. Although complex tutorials with good quality tracking and mapping layers may represent a more successful approach to a given learning problem than drill or tests, IMPS provides for all the simpler local structures. These can be implemented on 8-bit micros inside the framework of a standard courseware development methodology.

10 Site Implementation

As true networks become more common, and as mid-range machines come down in cost to the current level of 8-bit versions, then any courseware created using IMPS can be re-implemented. In most cases, re-implementation of IMPS courseware ought to be simpler than the complex and often futile attempts to make the languages themselves fully portable.

Languages are in constant change. If you have a bigger machine, why not move to a language tool that includes direct access to a relational database? If you have access to a relational database, then your courseware is going to change its nature to such a degree that a re-implementation is almost inevitable. Languages, after all, are only software tools. Many courses represent a larger investment and far more code than do the languages in which they are implemented.

What you want to avoid above all is the need to re-enter your data or redefine major aspects of your objectives.

DESIGN VERSUS IMPLEMENTATION

Courseware development can be quite straightforward or as complex as any other form of software development. The author can, therefore, experience a learning curve that moves from the simple to the complex. In each of the following sections, we tend to stress the starting levels, while keeping in mind that development can and should continue within each.

In addition, remember that IMPS is not a heavily "gated" system. The pattern that is presented is logical and natural, but not a one-way process like a salmon by-pass. You will move through the layers in various cycles. Implementation problems may mean that you have to redefine the conclusions of the presentation layer. A new piece of machinery may mean that you can write a new implementation with far more tracking functions than you had first considered possible.

HARDWARE FACTORS

Although language factors are intrinsically far more important than hardware factors, in practice, people tend to think about hardware first. There is some logic to this, since the hardware factors are more easily quantified. Many of them will have been dealt with in the presentation layer of your course: screen size, range of color, special input devices, graphic requirements. It is fairly straightforward to make a table of these requirements and match them to those available on the chosen machine.

Where matches of hardware and presentation requirements are not possible, you have to trace out the implications for the other layers. These implications can range from minor to major. If major, it may not be possible to implement the course at all. If minor, there may be quite simple ways around the problem.

The Elements of CAL

In practice, when the design is done locally, the known presentation limitations of the hardware are built into the development of the first three layers. When courseware is transferred, however, some major reconstruction of the presentation and local structure layers may be necessary before the course is functionally possible.

A number of other hardware factors can also be quantified.

Core Memory

It is always a good idea to estimate the memory needs of your program in advance. 8-bit micros have at most 64K of "core" or main memory. If you find you are not going to have enough space, you may have to cut certain functions from the tracking or student support layers. You may also want (if your language permits) to implement the course in a structured fashion so that the least important functions can be implemented last. Our sample course demonstrates how some desired functions may have to omitted from a 64K micro implementation.

Storage Memory

Again, the definitional layer will be of major use in estimating possible restrictions here. It is fairly easy to develop some rules of thumb about how many average length words you can store on your machine at a time. If you are limited to one or two floppy discs and have a good deal of example data, then you may want to organize your local structures somewhat differently than if you have access to a shared hard disc.

The separation that IMPS insists on between control code and data makes this kind of restructuring relatively easy. Always leave yourself a good buffer for storage memory. One of the best ways to improve a course is to extend the variety of examples. Storage memory is becoming cheaper and cheaper. Any implementation that uses data should be structured in such a way that further examples can be added with a minimum of fuss.

Interaction Speeds

By the very definition of a site implementation, the problems in this area are less complex than they are in a network implementation. In general, the only limitations you have to worry about occur with graphics and with control of external display devices such as VTRs. If your site does use communication links such as modems, make sure that you take into consideration any loss in speed caused during the communication cycle.

In any case, it is often a good idea to run through the design of the course looking for potential problems. As Chapter Five makes clear, no graphic at all may be better than an image that takes two minutes to form. As a number of site

10 Site Implementation

implementations are completed, the range of graphic possibilities will become clear and these can be made known to all site authors.

Keyboards and Other Input Devices

On low-range machines, the keyboard is often the weak link. It is an easy place for the product engineers to save money, but for foreign language alphabets, chemical symbols, graphic design or music skills, the limitations of certain keyboards may make it impossible to implement your course. The presentation layer should be quite specific on all input requirements.

If you are working on a translation of an implemented course, however, some of these problems may be less obvious. It can save a good deal of time if you have a table of keyboard limitations of all machines at the site and check this before beginning the coding.

Display Devices

Graphic displays are an area where non-standardization is rampant. Those devices, such as TELIDON, which represent an attempt to develop a standard, often only confuse the matter by being non-standard in all other aspects (such as keypad input, modem speeds, etc).

There has been a good deal of talk by groups such as SIGGRAPH about developing standards for portability, but we are unlikely to see much real effect until the late 80's. If a course has heavy graphic requirements, then the implementation may be very machine specific and its re-implementation costly. The presentation layer should be quite specific about the degree of complexity required and it may be practical to examine this layer in some detail before attempting even a prototype implementation.

Conversely, many sites that have heavy graphic requirements may find that this becomes the central focus of their development activity, strongly affecting decisions about hardware, software and development methodology.

Kludge Systems

It is possible to build some rather extraordinary hardware configurations for specific courses. Beware of courses that have requirements that look like this:

    one 64K Apple
    Mountain Man Synthesizer in slot two
    Z-80 card in slot three
    Zipper Dipper 80 Character card in slot four
    Zylon Graphic Display in slot four
    Hillside Clock in slot five
    M&M Memory-Disc in slot six

The Elements of CAL

    Curved Space hard disc controller in slot seven
    (using Bighead extensor board)
    etc.

It may be that this is the only way to present the course material, but the odds are that it is not. If there are indeed no alternatives then you had better be sure that you have sufficient demand to justify what will become a dedicated machine and sufficient funds to pay the hardware maintenance bills.

LANGUAGE FACTORS

The preparation of good courseware depends very much on language factors: which language you have chosen to work with (this time); how experienced you are as a programmer; what language and software development environment you work within.

Later, we summarize the available languages used for CAL. For those who are just beginning, it may be useful to establish the polarities.

You may very well be a parent, or a student, or a trainer in small firm, and have only recently learned BASIC. BASIC may well suit your purposes. Just remember that there are two processes underway and they ought to get equal time: you are learning about programming (in BASIC) and you are learning about CAL.

The fundamental rule is not to be too ambitious in either direction. You have to be able to distinguish among the following: problems with your full understanding of BASIC; problems with BASIC as a language; problems with your version of BASIC (and there are many versions); problems with CAL in general; problems with your current understanding of CAL; problems with the particular course you are writing or adapting.

On the other hand, you may exist in a friendly CAL environment where there are several major languages being used, where IMPS or an IMPS-like system has been installed for courseware preparation and where you have an option to program or just pass on your design and data to the programming experts.

The danger here is the high priest syndrome. If you do not know a fair amount about programming and the various choices open to you, then you may well end up under the influence of a high-priest of some large and elaborate system who will insist that nothing you wish to do is possible without great cost and vast contortions. If you become proficient in one or more languages, then you run the risk of joining the priestly class yourself.

Most likely you will find yourself somewhere in the vast middle. You probably have friends or associates who have somewhat more or somewhat less experience with languages than you do. At least one of these is probably a PASCAL or APL or LOGO or SMALLTALK or FORTH or C or DOUBLETHINK

10 Site Implementation

adherent. The single common characteristic of all such afficianados is that they scorn BASIC and are eager to convert you to "their" language as quickly as possible.

Basic BASIC

Tell yourself that they cannot all be right. There is a good deal that BASIC can do and it can certainly provide enough functionality to let you learn about most of the local structures described in Chapter Four and how to apply them to your own training materials.

In reality, you may well have to deal with a few dialects of BASIC. Perhaps various computers have been purchased in your environment: two Apples, an Atari 800, three PETs and one SuperPET, one TI and a Timex. This may not be as unusual a combination as you think.

In fact, learning a few dialects of BASIC is good practice for the process of learning a few languages. Remember two home truths. The preparation of code should represent no more than 10% to 20% of the total effort involved in getting a particular course or course segment working. Thus, assuming you know a number of languages or dialects, implementing a second version of the same piece of courseware should take less than a third of the time spent on the first version.

Secondly, it is the nature of language development to be piecemeal. A language is just another piece of software. Although at first even dialects may appear to differ significantly, in fact, the languages themselves are quite similar. The only way to see this is to learn a number of them.

Living in the Tower of Babel

Historically, those who were very unhappy with the nature or productivity of software development often put their efforts into the development of a new language that would solve the problems they faced. Creating such languages was a lot of fun, promoting them was less fun, and solving the problems that other people faced when using them was no fun at all. Another solution was to refine and/or approve a standard for a language (such as COBOL) which people could not easily abandon because it had a large amount of application software written in it.

In an ideal world, you might be able to accept this, learn some chosen group of languages, and treat them all as handy tools for creating courseware. Unfortunately, many languages do not really talk to one another even in terms of their output and collections of data. You may have a good graphics package (in PASCAL), a decent file-handler in FORTRAN, and a inexpensive but acceptable text-editor in BASIC. You can expect to be able to use them for a common project the way you would use tools in a toolbox.

The Elements of CAL

Language One

For those just beginning, the process we recommend is as follows. Learn a single language that is widely available (BASIC, PASCAL, C), or a special purpose language if you have access to one (LOGO, SMALLTALK, LISP, PROLOG, ADA, APL).

Then, implement some simple courseware in this language. All of the languages will be able to produce the basic local structures. There are numerous available examples of courseware written in BASIC. Chapter Fourteen demonstrates the way in which courseware can be developed using PASCAL.

Next, implement some more complex courseware in the same language, paying special attention to the kinds of features you wish to stress. This process will begin to point out any limitations in the language you have chosen.

Adapting courseware written by another author in the same language is also good practice. There may be techniques of design, presentation or implementation that you can borrow. (When trying this, however, make sure that you backtrack from the borrowed code to the first stages of IMPS if they are missing.)

A further option is to work in another dialect of the first language. BASIC dialects are very common, but even languages like PASCAL and LOGO already have varying implementations. Try to pick a more powerful option, especially if you see that your implementations are facing language constraints. There are some reasonably powerful dialects of BASIC. Some are compiled; some permit modular construction of code.

If these steps in the process allow you to produce functional courseware of the desired quality and complexity, then stop. For many people, the best way to improve short-term productivity is to learn one language very well. This separates out the problems of language learning from those of CAL production. As our two examples demonstrate, similar modules can be used for courseware of quite different kinds.

Language Two

If this process does not allow you to produce functional courseware at all, then you may want to take some time to examine the nature of your problems and to discuss them with people knowledgeable in a variety of languages and aware of any hardware constraints you may be facing. Here, the early stages of your IMPS-based design will help, as they will allow the language expert to see what you are aiming at and why you may be missing the target at the implementation layer.

Another possibility is that your first implementations are functional, but lack the quality or some features you feel necessary. Or, your environment may have different machines or different input devices that require some knowledge of a second language.

10 Site Implementation

It is probably worth learning a second language just for the sake of learning if you intend to continue playing a role at implementation time.

Whatever the reasons, we recommend the following process. Once you have mastered the basics of the language, start with some new courseware. All languages differ and tend to impose their nature on programs written in them. Starting with new courseware allows you to clear your head of the old implementation methods you have become accustomed to.

Then, adapt some courseware, your own or another author's, using the new language.

Finally, unless you have written off your first language, prepare some new courseware materials and write implementations in both languages in order to clarify the differences. Which one has the cleanest code? Which one comes closest to your ideals? Which one will be easier to maintain or expand?

It is usually best to put off for a year or two any decisions about the nature of involvement you are going to have with CAL in your environment. The available tools are changing rapidly and the only certain factor is that you must be prepared to adapt to change.

If your involvement means that you're probably going to be the programmer, then you should ultimately select a first-choice language, ideally one that is going to suit most of your requirements and/or grow and expand as the general level of understanding of software development grows and expands. The following brief descriptions of available languages stresses their general suitability for CAL.

LANGUAGES AND CAL

A number of factors have to be taken into consideration when choosing a language to work with. These include: price, availability, related tools, utilization rate, ease of learning, productivity, and special features. There are numerous good books on most languages. We list the favorite reference works in our shop.

BASIC

Somewhat reluctantly, we have to admit that this is probably the language of first choice for many of those involved with CAL. It is cheap, it is widely available, it is widely used, and it is easy to learn. Until its users learn another language, however, they are unlikely to see the advantages in terms of productivity, related tools and special features. *The BASIC Handbook* [Lien] is one of many useful additions to the specific texts and addenda that come with your machine.

The Elements of CAL

PASCAL

Like BASIC, PASCAL was designed as a tool for teaching programming. Its emphasis is on structured programming. It insists on very stringent definitions of variable types and is rather weak in input/output handling. It does, however, permit the creation of data structures, which is very important, almost crucial, for efficient courseware.

At the moment, it is probably the pragmatist's best choice for a second language, although some of its momentum seems to be dying. Because of some important missing features in the first versions, a wide variety of "supersets" were created in order to make the language more functional. These additions, of course, also guaranteed that courseware in PASCAL is only slightly more portable than courseware in BASIC.

However, learning PASCAL will at least insure that you learn to use some powerful programming tools not available in BASIC and that you can rid your programs of unnecessary **goto** statements. Most of the underlying theory of PASCAL can be found in two books of general interest: *Systematic Programming* [Wirth] and *Algorithms + Data Structures = Programs* [Wirth]. For PASCAL on Apples we have a slight preference for the *Pascal User Manual and Report* [Jensen] or *APPLE PASCAL: A Hands-On Approach* [Luehrmann and Peckham] over *Pascal Programming for the Apple* [Lewis].

C

If you are serious about programming, or if you have access to a UNIX system, then C ought to be your language of choice. The kernel of C is quite a small language and fairly easy to master. UNIX itself is written in C and there are extensive libraries in C that make CAL possible. The growth of C will be to a large extent dependent on the growth of UNIX. We recommend two other books by Kernighan later; however, his introduction, *The C Programming Language* [Kernighan], is by no means a model language manual, being poorly organized and difficult for the beginner to grasp. This language will require a number of good texts before it gains the popularity it deserves.

NATAL

The only high-level, portable language specially designed for CAL, and potentially widely available, is NATAL [Brahan]. Developed at the National Research Council of Canada, and currently running on a number of mainframes, NATAL has not, as yet been commercially exploited. Although Honeywell is in charge of marketing CAN-8, a language developed at the Ontario Institute for Studies in Education which might be viewed as a competing product, the firm may decide, at some future date, to market its licensed version of NATAL.

Commercial versions of micro-NATAL, the version of NATAL designed to run on low- to mid-range machines, are expected to be available in 1983.

APL, LOGO, LISP, ADA, SMALLTALK and PLAIN

There are a variety of other languages which may be used for CAL. APL is a powerful language and certainly useful for statistics- or math-oriented courseware. LOGO is useful in certain situations as defined by Seymour Papert, who also insists that LOGO is not a language but a philosophy. Good research work on LOGO is being done in Scotland and France. [du Boulay, *CAL 81 Symposium*]

LISP is a typical special case language, difficult to learn but ideal for certain aspects of CAL connected with an artificial intelligence approach.

ADA may be the inevitable choice in certain military-related situations. It does appears to be a potentially useful general purpose language and the portability of ADA software is insured through the process by which all ADA compilers must be fully compatible and verified by the U.S. Department of Defense.

SMALLTALK is another special case in that its role is entirely dependent on the production of low-cost systems to compete with the current BASIC and PASCAL machines.

PLAIN is typical of the many special case languages that might be useful for CAL. PLAIN was designed by Anthony Wasserman for use in interactive information systems. Interestingly enough, it contains many of the same features as NATAL in terms of string and response handling. In addition, it contains a set of relational database access commands. However, most people have not yet heard of it. [Wasserman *PLAIN*]

STANDARD CONCEPTS

Whatever the language or languages you select, there are some standard concepts that may or may not be obvious while you are learning your first language. Although *The Elements of CAL* is not intended as an introduction to programming, the following eight concepts are important if you are going to become seriously involved in creating courseware. We provide only a brief overview; eventually, you will have to deal with all of them in some detail.

For a quite different examination of a number of these concepts, an unusual but interesting point of view, and an excellent bibliography, we recommend Shneiderman's *Software Psychology: Human Factors in Computer and Information Systems* very highly. Shneiderman is an exceptional researcher; few programmers seem able to achieve the kind of humanistic and disinterested approach to information systems which he provides in this work.

The Elements of CAL

EIGHT STANDARD CONCEPTS

1. System Software versus Languages.
2. Terminal Handlers.
3. File Systems.
4. Procedures and Functions.
5. Compilers and Interpreters.
6. Concurrent Processes.
7. Libraries.
8. Graphics Languages.

1. System Software Versus Languages

In a few instances, these are related (e.g. PASCAL on the Apple, UNIX in C). Normally, however, they are distinct in construction as well as in nature. On low-range machines, the operating system provides limited functions and attention is focused on the language or application package.

On larger machines, however, the nature of the operating system becomes very important for large-scale CAL. In fact, a good deal of what you need for CAL is as dependent on the operating system and its components as it is on the particular language chosen for implementations. Portability of courseware thus becomes not simply a matter of language portability. Mastery of some of the functions found at the operating system level eventually becomes as important as language mastery.

There are a number of major contenders for hardware independent operating system software and authors interested in CAL should pay as much attention to the system software as to the first language of choice.

CP/M AND VARIATIONS

This is the most popular of the low-range operating systems. It lacks the flexibility of the other two contenders, it is crude and rude, but it is widely used. Digital Research, its manufacturer, is developing extensions and improvements and is trying desperately to keep all versions as compatible as possible.

The acceptance of CP/M by IBM, DEC, Osborne and other major manufacturers of 8-bit systems probably makes it the operating system of choice for simpler CAL courseware. Unlike UNIX, CP/M was originally implemented as a single-task, single-user system. MP/M indicates a multi tasking version.

For details on CP/M, MP/M II, and MP/M-86, you should consult current users. A useful annual comparative summary of all major microcomputer operating systems appears annually in the magazine *EDN*.

10 Site Implementation

UNIX

For anyone who started with CP/M and moved on to UNIX, the thought of being forced to move back is like one of those nightmares you have of being forced to repeat all your grade five examinations — under water.

UNIX is friendly and logical. Originally developed at Bell Labs, it was distributed in a strange fashion by the parent, AT&T. Non-profit groups paid $300 for a license to use it, and profitable ones paid $30,000 plus. Since UNIX is a multi-user, multi-task system, and was reasonably portable from day one, research groups jumped at the carrot. In 1981, AT&T began a new method of distribution which basically allowed all users to purchase the software package for less than $1,000.00.

Because UNIX stressed text handling facilities from the beginning and because of the wide range of facilities available, including relational database systems, we believe that UNIX and its look-alikes and official variations (such as Coherent and Xenix) will become the operating system of choice for CAL authors using any except the lowest range of machines. For an introduction, see the *User Guide to the Unix System* [Yates and Thomas] or *Using the Unix System* [Gauthier]. Both provide references to more technical documentation and articles.

SMALLTALK

SMALLTALK has hovered like a golden balloon just off the horizon for the past ten years. First developed as a research project by XEROX, it offers a simple user interface and high resolution graphics. These are certainly major requirements for any CAL system. Some experts predict that SMALLTALK will be the operating system of choice for the 16-bit machines, closing off any window of opportunity that CP/M and UNIX might have gained. Conceptually, it does have advantages and its adherents tend to be devoted.

However, as CP/M well demonstrates, logical superiority means nothing and practical availability means everything. Almost anyone could have written a better operating system than CP/M, just as the most popular micros are not necessarily the best. There is a market momentum which must be developed and maintained and that momentum is far more important than conceptual superiority.

Our own prediction is that the odds are only 1 in 10 that SMALLTALK will be given the market push to insure that it becomes anything more than something odd and special but not popular, like LISP. A reasonably accessible introduction is to be found in *Byte* Magazine. [*BYTE*, Aug. 82]

The Elements of CAL

THE G5 CONTENDER

It must be borne in mind that we can expect developments at the hardware level to continue at the current rate. Eventually, the expanding hardware capacity will create the need for an operating system that is to UNIX as UNIX is to CP/M. At the moment, only the Japanese with their fifth generation computer research and development work are really addressing the problems connected with such a system. [*Japanese Information*]

The questions addressed by the Japanese research: voice input and output, artificial intelligence, associative searching of very large databases, and automated processing, are all questions which have important implications for CAL. If the Japanese researchers solve the problems they have outlined, then we will at last have the proper tools to produce the kind of CAL that now exists only in our imaginations.

2. Terminal Handlers

The problems of multiple terminals do not arise with low-range, single user CPU implementations. If we stick to our definition, however, a site implementation can include a large computer with many terminals.

Usually, there will be several types of terminals (and micros that can switch into terminal mode) which your course may have to use as a display mechanism. Each terminal type will require different codes and sequences to control it intelligently at the physical level. Some systems, such as UNIX, and some CAL languages, such as NATAL, have dealt with this problem in advance. A terminal handler is a software package which permits authors to address a "virtual" terminal instead of a whole range of specified devices.

At the implementation stage, it is very convenient not to have to worry about whether your courseware can be run using the wide range of ASCII terminals, but to let the language or operating system take care of these problems. However, if your operating system or language cannot solve the problem, you must deal specifically with the different terminal types attached to your computer. Make sure that you have considered this problem before you start coding.

3. File Systems

CAL, almost by definition, is an extensive user of data. Before beginning any implementation which obviously requires a good deal of data, be certain that you have a thorough understanding of the limitations of the file system on the intended machine.

Questions to ask:

- What is the total available storage space?

10 Site Implementation

- What is the largest number of available files?
- Can you have access to records in files and fields in records?
- What are the limitations on length or number of records or fields?
- What are the limitations on the number of files in a directory?
- Is the file system hierarchical or sequential?

4. Procedures And Functions

Most modern languages are procedural. That is, they permit the creation of modules of code which stand as self-contained components of a larger piece of code. It is far simpler to create CAL in a procedural language. Procedures work by hiding information. Any procedure should only know about its *own* information and not, for example, about the many variables required in other modules.

Each procedure can have zero to *n* arguments (containing information), each of which, when the procedure is called, can be passed "in" only, passed "out" only, or passed "in and out".

In addition to these arguments, procedures may or may not return a value: a number, true or false, or a pointer to a more complex item. Functions are simply procedures that always return such a value. In many cases, especially in the sciences, their role is very important. Both procedures and functions are used and demonstrated in our sample courseware.

5. Compilers And Interpreters

As we indicated when discussing debuggers in Chapter Nine, languages can be compiled, or interpreted, or compiled into an intermediate language and then interpreted.

The trade-off is quite simple. Compiled languages in general produce programs that run more quickly. Interpreted languages in general appear easier to learn since you can write a line of code and then see the results.

BASIC is available as either an interpreted or compiled language. PASCAL is compiled. In the long run, for almost all implementations, compiled languages are preferable because of their efficiency, but make sure that you pick one with good debugging facilities. If you are interested in the underlying concepts of compilers, we recommend *Principles of Compiler Design* [Aho and Ullman] for further study.

6. Concurrent Processes

Most languages are sequential in that they only initiate a single process at a time. They leave it up to the operating system to deal with questions of concurrent processes. ADA, however, is designed to permit concurrent processes

The Elements of CAL

which allow several tasks in your program to execute in parallel. The major difference between a procedure and an ADA task is that the body of a task is not executed until the task is activated by another procedure or task. Tasks can contain entries, which look like procedures but specify synchronization and communication between a calling and a called task.

For many aspects of learning, the potential of concurrent processing is very important. ADA is designed to enforce portability by being a designated standard for a very large user, the American military. Its use will have major impact on CAL since much of its functionality meets the general specification of a high-level courseware authoring language. [Ledgard].

7. Libraries

Languages such as C have gained much of their acceptance through the use of libraries. These are standard functions and procedures which can be stored in either system or user areas and included within specific programs at compile time. Compared to many versions of BASIC, C provides excellent productivity. Often, over half of a given course can be drawn from earlier libraries of functions and procedures. This saves hours of programming time and shortens the final code considerably.

8. Graphics Languages

For some learning areas, nothing holds as much promise as low-cost, high-level graphic capabilities. Most current sites have graphic capabilities which can only be described as primitive. Unfortunately, there is little hope for any quick solution.

The SIGGRAPH CORE specification [*Computer Graphics* Aug. 79] is the probable software solution and the TELIDON or Presentation Level Protocol is the probable hardware implementation. For an introduction to the TELIDON version of graphics on computers, see *The Telidon Book* [Godfrey and Chang].

However, for most low-range micros, it is unlikely that either of these solutions will arrive in a practical and standardized form. At the moment, arcade games are a driving force in lowering costs in the graphic field, but these solutions tend to be proprietary and idiosyncratic, as anyone who has worked with the Atari graphic facilities knows. Major research on graphics is underway at many universities and some of this may reach the marketplace fairly soon. If you are interested in graphics and CAL you should join the SIGGRAPH section of ACM, if only for the publications.

TRANSLATORS

Rather than insisting on the use of a single common and portable language a number of researchers have faced the question of portability in a different manner. They have created a very general purpose interface to a large machine and then developed a set of translators to operate on existing source code in various languages. The purpose of such translators is to make the large body of courseware written for machine and language-specific systems, such as CDC's PLATO and IBM's COURSEWRITER and derivatives, available in what is in essence a *portable* environment.

The most promising of these is ELF, Educational Language Facilitator, now in operation at Steve Hunka's Division of Educational Research Services at the University of Alberta in Edmonton.

ELF can operate on COURSEWRITER† source code and yet drive a DEC VAX as the delivery machine. Translation facilities for NATAL and other languages are underway. This is a very promising development.

DATABASE MANAGEMENT SYSTEMS

The software facility with the greatest potential for CAL in a majority of fields is database management. We have already introduced these systems as a useful tool for the author support layer. Within courses, they can be used in three major ways.

1. INQUIRY MODE COURSES

As the major resource for large inquiry mode courses, a DBMS can model that part of the learning process which consists of finding, gathering and organizing information. In this mode, students should be able to create their own sample databases.

2. RESOURCE FOR SUPPORT STRUCTURES

As a resource within other courses, a DBMS can support local structures of any type by storing large quantities of data in a readily accessible form. They can also be used to maintain student support structures such as glossaries and dictionaries and to facilitate rapid transfers from local to support structures.

---

†COURSEWRITER itself is an earlier version of IBM's current CAL language. There is nothing to recommend either the earlier nor the current version except for the fact that they do work on some IBM hardware. The COURSEWRITER used at DERS has many local enhancements that greatly increase its functionality.

RESOURCE FOR COURSE CREATION

As a resource for course creation, the DBMS can store all of the pre-implementation data in a form that should make the transfer as nearly automatic as possible at implementation time.

At the moment, such facilities represent an area of computing that has not really been shaken out by market factors. Many products are announced for the low-range machines, but most of these are not really very effective. As indicated in Chapter Nine, buyers must beware.

We expect that proper relational type database management systems will be part of the standard software of UNIX-based 16- and 32-bit machines. CAL languages will have to adapt the PLAIN strategy and provide relational database access at the language level. For references, see Chapter Nine.

STRUCTURED PROGRAMMING

This topic is an important one. One of the best general books for CAL authors is *The Elements of Programming Style*. [Kernighan and Plauger] Their other work *Software Tools* is more advanced but still useful. An earlier but important general work is *A Discipline of Programming*. [Dijkstra]

SOFTWARE ENGINEERING

There have been numerous attempts to make programming less of an art and more of a science. These efforts are summed up in the term software engineering.

Although the goals are excellent, the terminology and definitions lack a certain clarity and coherence. There are any number of more or less useful summaries and collections. An example is *Tutorial Software Methodology* [Ramamoorthy and Yeh]. A broader view is given in *Software Development Tools* [Riddle and Fairley].

ABSTRACT DATA TYPES

One of the more useful ideas developed during these attempts to remove art from programming is that of the abstract data type. An abstract data type is a collection of objects and operations on those objects. It is implemented by defining both a storage structure and procedures to carry out the operations. Based on the more general concepts of information hiding, the abstract data type addresses a number of problems, including maintenance of software, that currently make life difficult for CAL authors. Given the emphasis in CAL on information transactions and the widespread use of high-level operations which we term local structures, the abstract data type may be a useful concept for CAL development.

10 Site Implementation

For an excellent introduction to what is admittedly a complex subject, see a recent article by Levy [*Communications of the ACM* Aug. 82].

PROLOG AND AI

One interesting general development for CAL authors is PROLOG. This is a language written in LISP and designed to forge a more direct link between logic and programming. Until recently an underground phenomenon, there is now a decent text available [Clocksin and Mellish].

PROLOG would be extremely useful for teaching logic, as an introduction to database practice, for word games, and for demonstrating the difference between regular and context-free grammars. It is interesting to note that the Japanese have selected PROLOG as their initial language to use during the specification period of their fifth generation projects.

SOME IMPLEMENTATION GUIDELINES

Whatever the language chosen, authors and teams will develop their own patterns of moving from specification to implementation, and those patterns will vary greatly depending on the hardware, language, and software development facilities available. A few general patterns are often useful. A detailed example is provided in chapters Twelve to Fifteen.

Prototypes

The separation of data and control code in IMPS make it fairly simple to build a prototype of the course which uses only fake data. Build those parts of the course which the learner will see as structure and then "walk through" them to make sure that you have what you want.

To this structure, you can then add samples of all kinds of generated and accessed data. When this prototype is debugged and has been viewed by a reasonable sample of students or instructors, then you can add in the larger bodies of data and any tracking mechanisms.

Bullet Proofing

Every CAL author should have a friend who delights in blowing up programs. It is almost impossible for a programmer to see the potential flaws in his or her own program. You know so well the intended paths and responses that it really is difficult to see even simple problems in some cases.

If you lack such a friend, then the only sure solution is to pretend that you are an absolute idiot who delights in random responses. Ignore the structure, ignore all instructions, develop a distrust of machines and a hatred of the course. Then go through the prototype and see what happens.

The Elements of CAL

Errors often occur when there is unexpected input. Make sure the program can handle it if the learner keys in blank spaces, strikes the reset, escape and/or control keys, creates long strings or out of bound integers, or becomes confused and uses upper case when lower is expected, letters where numbers are expected, or numbers where letters are expected. You know what the "proper" input is. Think of all the other possibilities and try them on your prototype and on the final course as well.

Maintenance

A good CAL course, like a good lecture, is one designed in the knowledge that it will never be completely finished. It is important to implement the course in such a fashion that it can be edited and upgraded as easily as possible.

This may be a hard concept to accept when you are starting out. Then it appears difficult enough just to get the thing working at all. However, once you have mastered a language or two and a development method such as IMPS provides, a good deal of your effort will go into maintenance.

The danger, of course, is that most creators are far more interested in creating than they are in maintaining. One of the prime advantages of team development of CAL over the one-man band method is that the team often contains people who enjoy developing the skills required for high quality maintenance of courses. One of the real advantages of high-level languages is that they facilitate maintenance because they are easier to comprehend, especially by programmers other than the original author.

Evaluation

Although a good deal of evaluation is external, provision must be made during the implementation for the internal aspects of evaluation. On low-range machines, there may have to be trade-offs. The evaluation factors should be listed in the tracking layer of the IMPS specification and should be ranked by priority there. With experience, some of the suggested tracking components listed at the close of Chapter Six can be implemented on low-range machines. Those that are considered most important can be stressed. The techniques for handling this layer within the implementation will be very similar for all courses.

SUMMARY

At the moment, despite two decades of fairly intensive research, a great deal remains unknown and unpredictable about the creation and use of courseware. It is hard to deny, however, that programming skills are still important. Unless you are part of a team which contains people with all the necessary programming skills, it is better to admit from the start that you must attain a fairly high degree of mastery of all the skills a regular programmer must master.

10 Site Implementation

This is certainly not an impossible task, indeed it is often an exciting one. But it is best accomplished as a recognized task and not as a subsidiary activity. At the moment, if you are going to create top-notch courseware, you are probably going to have to learn a great deal about software development. You might as well do it properly from the very start.

Chapters Twelve through Fifteen provide two detailed examples of how site implementations take place in our shop, and make clear the relationship between writing courseware and good software tools.

11 Network Implementations

ONE	Definitional Layer
TWO	Local Structures
THREE	Presentation
FOUR	Tracking
FIVE	Mapping
SIX	Student Support Structures
SEVEN	Author Support Structures
EIGHT	Site Implementation
NINE	**Network Implementation**

INTRODUCTION

In general, network implementations are more complex than site implementations, although they can be more cost effective. Almost everything said in Chapter Ten (and demonstrated in chapters Twelve through Fifteen) applies to network implementations also, but in addition a number of other possibilities are open to authors.

We use three terms to describe the concepts which must be defined in this layer: network, termnet and lattice.

NETWORK

A network is as defined previously: a set of linked, multi-user computers. At the moment, most of such networks belong either to large universities, large corporations or governments. This situation is rapidly changing.

Although one can network single-user, low-range computers, little is gained except to provide the possibility of mail and shared resources such as printers and discs.

125

The Elements of CAL

TERMNET

We will use the word *termnet* to describe an array of terminals hooked up to a single master computer. Obviously, a network is likely to have at least one termnet attached to it. The problems that arise when implementing CAL on a termnet are usually less complex than with a true network.

LATTICE

We use the term *lattice* to describe a human network, a group of teams or individuals working on related CAL projects. There is no necessary relationship between any lattice and a multi-computer network. A co-operative exchange group, linking a number of local sites and designed to evaluate and distribute PET software, would be an example of a lattice. They might or might not use a computer network to store and distribute the code and documentation.

However, network implementations always tend to form lattices among their users. Such lattices facilitate the exchange of design, data, and code throughout the physical network.

HARDWARE FACTORS

It is relatively straightforward to describe an ideal configuration for CAL in a network environment. One large computer would be dedicated to CAL and used for the major design, development and maintenance work by various teams and individuals. Some courseware could be distributed to other large computers in the network, especially courses with a high access rate or those tied to the operation of specific computers or applications.

This hardware complexity would remain invisible to all authors and learners. If they were on computer A and asked for a course stored on computer B, they would automatically be switched to that computer for the duration of the session. As mid-range computers were purchased and installed locally, these would be merged into the network to encourage diversity and decentralization.

Unfortunately, as is true with graphics, network development is still largely in the dream and design stage. Although many firms and institutions have various brands of mainframe computers, most have not even begun to get them talking to one another. The majority of senior trainers, if they have access to a computer, are limited to master-slave termnets on big, old machines with archaic operating systems.

Fortunately, the need for the ideal networks is widely recognized. A useful first step is the Open Systems Architecture. As described by the International Standards Organization in their Open System Interconnection protocols, this set of network standards has already begun to help solve some of the technical problems inevitably associated with networks. The necessity of such international standards for the long-term health of CAL cannot be over-emphasized. For a useful discussion, see Abell in *The Telidon Book* [Godfrey and Chang].

Computers, Terminals and Work-stations

In the past, it was possible to make a simple distinction between a computer and a terminal. Now most microcomputers can easily become terminals. Many terminals, such as the Northern Technologies Vision Series, or the DEC VT-100, can also be transferred into microcomputers with very little work. *work-station* is becoming the term used for terminal-computers which have a good deal of local computing power.

However, the meaning of the term *work-station* remains vague. We define a work-station as a mid-range machine used by an individual. For the moment, at least, work-stations are similar to terminals in that they do not act as hosts to other terminals. But that will surely follow.

The inroads made by personal computers only prefigure the inroads to be made by work-stations. The difference between a work-station and many existing minicomputers is minimal. Even in large firms, training is often very decentralized. Once a senior trainer can purchase a mid-range system (a 40 megabyte disc, 1 or 2 megabytes of main memory, 8 to 16 ports, UNIX and five languages, and tape back-up) for under $25,000, then the way will be open for rapid growth in the courseware field even within decentralized firms. Such systems are already on the horizon.

Local Area Networks

A related development adding to the confusion are the hundreds of variations of Local Area Networks (LANS) springing up. We see these simply as a practical way of connecting resources to a number of single user machines. It is probably not practical to attempt clear and hard definitions, as there are already too many models on the market, but there is a fairly steady stream of articles in the technical magazines making some useful distinctions. [*BYTE*:Oct. 81]

But however they are defined, the important thing about Local Area Networks combined with work-stations is that they offer schools, businesses, divisions of large firms, colleges, and smaller universities, for the first time, the kind of network facilities previously utilized only by large, centralized firms and institutions.

Work-stations and LANS suggest how hardware changes will affect CAL, even though it is hard to predict the exact rate and direction of the changes. At some point of hardware complexity, 8-bit microcomputers fade from the picture and CAL changes complexion. The factors which need to be considered when CAL is implemented within such networks are covered in the following sections.

The Elements of CAL

THE CAL ARCHITECT IN NETWORK IMPLEMENTATIONS

One sure way to distinguish true network implementations is that the need for an *architect* becomes apparent. The architect may be an individual or a team, appointed or elected, but the problems remain the same.

The advantage of networks is that more choice is possible: more raw computing power, more languages, more sharable records, more experience with design strategies, more prototype courses and procedures.

The role of the architect is to develop a functional model and some guidelines for the CAL activities of the group. This model might include some formalization of the lattice or human network, some coherency in the courseware development methodologies, some limits to the possible languages, and some co-ordination of text editors, DBMS, graphic and network protocols, and other supporting tools used within the lattice. The formalization might be strict or consensual. In either case, the architect must deal with a number of problem areas which we now summarize.

Language Factors from the Architect's Perspective.

The architect must deal with all of the questions covered under language factors in Chapter Ten, and may have to do so in a consistent and comprehensive manner. The central question remains: what is the best way to bring existing expertise and the implementation problems together? Much effort over the past two decades has gone into bridging the gap between experts and courseware. These efforts may be categorized as follows:

Subject Expert	+	*Easy To Learn Language*	=	Courseware

Here, the choices remain the same: BASIC, PASCAL, C. And perhaps NATAL and SMALLTALK if they are made available in inexpensive versions. However, in a network environment, the limitations of BASIC are likely to be obvious. A recent study by Martin Lamb for the Ontario Ministry of Education points out the potential advantages, for CAL, of some combination of the facilities of NATAL and C.

Subject Expert	+	*Rest of Design and Program Team*	=	Courseware

A typical CBT team consists of experts in instructional design, evaluation, presentation and programming. This is a useful method in the network environment, even when the teams represent authors working co-operatively rather than as employees. This method permits systematic design and opens the range of language options. If there are APL, LISP, PLAIN, PL/1 or PROLOG experts on the team, then different courses can be prepared in different languages. IMPS or a similar system can maintain courseware consistency.

| Subject Expert | + | Fixed Method Language | = | Courseware |

Another probable option is a system such as PLATO or TICCIT where the instructional design theory is virtually embedded in the language. We do not recommend either of these systems because of their high cost and low adaptability to current hardware developments, but they often appear to be the only choice to architects who must deliver results immediately.

A good network does permit a role both for TICCIT and for other options and we will discuss this under cost-benefit factors.

| Subject Expert | + | Automated Courseware Generators | = | Courseware |

As Kearsley makes clear in a recent article, *Authoring Systems in Computer Based Education* [Kearsley] CAL represents one of the major development areas for automatic code generation. Courseware may appear to be somewhere between a known application, which just requires a production package, and a situation which requires individual programming of individual courses.

At the moment, all that can be said with certainty is that some course generators provide a reasonable introduction to CAL for those who are considering whether or not to learn a language; most, however, are not very useful.

| Subject Expert | + | Portable Selected Software | + | Optional Editing | = | Courseware |

As long as companies like IBM, DEC, CDC and Honeywell were in charge of developing facilities such as languages, text editors, DBMS, and accounting packages (almost all of which worked only on their own machines), prices tended to start at ten thousand dollars a package and head up to the quarter million dollar mark. The same held true for their CAL facilities, except that the vendors tended to spend even less time developing and refining them and certainly refused to make them portable.

The Elements of CAL

The great advantage which 8-bit micros brought with them was in the software field. Products such as CP/M and Visicalc, whatever their limitations, demonstrated that there was a market for low-priced facilitative software.

Good CAL courses, like good DMBS packages, require a mid-range machine. What is happening now is that the software emphasis is shifting from the low-range to the mid-range machines. Even in network environments, the future probably lies with this fifth option. As teachers and trainers find workstations available that can handle four to sixteen learners at a time, then the potential of portable CAL languages and courseware will begin to be realized.

Portability Factors from the Architect's View

It is our observation that a great deal of the research effort connected with trying to attain courseware portability through language portability has been useful, but misplaced. The difficulties in creating inexpensive, effective CAL may arise in any layer or combination of layers in our nine layer process.

However, all five solutions above tend to assume that the real problems are somehow connected with the programming level. The general theory seems to be that if you solve the programming snags the rest of the problems will drift away.

- Solution 1 says that the Subject expert should become a programmer but learn an easy language.
- Solution 2 says that even this level of programming is a waste since only the computer experts can handle programming.
- Solution 3 says that programming should be tied very explicitly to a single learning method so as to appear somewhat invisible.
- Solutions 4 and 5 say that the Subject Expert need know a bare minimum about programming.

Historically, there is justification for focusing on language and programming problems in CAL. Each small improvement, in fact, has tended to be embodied in a wholly new language. Larger scale improvements, such as those represented by the work done on NATAL, SMALLTALK and on the conceptual design of ADA, tend to take a very long time to implement, to be expensive, to be hard to utilize, or some combination of the three.

The recent improvements in programmer productivity brought about by the concepts of structured programming, software engineering and software development methodologies are, in many ways, more useful than improvements to existing languages or new languages themselves since the concepts can be applied to many languages and to the act of programming, for whatever purpose.

In a network implementation, it is possible for all those involved to encourage research, development and production, in different languages and on different machines. With IMPS, both design and implementation layers, and many versions thereof, may be stored and easily distributed to many sites for discussion, amendment or extension.

The role of the architect, or planning committee, or whatever, must be to keep all the participants talking, to keep the design and software variations within bounds, and to develop and implement some useful and reasonable evaluation methods. None of this is ever easy. If network implementations are to function, a number of background factors must be well understood.

THE TWO SOLITUDES

One of the reasons for the relatively slow spread of portable, professional level CAL has been the duality of effort by CAL researchers and software researchers.

A great deal of effort by each camp goes into research and development and testing, but the efforts usually remain separate. A group of course developers who have put 30 person-years into courseware development under PLATO or TICCIT or CAN-8 or whatever may recognize the goals and achievements of the SMALLTALK or ADA groups but, in general, the advances of one solitude are not available to the other.

COSTS OF LEARNING

The costs of transferring large amounts of courseware from one environment to another. are very high. Historically, these costs have prevented such transfers. PLATO courseware, for example, is not transferred to the TICCIT system, the courses are re-invented.

In this regard, however, it must be remembered that a site using a portable language such as NATAL may be as much of a "new" environment for a PLATO course as a site using TICCIT. There is a cost of transferring courseware from a fixed environment to a portable environment and unless a good number of sites adapt portability as a goal and begin to share courseware, the direct benefits of portable courseware may not be too apparent. It is this factor that has hindered the adoption of languages, such as NATAL, which have high portability.

THE FALSE 8-BIT FIX

The users of microcomputers are, in many ways, simply repeating the learning curves of those who earlier discovered the attributes and complexity of CAL on mainframes. Some jurisdictions and firms assume that courseware can be magically transferred from PETS to Apples, but they are now discovering the difficulties of transferring courseware even from one generation of a PET or Apple to another.

The Elements of CAL

The great advantage of the 8-bit micro, from a network point of view, is that it acts as a low-cost introduction to programming for those who might otherwise remain aloof. Some micros, in addition, make acceptable terminals. Machines like the SuperPET with their variety of languages represent very good value as a programming tool. However, except for cases where the objectives are quite limited and courseware can be created on an algorithmic base, the 8-bit micro is seriously limited by its lack of storage and is rarely a useful machine for professional CAL.

IMPS FROM THE ARCHITECT'S VIEW
A Balanced Diversity

From the architect's point of view, the adaptation of some version of IMPS permits a systematic approach to the development of courseware without unnecessary restrictions. Even though programming is a difficult area of CAL, this difficulty does not justify the tendency for other problem areas to be ignored or down-played and for creativity, variety and adaptation to be stifled simply because it takes so long to get the course running.

Programming problems should never divert attention from the true task of creating good CAL. Yet many good courseware developers have either become deeply involved in producing the new, ideal language, or system, or computer, or hardware tools or else have limited themselves to one particular system and thus ended up producing fairly similar packages over and over again. All of this remains a drag on the momentum CAL requires.

Even those who remain true to courseware development goals must somehow deal with the rapid evolution of hardware and changing cost-effectiveness parameters. In the network environment, a software development methodology such as that represented by IMPS is of major importance in helping to maintain the balance between courseware design and the problems and constraints of various languages. Controlled experiments with hardware, languages, tools, systems and software development methodologies can be carried out in a functional manner and a good deal of the comparative data captured during each design and implementation process.

The Family of Programs

In our experience, the architect is likely to discover eventually that the five strategies detailed above, when adopted, suffer from at least two serious flaws. First, they stress the implementation layer as the main source of problems when in fact it is only one of many sources. Secondly, they tend to look on implementation as "a" task that requires "a" solution.

Parnas has dealt with this assumption in more general terms [Ramamoorthy and Yeh]) and has developed the concept of families of programs

11 Network Implementations

as another way of looking at the general problem. A set of programs, in these terms, is a program family if the programs have so much in common that it pays to study their common aspects before looking at the aspects that differentiate them. As even our two small examples of courseware will illustrate, this concept is particularly useful for CAL. CAL courseware is definitely *familial*. The layers in IMPS are designed to emphasize the aspects of CAL common to many courses.

Teams and Lattices

It is most important that the architect build up within a given team or lattice extensive experience at all nine layers of IMPS. The choice of hardware and software is important, but not nearly as important over the long-term as the building up of experience and expertise within the various teams.

Although the team strategy is the most practical one for network implementations, the roles should not be kept too specialized. Courseware designers function more effectively when they have mastered at least one programming language. The same need for general experience holds true for programmers; they should at least try their hand at course design, data analysis and preparation. Only such shared skills can help identify the "family" nature of courseware in a productive and accurate manner.

Consistency of Tools

It is the fourth through seventh layers of IMPS that can benefit most from the potential of networks and the concept of families of programs. One of the major roles of the architect is to insure that the design and coding tools remain as constant as possible.

Many of the facilitative tools within a CAL environment remain the same whether the content is scientific, humanistic or artistic. Tracking, student support, and author support layers all have far more that is common across disciplines than one might expect from looking at current conditions.

At the implementation level then, the architect must coordinate the way in which the various teams maintain a coherent approach – in all courses – in terms of the tracking, mapping, student support and author support layers. Much of what was covered in chapters six through nine can very effectively be implemented on all the mid-range and high-range machines common in networks.

IMPLEMENTING TRACKING

Network implementations should make tracking possible and straightforward. For the majority of courses, the elements that one wishes to track remain the same. A set of procedures or facilities can take care of the standard grading options described in chapters Four and Six, leaving room for development of a particular version of the descriptive model.

The Elements of CAL

Network implementations do, however, create some difficulties for tracking in that there may be many different courses and versions of courses. Nonetheless, the architect should be able to gain some consensus about a core list of tracking elements which will be recorded in all courses, no matter what the software and hardware factors.

IMPLEMENTING MAPPING

One of the concepts from database theory that can be usefully transferred to the CAL domain is the notion of *user views* of the data. In network implementations of CAL, you can conceptualize a user view of a course when the user is an instructor. Given high level languages and good separation of data and control, the network ought easily to be able to provide quite differing versions of the same course to different instructors.

These versions are somewhat different from different site implementations in that they may well share the same large-scale program. The variations are internal to the program. Instructors may wish leaners to take a more fixed path, to cover some objectives in non-CAL mode, to pass all tests at a given level before carrying on, to be spared certain "ambiguous" examples, etc. If a network implementation is planned, then many of these distinctions can be made at the mapping layer and it is up to the implementors to make the versions available in the most effective manner.

IMPLEMENTING STUDENT SUPPORT STRUCTURES

Obviously, many of the limitations present in low-range machines keep the learners from fully benefiting from CAL. They see a part of a course at a time, and the range of support structures available is very limited. On a network implementation, you have a responsibility to make provision for access to such support structures as: prerequisite courses, dictionaries and glossaries, mail, access to past results, bibliographies, and skill development packages.

Networked machines should deliver languages and facilities that make the addition of these structures to any given course relatively simple. Because all such structures should be available to as many potential courses as possible, the architect will soon recognize the need to gain some consensus about limitations on the use of unusual hardware and languages at an early stage.

IMPLEMENTING AUTHOR/INSTRUCTOR SUPPORT STRUCTURES

Provision of author support facilities such as text editors, report generators, DBMS, and special purpose display devices is an ongoing process which is both aided and complicated in network environments. On the one hand, general tools are common and accessible in networks. On the other hand, a network with many different machines, languages and operating systems may have difficulty in communicating at any level higher than messages and file transfers.

Simply because two or more machines are networked does not mean that any user may access any tool on any portion of the network. This layer is the one where major savings can be made if common, effective tools are provided to all involved. Justifying expenditures made to gain those savings (when the expenditures are always current and the savings longer term) is one of the more difficult tasks facing the architect, authors and instructors. The problems are especially complex in training environments since almost invariably the network is used for and supported by non-CAL activities which themselves form, in part, the subject matter of the courseware. There must, therefore, be some match between the CAL languages and the general languages used for the specific applications.

COST-BENEFIT FACTORS
What does Training Cost?

We have stated the strong relationship between CBT and cost-benefit studies. As is true with the design and methodology considerations, the emphasis in these studies is usually (and wrongly) placed on the implementation layer: CAL is expensive because programming is expensive. In fact, CAL should be able to reduce training costs by at least 20% and also increase the effectiveness of the training.

Yet the fear of the high costs of CAL remains. This is true both in many educational institutions, where the implementation layer appears to be all that CAL consists of and is considered a costly mystery, and in many firms, which have cost benefit methods well established elsewhere, but fail to apply them to the training domain.

Training is an area whose true costs are little understood. In the majority of firms, there is probably no other aspect of business which absorbs an equal share of costs, affects both morale and long-term survival as strongly, and yet is as thoroughly lacking in examination as training. Yet the techniques for gaining such information are readily available. Finding out what training costs and what its benefits are is no more difficult than a similar examination of production or marketing activities. A basic methodology for firms is suggested below.

The Four Objectives

COST BENEFITS OF REGULAR TRAINING

You should always have the costs of your training programs as a baseline; they are the simplest to establish since the various factors involved are well known: cost of trainers, space, materials, overhead, student travel, student wages, etc. Once you have established a model for determining costs in current programs, it is simple indeed to apply it across the board to costs involved with CAL.

The Elements of CAL

The benefits side of the equation are two-fold. If the learning objectives are well-established, then mastery by the students of these objectives is the primary benefit. There are well established ways to evaluate these benefits.

Secondary benefits include better morale among employees, higher productivity, and a greater willingness to expand horizons and take on new projects and areas of expertise. Although these secondary benefits are difficult to quantify, they should not simply be ignored. The manner in which they are included within the training cost-benefit methodology will depend on the firm's general model of dealing with this level of benefits. Many large firms now face the need for constant training as they have adopted some variation of the Japanese model of long-term employment patterns.

NORMS FOR CAL

There is a growing body of work consisting of general and case study examination of the costs and benefits of CAL (although these usually speak of CBT and CMI specifically). Examination of such studies, done with some care, can let the firm establish a set of norms that ought to apply to its own use of CAL.

Although all of the hardware and software costs are already quite dated, the most useful introductory work on the cost-benefits of CAL remains *The Cost of Learning with Computers*. This long term study of The National Development Program in CAL in Britain during the 70's covered over 35 projects with close to seven hundred teaching staff involved at 47 institutions. Prepared by Peat, Marwick, Mitchell & Co., the study provides a general methodology, some varied case studies, and very useful discussion of the more complex questions involved. [National Development Program]

CAL OR CAL

In network implementations, it is possible to compare varying methods of CAL. You may want to start, for example, with a TICCIT system and a number of widely-used courses. You can then demonstrate the cost-effectiveness of the general method and pay off both the original hardware costs and some of the general development costs. Then, a second system might be purchased as hardware and software improvements reach the market.

When comparing costs of newer systems and the original system, however, it is important to keep separate the various categories of costs. You may eventually want to be even more detailed, but the layers within IMPS may be used as a starting point.

Layer One should be costed separately. Often the results of this layer can be used in non-CAL modes and can certainly be used in all computer implementations.

11 Network Implementations

Costs of layers two and three may be combined as there is usually a significant interaction between the two. Design and development costs on layers four through seven should be kept separately and carefully, however, as much of what is done in these levels applies not only to all implementations of the course but to many other courses.

Naturally the implementation costs should be kept separately for each implementation of each course. You should know not only the average costs of developing an hour of courseware but the costs of developing similar implementations in different languages. You should also be able to track across types of courseware so that reasonably accurate predictions can be made about transferring various categories of courses to a CAL mode.

Fair practices have to be developed to allocate out the pre-implementation costs against all actual implementations. Using IMPS, any second implementation should cost less than 30% of an initial implementation. Careful attention to this step will usually demonstrate that implementation costs are not the major factor in developing good courseware. If they are, you should examine the nature of your software tools and consider more closely some of the options outlined in Chapter Ten.

In addition, validation and maintenance costs must be detailed and allocated over the life cycle of any given courseware. These may vary with use and with content changes, of course, but they may also vary with the nature of the tools used during development

COST BENEFITS OF LEARNING ABOUT CAL

Equally important but more difficult to quantify are the factors associated with learning about CAL itself. These may be divided into three phases: initial learning, development of productivity, and expansion of horizons and skills. There are costs associated with each phase and these costs must be accounted for separately from the costs associated with development of specific courses.

SUMMARY

For many teachers and trainers, the establishment of CAL facilities encourages that "basic change in attitudes" which we spoke of much earlier. Network implementations intensify the underlying change since they have such major potential for structural innovation in the training of many different kinds of workers.

In the electronic world which we now inhabit, a world of extreme change, these new skills and attitudes may be of great value to firms and institutions. In some cases, they may be all that insures the survival much transformed, of individuals and groups greatly affected by the electronic whirlwind.

12 Curriculum Four

Curriculum Four is a practical application of the IMPS system. It is also functioning CAL, which you can key in and run on an Apple II Plus with PASCAL.

The Curriculum includes two courses, each pointing out a different approach to CAL. FRACTIONS is a pre-structured mathematics course designed to drill and test in one aspect of fractions. The structure of the course and presentation methods are based to a certain degree on the nature of the material to be taught. WORDS can be used in any situation where the learner wants to memorize basic terms, learn to spell, expand her vocabulary, learn simple facts, or any other similar activity. While the structure and presentation of the WORDS course are independent of the data, FRACTIONS is a single-use course. Once the learner has mastered the objectives, FRACTIONS is of no further use except for review. WORDS can become valuable to all learners on an ongoing basis. The design and coding time for each course were almost equal.

Layers 8 and 9, this chapter, outline possible implementations of Curriculum Four. Chapters Thirteen, Fourteen and Fifteen provide all the information, data, code and documentation for a specific Apple/Pascal implementation. Note that the Apple/Pascal implementation does not contain all the facilities described as desirable for the courses in the following description. Those aspects not implemented are marked for your convenience.

CURRICULUM FOUR
1: The Definitional Layer

The overall goal is to provide a young learner with CAL in two different subject areas: mathematics and language skills. Target learner:
- In grade four or five.
- Able to read at the average level for grade four.
- Familiar with the terminal.

The Elements of CAL

This goal is best reached by creating two separate courses: WORDS and FRACTIONS. At this point it is best to deal with each course separately, moving through the IMPS layers, defining the needs of each course. Once that is done, we can return to the mapping, tracking, student and author support structures, and implementation layers to form a picture of what will be required by the curriculum.

WORDS

1. Definitional Layer

The goal of WORDS is to increase the learner's vocabulary.

OBJECTIVES

Objective 1. The learner will be able to use the computer as a resource. This objective will be reached if the learner can look up the meaning of a word contained in the database.

Objective 2. The learner will become familiar with a specified subset of the database. The instructor will identify a subset of the database (five words). This subset becomes a segment of the course. Segments will have to be accounted for in the mapping layer. There will be a maximum of five segments in the course. Five words and five segments have been chosen as the correct number to challenge a learner, yet stay within the time limits which allow the learner to have a sense of accomplishment within each learning session. Use of the course may indicate the need for a change in the number of words and segments needed for optimum results.

The learner will be offered a choice of two different local structures designed to meet this objective. One structure will offer a inquiry browse; one structure will offer a tutorial. This objective will be fully met if the learner sees each rule in each segment at least once in either local structure.

Objective 3. The learner will be able to respond with the correctly spelled word when the meaning is displayed. This objective will be met when the learner can answer all questions from all segments correctly.

Rules

A rule will be a word and its definition. All the rules will be available for a learner working toward Objective 1, but not all rules must be accessed for the objective to be met.

The rules comprising objectives 2 and 3 will be defined by the instructor when the segment is defined.

Examples

An example will be the word used correctly in a grammatically correct sentence.

Questions

A question will consist of a display of the definition. A correct response would be the learner's typing in the correctly spelled word which matches the definition.

2. Local Structures

DICTIONARY

The learner types in the word she wants to read from the dictionary. If there is an exact match, that is displayed. If there is no exact match, the words that are the closest matches are displayed as a menu. If there is no match, all the words in the dictionary are displayed as a menu. When the database is large, this menu will extend over several screens. This may not be desirable, the menu may work better displayed in segments. An optional expanded definition and examples will be available for each word.

This is a simple inquiry local structure. If the learner can look up a word using this system she has reached Objective 1. Figure 12.1 shows the dictionary local structure.

MEANINGS

The student is presented with a menu of the words in a single segment, from which she may select one. The initial display of the selected word will include the word, with a basic definition. A further definition and examples are optional. The learner can see the same word as many times as she likes.

This local structure is a type of inquiry (inquiry of a pre-selected part of the database) and is one of two local structures the learner may use to meet Objective 2. (Figure 12.2.)

PRACTICE

The practice local structure allows the learner to answer questions on the rules in a single segment. The questions will be based on rules selected in random order. If the learner makes an error, an attempt will be made to diagnose the source of error. When all questions are answered, the learner will receive a reinforcement message, but may continue practising. If the learner leaves the local structure before answering all the questions correctly, a reinforcement message to that effect will be provided.

Practice is a tutorial local structure and is one of two local structures the learner may use to meet Objective 2. (Figure 12.3.)

The Elements of CAL

12.1 Dictionary Local Structure

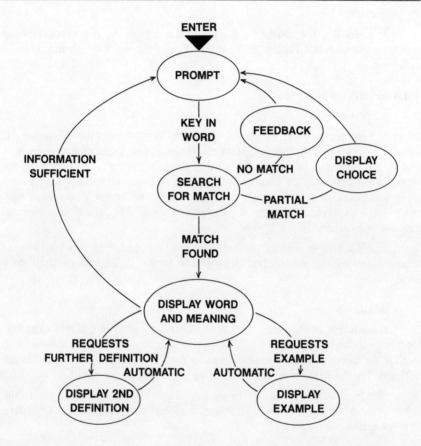

In all diagrams, an asterisk (*) indicates a point of reinforcement.

12.2 Meanings Local Structure

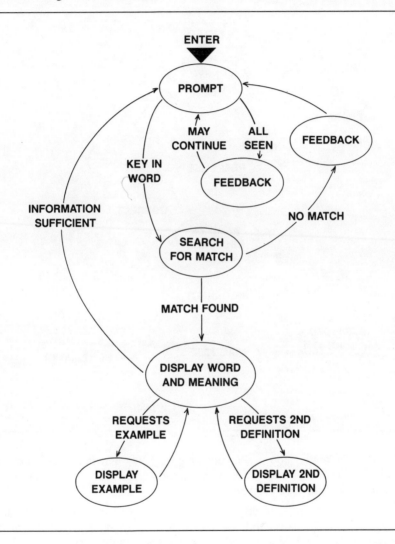

The Elements of CAL

12.3 Practice Local Structure

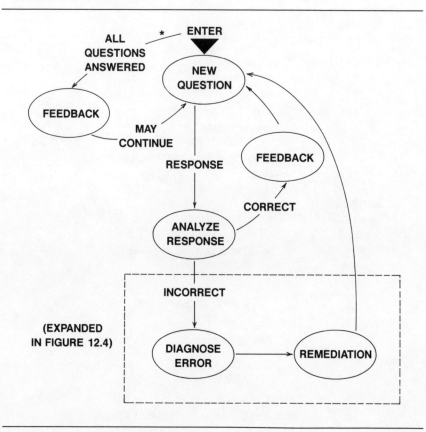

The diagnostic loop of Practice (Figure 12.4) will first determine how many times the learner has answered the question incorrectly. The first error will result in a display of the correct answer.

The second error will display the correct answer, then ask the learner if everything is now understood. If the learner responds *yes,* the diagnostic sequence will end and the learner will be presented with the next question. If the learner responds *no,* she will be offered a choice of an example, another definition or information on how to answer the question. After the display of any of these choices, the learner will again be asked if she now understands. If the answer is yes, the diagnostic sequence will continue, if the answer is no, the diagnostic menu will be re-displayed.

12.4 Diagnostic Loop in Practice

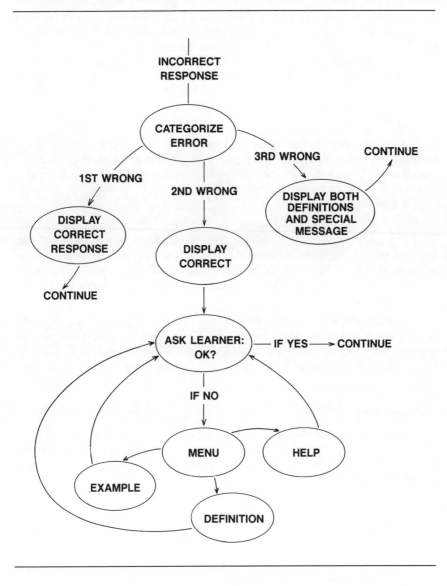

The Elements of CAL

The third error for the same question will display a special warning to *pay attention*. The fourth error will take the learner back into the diagnostic sequence. This pattern of diagnostic sequence – warning – diagnostic sequence will continue until the learner finally enters a correct response. There is the possibility that the learner will be left with one word and move back and forth, never providing the correct response. Mapping will have to make sure there is a way out if the question is never answered correctly. If this happens to many learners during trials of the course, some alterations may have to be made to this local structure.

TEST

Test randomly displays questions based on the rules in one segment. (Figure 12.5) Feedback is limited to acknowledging receipt of a response. On completion of all five questions the learner receives a reinforcement message and a score. If the learner leaves the test without answering all questions she will receive a message to that effect.

Test asks questions and provides feedback to the response. This is a Test local structure. For this test to be effective, the feedback to a wrong response must not include the correct answer. If the learner saw the correct answers it would be too easy to figure out the answers to the remaining questions by the process of elimination. Successful completion of Test will indicate that the learner has reached Objective 3.

Because the learner is free to access the test local structure at any point, this test can be either for evaluation or diagnostic purposes. That is, the learner may first test to see which words she does not know, then practice the ones not known, or may choose to practice, then test. Mapping will have to allow for this choice.

3. Presentation

Words will be presented to the learner on a screen with a standard keyboard. Graphics are not required. A printer to print out examples and definitions is a optional asset, but not required. Upper and lower case characters are definitely preferred.

Screen design must allow for:

pathway information
menus
choice bar
room for definitions of varying length
room for examples of varying length
an area for messages to prompt the learner which does not vary

Figure 12.6 shows the preliminary screen design for a screen size of 40 × 24.

12 Curriculum Four

12.5 Test Local Structure

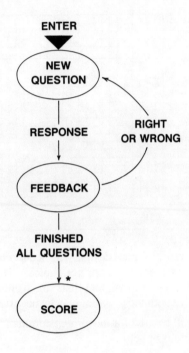

The Elements of CAL

12.6 Screen Design for WORDS

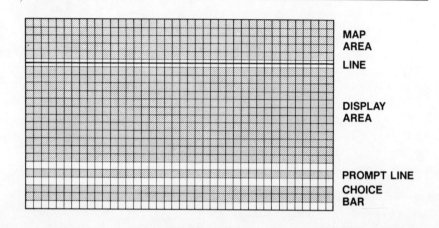

A potential problem in screen design will occur when words are listed to show the content of the segment, but are not choices. This will be resolved by keeping all menu displays vertical and lists of words horizontal. Specific response feedback to deal with the problem may be necessary.

The choice bar will be used for movement commands, and to request additional examples, definitions or help.

4. Tracking

LEARNER PROGRESS REPORTS

[Not implemented.]

- which segments the student has accessed in each session
- time spent in each local structure or support structure
- which objectives were reached
- average length of response time
- length of each session
- comparative figures (how individual compares to the group, how one group compares to another.)

This information will be for instructor use only. The learner only receives scores and feedback as indicated in the local structures.

12 Curriculum Four

COMMENT

[Not implemented.] The instructor must be able to read the results of the Comment support structure. The report must include:
- which learner made the comment
- where the learner was when the comment was made
- when the comment was made

It would be beneficial to have the comments collected according to category. For example, print all the comments related to a particular rule, segment or local structure.

The instructor must report to the learner about the action taken on the comment. This should occur on-line, either upon entry to the course, or through a mail system.

5. Mapping

The key concept underlying the mapping for WORDS is that the selection of objectives will be learner controlled. Any of the local structures may be accessed for any length of time, in any order, by any learner. Once a learner has selected Learn, however, the Dictionary local structure is only available by exiting Learn and selecting Dictionary from the first menu.

WORDS is menu driven. The instructor must "initialize" the course by naming a segment and listing the words in the segment. The following description of the main pathways will be easier to understand if you use Figure 12.7 as a guide.

- The learner must first choose whether she wants Dictionary or Learn.
- When the learner is finished with the Dictionary or Learn, she is returned to the menu which offers a choice of Learn or Dictionary.
- If the learner selects Learn, she must then choose a segment, one of five offered in a menu.
- After selection of a segment, the learner must choose one of Test, Practice or Meanings. When finished with any of these local structures, the learner is returned to the Test, Practice or Meanings menu.
- Return from a support structure will be to the spot from which the structure was accessed.

CONTROLLING MOVEMENT

The learner controls or her movement *down* through the course by either making a selection from a menu, hitting the return key, or (in some cases) selecting *X* for a new word. In all cases, the prompt will clearly indicate which choice is expected. Movement up is made at any point in the course by selecting *M*.

The Elements of CAL

12.7 WORDS Map

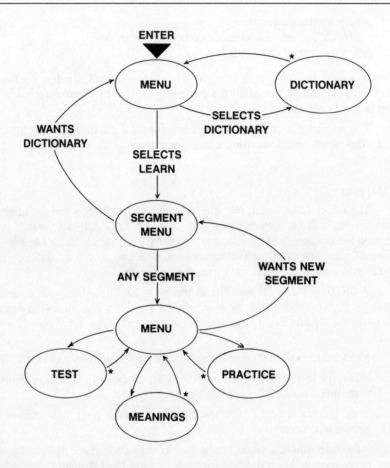

The learner may exit from the course completely by selecting *Q*.

Menu, Quit, Help and Comment will be valid in all local and support structures, and will therefor always appear on the choice bar. In Practice, Dictionary and Meanings, Example and Definition will be added to the choice bar. X for *new word* will appear in Dictionary and Meanings.

12 Curriculum Four

MAPPING INFORMATION

A record of the learner's location will be kept by a message in the upper left-hand corner of the top section of the screen. This will be continuously updated, with the current location the last item on the list.

Directions on movement and possible pathways open to the learner will be found in Help.

6. Student Support Structure

HELP

There will be four types of help messages in WORDS. The actual wording will vary depending on the local structure and the learner's position in the local structure.

- An introductory message can be accessed from the first layer. This will explain the basic WORDS map, and choices open to the learner.
- Dictionary will require a help message which tells the learner what to do in response to the initial prompt for a word.
- If the learner is at a menu, the message will explain each item on the menu, and how the learner can access that item.
- If a learner is in a local structure which asks questions, Help will include instructions on how to answer the question.

COMMENT

[Not implemented.] Comment will prompt the learner for input. The learner should be able to type in several lines for each comment. Comment should end with a reinforcement message which indicates to the learner when she can expect action on the comment.

A learner should be able to access the comments she has made and make alterations.

SUPPLEMENTARY MATERIALS

[Not implemented.] Each learner should be able to obtain a print copy of the current database organized alphabetically and/or by segment.

SUPPLEMENTARY ACTIVITIES

The following are suggestions for activities that can be used to integrate words into a broader goal.

- Learners could create sentences or paragraphs using the words in one or more segments of the course.

The Elements of CAL

- Groups or individual learners could share off-line research with other learners by being allowed to enter words or segments into the database.

- Words from various segments could be regrouped into new segments to illustrate variations in meaning.

7. Author Support Structures

REGISTRATION

[Not implemented.] Learners must be able to be registered as individuals or part of a pre-defined group. The instructor must be able to add learners, delete learners, create and alter groups.

EDIT THE DATA

The instructor must be able to add, delete or edit words or segments with their examples and definitions.

8. Site Implementation

As noted in the introduction, WORDS is essentially a tool, here configured for use by target learners at the grade four level. With changes to the data, it could meet the needs of a variety of learners.

The course is large for the main memory capacity of low-range machines. A skilled programmer could get around this problem. (See Chapter Thirteen for a more detailed explanation of approaches to programming Curriculum Four.)

VARIATIONS

One solution to the memory problem would be to create many copies of WORDS. That is, rather than run a course with a large database, a series of diskettes could be prepared using the same modules of code but with different data.

Alternatively, WORDS could be split into courses built on the Dictionary and Learn options. The smallest possible course would be one segment of five words from within Learn. If Dictionary were a course on its own, it could function with one or more segments. On low-range machines, separate diskettes could be prepared for the specific vocabulary required by each group of learners.

Both of these solutions could create problems with registration, tracking and editing facilities. It could become difficult to follow the path of a learner over several diskettes.

Level 9. Network Implementation

Network implementation of WORDS would depend very much on the nature of the network. Authors or instructors at sites in the network could create customized versions of the course by changing or adding to the data. These versions could then be catalogued and centrally stored, to be either down-loaded to microcomputers or accessed via a termnet.

If the design proves rugged and acceptable, then an author support structure which permitted virtually automatic creation of new versions would be very useful. Because the data is stored in a separate file, you would only have to write a front-end process which named the version and prompted for data for that version.

On larger networks, implementation would depend very much on the nature of the DBMS available. The relationships among the segments, the words, definition, examples and content of the diagnostic structure are easy to understand. It is possible that with a different target learner the instructor may feel each segment should be larger. Our feeling is that this could be tried, but that five words per segment will be the most comfortable limit for learners of any age in any subject.

Definitions of terms play an important role in learning any subject. In general, instructors will agree about basic definitions. However, network implementations of WORDS should provide for instructor variation of both definitions, content and examples.

FRACTIONS

The goal of FRACTIONS is to teach the learner how parts of a region can be expressed as a fraction.

1. Definitional Layer

OBJECTIVES

There are three objectives in FRACTIONS. The objectives are designed to be mastered in sequential order. The content of each objective builds on rules assumed to be mastered in the preceding objective(s).

Objective 1 The learner will be able to count the number of squares displayed on the screen.

Rule

The rule for this objective can be expressed as a table. Beginning with the integer 1, 1 corresponds to one square on the screen, 2 corresponds to two squares on the screen, and so on up to and including 9. For this target learner, fractions should be limited to greater than 0, less than 10.

The Elements of CAL

Questions

All questions for all rules will be generated randomly according to an algorithm. A question for the rule in this objective will take the form of squares displayed on the screen. The learner will be prompted to type in the number corresponding to the squares on the screen. The number must be exactly correct and must be an integer. That is, *four* does not equal *4*.

Examples

Examples will be in the form of questions, with the correct answer supplied. Such examples will occur as feedback to incorrect responses.

Meeting the Objective

This objective will be met if the learner can answer five questions in a row correctly, of ten questions asked.

Objective 2. The learner will understand the difference between a region and its parts.

Rules

Rule 1: A region is an area drawn on the screen.

Rule 2: A part is an area inside a region.

Questions

Each question will have two parts. First, a single square will appear on the screen. The learner will be prompted to type in the number of regions. Then, the square will be divided into parts. The learner will be prompted to type in the number of parts. In both cases, the learner must type in an integer.

Examples

An example will use the same graphics display as a question, except that the number of regions and number of parts will be provided. Such an example will occur as feedback to an incorrect response.

Meeting the Objective

This objective will be met if the learner can answer three questions correctly in a row.

Objective 3. The learner will be able to provide a fraction which represents the relationship different colored parts have to the whole of a region.

Rule

The relationship between a subset of the parts of a region and the total parts of a region can be expressed as a fraction.

Questions

Some of the parts of the region will be in a contrast color. The colored parts will represent the numerator. The total number of parts will represent the denominator. The learner will be asked to provide both the numerator and the denominator.

Examples

Examples will take the form of questions with the correct answer provided.

Meeting the Objective

The objective will be met if six questions of six questions asked are answered correctly.

2. Local Structures

COUNTING

The learner is presented with ten questions of the type described under Objective 1. If the response is correct, a message to that effect is displayed and the sequence continues. If the response is incorrect, the correct response is displayed and the sequence continues.

The sequence will ask a total of ten questions. If the learner gets five correct in a row, she receives a reinforcement message and leaves this local structure. Objective 1 has been met. If the learner does not get five correct in a row, she leaves the local structure with a message indicating problems. Objective 1 is not met.

Counting is a simple drill local structure. (See Figure 12.8.)

REGIONS AND PARTS

The sequence begins with an example of the rules of regions and parts. The sequence will then display questions of the type described under Objective 2. If the learner provides the correct response, a message to that effect is displayed, and the sequence moves to the next question. If the learner provides an incorrect response, the correct response to that question, in the form of an example, is displayed. If the learner gets three responses in a row correct, she leaves this local structure and receives a reinforcement message indicating that Objective 2 has been met. If the learner gets three incorrect responses altogether, she leaves this local structure, with a message indicating that Objective 2 has not been reached.

Regions and Parts is a drill local structure. (See Figure 12.9.)

The Elements of CAL

12.8 Counting Local Structure

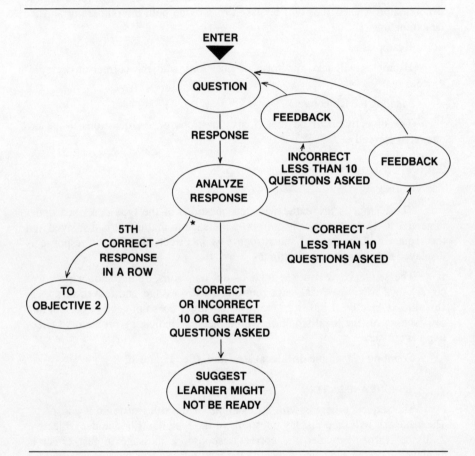

12.9 Regions and Parts Local Structure

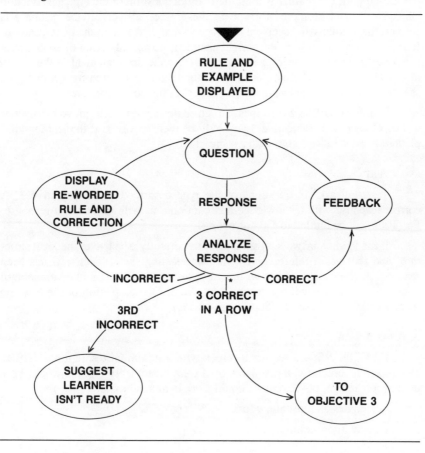

FRACTIONS DRILL

Fractions Drill is a local structure designed to first teach the rule concerning how fractions relate to regions and parts, then give the learner an opportunity to practice answering questions based on the rule. (See Figure 12.10.)

In the first part, the sequence will display an example, then ask the learner to copy the correct answer from the example. If the response is incorrect, the learner is given the correct answer in the form of an example and next question is displayed. If response is correct, the learner is given a message to that effect and the next question is displayed. If the learner gets 3 incorrect in a row, the sequence will end, and the learner will not have met Objective 3.

The Elements of CAL

If the learner makes three correct responses in a row, she receives a reinforcement message and continues with the second part of the local structure. In the second part, the learner is presented with a question of the type described in Objective 3, and prompted to type in the correct answer. If the response is correct, the learner will receive a message to that effect, then the next question. If the response is incorrect, the correct answer is displayed. After three incorrect responses in a row, the learner is moved back to the first statement of the rule in this local structure and must start over. If the learner gets three correct in a row, she receives a reinforcement message and leaves this local structure.

Fractions Drill is a drill local structure designed to help move the learner toward Objective 3. Objective 3 will only be met, however, if the learner completes the test local structure with a score of 6/6.

TEST

Test will ask six questions of the type described under Objective 3. A correct response will acknowledge and continue, as will an incorrect response. Feedback will be limited to right or wrong.

If the learner answers all six questions correctly, she leaves the local structure, and receives a reinforcement message stating that Objective 3 has been reached. If the learner makes an incorrect response, the test will continue until completion, but she will not reach Objective 3. On completion of the test, the learner will receive a score. (See Figure 12.11.)

3. Presentation

FRACTIONS will require a screen with a minimum resolution of 279 × 191 pixels in order for the squares to display adequately. Color would be a definite advantage, but the course could work in monochrome.

Screen design must allow for:

pathway information
menus
choice bar
room for both graphics and text
a prompt area which is constant

The basic screen layout will work for this course, but care will have to be taken that there is room for the graphics and any prompts or messages. Figure 12.12 shows a preliminary design for a screen of 279 × 191 pixels. Depending on the screen size, the screen may be too cramped to display a lot of mapping information.

12.10 Fractions Drill Local Structure

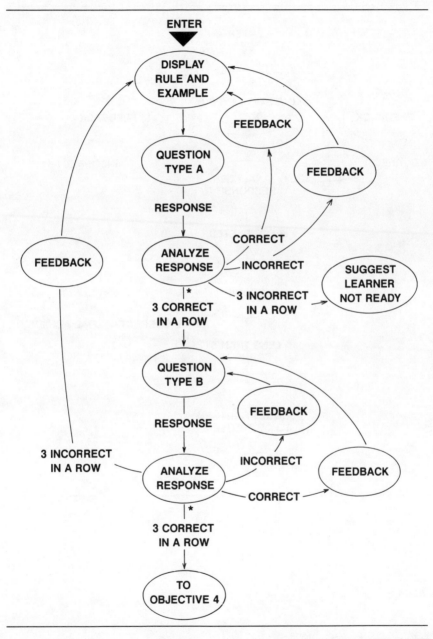

The Elements of CAL

12.11 Test Local Structure

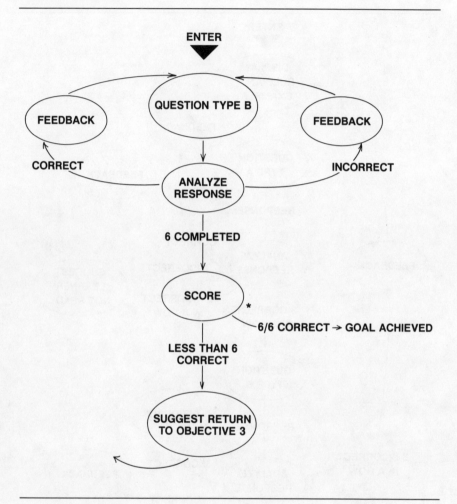

12.12 Screen Design for FRACTIONS

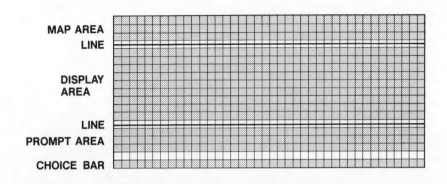

4. Tracking

[Not implemented.] Because FRACTIONS is a pre-structured course which progresses in a linear fashion, tracking must record the progress of each learner for each session. When the learner starts the course again, she should be brought into the point she had reached during the last session. The progress to that point should be displayed for the learner's information.

The instructor will also require the following information in order to assess the effectiveness of the course:

- which local structures accessed in each session
- time spent in each local structure or support structure
- average length of response time
- length of each session
- comparative figures

5. Mapping

FRACTIONS will work best divided into four segments. Segment 1 will contain the Counting local structure. Segment 2 will contain Regions and Parts, segment 3 will contain Fractions Drill and segment 4 will be the Test. (See Figure 12.13.) The pathways between segments are linear. Segment 1 must be met before the learner can continue to segment 2, etc. Once a segment has been completed, the learner may review a completed segment, or move to a new segment.

The Elements of CAL

12.13 FRACTIONS Mapping

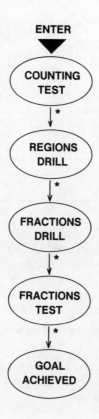

This structure will be made clear to the learner by presenting a menu when the learner leaves a local structure. When the learner leaves the Counting segment without achieving Objective 1, the menu will only contain: 1. Counting. If the learner has achieved Objective 1, however, the menu will contain:

1. Counting
2. New Segment

The learner can choose to review counting, or choose to move onto the new segment, which is Regions and Parts. If the learner leaves regions and parts without achieving Objective 2, the menu will contain:

1. Counting
2. Regions and Parts

If the learner achieves Objective 2, the menu will read:

1. Counting
2. Regions and Parts
3. New Segment

And so on.

CONTROLLING MOVEMENT

In FRACTIONS, the learner is given only limited control over movement. Selection of an item from the menu can be used to move up or down in the course. As explained above, however, the selection on the menu will not always include all the segments of the course.

Help, Quit, Menu and Comment will be valid at any point in the course, and thus will always appear on the choice bar. If the user is within a local structure, Menu will take her to the menu. If the learner is at the menu, Menu will take her out of FRACTIONS. Return from Help or Comment will be to the point at which it was requested. Quit will also take the learner out of FRACTIONS. Reinforcement will be used to emphasize the completion of or exit from segments.

6. Student Support Structure

HELP

FRACTIONS will require a variety of help messages, depending on the learner's location when this support structure is accessed.

- Help messages will have to provide mapping information when the learner is at a menu. The structure of the course may not be readily apparent unless the learner accesses some of these helps.

- A different help message will have to be written for each type of question, to give the learner information about how to answer the question.

COMMENT

[Not implemented.] Comment will prompt the learner for input. The learner should be able to type in several lines for each comment. Comment should end with a reinforcement message which indicates to the learner when she can expect action on the comment.

The Elements of CAL

The learner should be able to access the comments she has made and make alterations.

SUPPLEMENTARY MATERIALS

[Not implemented.] Supplementary materials could include worksheets generated by the computer.

SUPPLEMENTARY ACTIVITIES

The learners could create their own fractions using paper cutouts and or crayons.

7. Author Support Structures

REGISTRATION

[Not implemented.] Learners must be able to be registered as individuals or part of a pre-defined group. The instructor must be able to add learners, delete learners, create and alter groups.

EDITING THE DATA

Because the data for FRACTIONS is generated according to an algorithm, editing of the data will be restricted to changing the parameters of the questions and examples generated. Instructions for changes, or restrictions on changes will have to be made to take into account the graphics limitations of the screen used for output.

8. Site Implementation

FRACTIONS could be implemented as designed on a high-range or low-range machine. The student and author support structures are likely to take more space than the local structures, but they are important to this course and should be implemented wherever possible.

If necessary, or desired, the course could be separated into four smaller courses, one for each of the four segments. Each course could then be stored on a separate diskette.

9. Network Implementation

It is not likely that FRACTIONS will lend itself to variations in content. However, the objectives are common and versions based on different low-range microcomputers are likely to develop. For networks based on a lattice of micro users (if there were consensus in the lattice), it might be useful to keep the variations to such machine-dependent alterations.

It is also possible that one segment of FRACTIONS, the Counting Test, for example, would be useful in another mathematics course for young learners.

THE CURRICULUM

Now that we have a good idea of what is required by each course, we can examine how the courses will fit together as a curriculum. Once again, IMPS acts as the framework for the explanation.

1. Definitional Layer

It is immediately evident that the goals for each course are totally independent. The objectives are not related in a meaningful way, and our original assumption of two separate courses is correct. Because, however, the target learner for each course is the same, both courses can logically be part of the same curriculum. (See Site Implementation, below.)

2. Local Structures

The local structures are designed to meet the objectives of each course, and are thus completely independent.

3. Presentation

Both courses require a screen for output and a keyboard for input. WORDS requires a screen which can display a lot of text. FRACTIONS requires a screen with high enough resolution to accommodate the graphics. The implementation will either have to be on a screen which meets both requirements, or have the ability to switch from one type of screen to the other.

The basic screen design, however, will work for both courses and the learner will be able to move from one course to another without problems of consistency.

4. Tracking

[Not implemented.] Both courses require the same type of tracking information, which suggests a single module of code could handle both courses. It is possible that a tracking system from another course could be modified for use in Curriculum Four. Tracking is a desirable part of WORDS, but more essential for FRACTIONS. Tracking reports would have to be able to handle two separate courses.

The Elements of CAL

5. Mapping

The conclusions drawn from the first layers would suggest that the learner's initial menu would offer a choice of FRACTIONS or WORDS, and that to change courses the learner will have to come back to this initial menu. (See Figure 12.14.) If, however, vocabulary used in WORDS were terms related to fractions, FRACTIONS could allow access to WORDS.

6. Student Support Structures

HELP

Both courses heavily rely on Help to provide information to the learner. This is good because it will be consistent when the learner changes courses. The programmer may decide to have one module of code handle the help facility in both courses. This might create problems of portability, however, should an instructor want to use just one course in another curriculum, or independently. If the curriculum is implemented at a site which uses two different screens, the problems of displaying the help messages could become quite complex.

It appears at first that one course will not act as a support structure for the other. This is certainly true if the words in WORDS have nothing to do with fractions. If however, the vocabulary in WORDS were terms used in FRACTIONS,

12.14 Curriculum Four Map

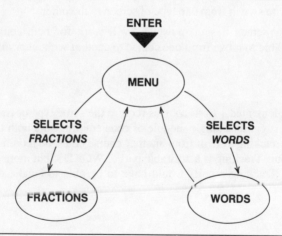

then you might want to allow the learner to access WORDS from within FRACTIONS. This would require an alteration at the mapping layer. [Not implemented.]

COMMENT

[Not implemented.] Comment would function exactly the same for each course. Comment would almost certainly be a common programming module for both courses.

7. Author Support Structures

REGISTRATION

[Not implemented.] The registration facility should be common to both courses, allowing the instructor to get an over-all picture of the curriculum, but should clearly separate which learner is in which group for which course.

EDITING THE DATA

Editing the data will be quite different for each course. In order to edit, the instructor would have to first specify which course. The procedure from that point on would be different for each course.

8. Site Implementation

It is possible to implement Curriculum Four at a site using a low-range machine. Chapters Thirteen, Fourteen and Fifteen detail such an implementation.

In fact, it is not likely that a curriculum containing these two courses would exactly meet the needs of many sites. We have decided to create the curriculum, however, to illustrate this higher level of mapping.

9. Network

It is not likely that WORDS and FRACTIONS would be implemented as a curriculum for a network implementation. Although each course in a network is likely to have a vocabulary support structure, it is more likely that WORDS would be part of a language arts curriculum and FRACTIONS part of a math curriculum.

SUMMARY

This is just the beginning of Curriculum Four. With this information, we are ready to plan an implementation. Chapter Thirteen reports the conclusions reached and decisions made for an actual implementation.

13 An Implementation

INTRODUCTION

Chapter Twelve provides the pre-implementation description of Curriculum Four. This chapter first discusses the process of implementation, then describes an Apple II Plus/Pascal implementation, and modifications which were made during implementation.

THE PROCESS

At the Softwords' CAL center, where these two courses were developed for the purpose of this book, we use the team approach to course development. A CAL team normally includes a programmer, an instructional designer, data editors, and data/researcher writers. In many cases, we also call in subject matter experts to help with either the content or educational objectives of the course being developed. Although you may not have access to such a team, you still must identify these separate functions in each course or lesson you develop.

Step One: Refining the Specifications

1. The state diagrams and IMPS description of the course go from the designer to the programmer. The state diagrams include the map and all the local structures.

2. Any special problems are identified by the programmer, who creates test modules where needed. Problems may be with graphic displays, or routines not currently found in the programmer's library. The programmer does any tests necessary to make sure available memory and equipment can meet the course specifications and creates a list of recommended hardware. This may reveal the need for changes in one or more layers of the IMPS description.

3. Key programming decisions are made; for example, whether to store the data in binary trees or fixed arrays.

The Elements of CAL

4. Alterations are made to the IMPS description, if required. In some cases, this may mean the objectives will have to be altered. Usually, however, alterations are in the area of presentation, local structures or support structures.

5. If the alterations made in the IMPS structure require it, go back to the beginning of Step One.

Step Two: The First Prototype

1. A functioning prototype to show main pathways is created. Sample data only is used. Many special messages used for debugging will appear.

2. The first prototype is debugged by the programmer for programming problems.

3. The designer goes through the first prototype with reference to the objectives. The first prototype may point out the need for small changes to be made to the state diagrams and IMPS description. Although at this step it is more likely that the program will need minor revisions so that the pathways will function correctly.

Step Three: Creating the Data

Data creation is begun on the basis of revised pathways and presentation decisions. The data is created using the system text editor and stored in editable files. Data creation can be very time consuming and will continue concurrently with the next stages.

Although some sources of required data will have been identified in the definitional layer, additional sources will have to be located. The original material will very likely not be in a form ideally suited for CAL, and certainly will not arrive broken into rules to fit your objectives. You will be using this original material to create rules, questions and examples. This is a process which will often cause you to cover the same ground more than once.

Begin by looking at the objectives you want the learner to achieve as being composed of a system of elements which are connected in certain ways. Remember that the connections between the elements are often as important as the elements.

Focus on a single idea, collect information, sort the information into workable blocks (rule, example, potential question), then focus on the idea that emerges from this exercise. You may have to do it all several times before you truly identify the essential building blocks of the objectives you are trying to reach.

Remember to work back and forth between the structure and the data, all the while keeping in mind the skills, vocabulary and interests of your target learner.

13 An Implementation

Any supplementary materials such as learner guides, or specially created references should be begun at this point.

Step Four: The Prompts and Messages

The designer creates a page-by-page copy of all prompts, menus, choice bars and mapping information which will appear. Again, the target learner must be kept in mind for the creation of appropriate messages. These messages and prompts are indexed to the state diagram.

The original state diagrams will not show a bubble for each page in the course. At this stage, any display which will take two pages must be entered into the state diagram as two bubbles, any introductory pages or transition pages must be clearly positioned.

AN EXAMPLE

A section of this stage of FRACTIONS has been reproduced here to illustrate the level of exact detail required to ensure accurate translation of the designer's ideas to the final course. Keep in mind that even if you are both designer and programmer, you must work back and forth between diagrams and programs to avoid getting muddled, wasting time, or going off down a road which will end up being a detour away from your objectives.

The layout of the prompts and messages should reflect the screen design. In this case:

mapping area
main data display area
prompt area
choice bar

The mapping area will record level as per specification. The choice bar will always contain: Q)uit M)enu H)elp. See Figure 13.1 for location of each message.

29.
(Display Area)
This is a Test on Fractions.
(Prompt Area)
Press Return to Continue

30.
(Display Area)
* * * (Question type B)
(Prompt Area)
What is the fraction?

The Elements of CAL

(This prompt line will require 3 lines. The learner
will type in the numerator, the program will supply
the line, and the learner will type in the denominator.)

31.
(Display Area)
Right!
(Prompt Area)
Press Return to Continue

32.
(Display Area)
Sorry, that is wrong.
(Prompt Area)
Press Return to Continue

33.
(Display Area)
Good for You.
You finished the test.

Your score: N

(Prompt Area)
Press Return to Continue

34.
(Display Area)
Well Done!
You have finished FRACTIONS.

1. Counting Review
2. Regions and Parts Review
3. Fractions Review
4. Test

(Prompt Area)
Choose One

35.
(Display area.)

13 An Implementation

You should do some fractions review.

1. Counting Review
2. Regions and Parts Review
3. Fractions Review
4. Test

(Prompt Area)
Choose One

Figure 13.1 Modified Test Structure for Fractions

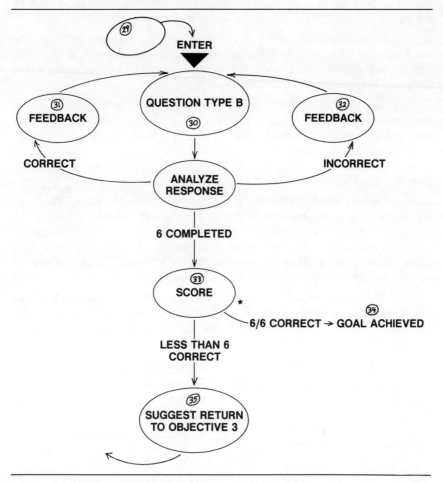

The Elements of CAL

These messages are created in an editable file and given to the programmer. In some cases, the messages will be hard-coded into the program. Alternatively, they will be stored in data files and called into the program when required. Usually, the help messages are also written at this point. In some courses, the help messages will be complex and portions of them will be generated according to an algorithm.

Step Five: Second Prototype

1. The second prototype is created, still with special de-bugging messages and sample data, but now with all transition pages, actual prompts, real menus. If possible, several people outside the development team are brought in to try and blow the program up. Any learner complaints, problems or requests are considered by both the designer and programmer. Any decisions to revise must be reflected in a revised IMPS description and state diagrams.

2. In some extreme cases you will have identified so many problems you will have to go back to the specification stage. In general, however, at the stage, you will only need to alter prompt messages, screen design and catch minor programming or typing errors in the prompts.

If, however, you do find a lot of problems, you must go back far enough in the process to identify the source of the problem. For example, if you do not have enough memory to create effective graphics, tinkering with the program will not help.

Step Six: The Course

1. Data is moved into the course. At this stage the course needs lots of testing. Every piece of data must be accessed through every possible pathway. You should allow for more learner input. No more alterations to the IMPS description should be necessary. The programmer may decide to fine-tune one or more aspects of the program. Data may need editing, or revision. This should be done through the author support structure designed for this purpose.

2. The debugging messages are removed and the programmer completes line documentation of the program. The IMPS description and state diagrams can stand as overview documentation, but additional documentation may be required.

3. Supplementary material such as user guides is completed.

4. Give the course to the learners. Record reactions, benefits, comments, problems. Wait a while. Revise and improve the course, or just keep the good parts for a new course.

13 An Implementation

THE IMPLEMENTATION
The Equipment
- 48K Apple II Plus
- memory card
- monitor
- Apple/Pascal System
- Apple disk controller with two 140K drives
- one Apple/UCSD PASCAL format single side, single density diskette
- Decwriter III printer (requires communication card in the Apple)

This equipment was selected because it is relatively common and meets the Curriculum criterion of being able to switch from a low-resolution text screen to a higher-resolution graphics screen. The Decwriter III is not essential for running the course, but was very important during development.

The Language

PASCAL was selected for the language of implementation as somewhat of a compromise. BASIC might be a more popular choice and NATAL would certainly have produced more precise code. However, the use of PASCAL allows us to demonstrate some of the principles of structured programming as they apply to courseware in a manner that most owners of microcomputers will be able to imitate directly, if they desire. All code is written in UCSD standard PASCAL and compiled on an Apple II Plus.

The Programs

The Curriculum exists as three *chained* programs: WORDS, FRACTIONS and the linking program called CAL. The programs are stored on one diskette. Each program is called into main memory as required. Because main memory is limited to 64K, certain desired but not essential aspects of the original IMPS description of the course were not implemented. The course as implemented reaches the limits of memory capacity. Depending on the pathways chosen, the course can be within 1/2 K of exhausting available main memory.

An alternate method of implementing this curriculum would have involved *segmenting* each program into smaller blocks.† We decided not to segment the Curriculum, however, because this is a complex programming technique which may have made it difficult for some readers to understand the important aspects

---

†Note that the term *segment* is used here as a programming term. It does not parallel our use of segment as part of the learner's view of the course.

175

The Elements of CAL

of structured programming and CAL which we hope to make clear in Chapters Fourteen and Fifteen. Also, because segmenting a course results in many more accesses to the disk while the course is running, the end result may be a slower running course. In order to demonstrate segmentation to those readers who might be interested, however, a small portion of WORDS has been segmented.

The Map

The Curriculum Map was implemented as designed.

WORDS

1. Definitional Layer

The goals and objectives were implemented as planned.

The sources selected for the data were two standard grade four dictionaries. We found that one basic meaning was available for each word, but that we had to write our own expanded definition. A young learner was brought in to approve the written definitions and write additional definitions where required. We also found that the definitions from the dictionaries, when put through our on-line reading level guide, were classified as being between grades five and seven. The decision was made not to alter the definitions at this stage because they could easily be altered after course trials.

The memory limitations imposed by this implementation meant that the database could not contain more than twenty-five words, with each definition limited to two hundred characters. Each word could have a maximum of two definitions. These character counts were also determined with the screen design in mind. The decision was made to use single-definition nouns only. We did not feel this limitation to the database altered the possibility of the objectives contributing to the goal, but it did mean there would be more editing for the instructor to provide the variety which will be required by learners.

Examples

The course was limited to two examples per word, with each example a maximum of two hundred characters in length. Young learners were asked to write the examples. This worked out well, with only slight editing to keep the definitions within character limitations required.

Questions

Questions were implemented as planned.

2. Local Structures

DICTIONARY

Implemented as planned.

Because the dictionary is limited to twenty-five words in this implementation, it is possible to display a menu of all available words if the learner does not select an exact match. Depending on the length of the words in the dictionary, the display may be quite crowded on the screen. Close matches are limited to words which begin with the same letter as that requested by the learner.

A decision had to be made about whether the definition would stay on the screen when the example was accessed, and whether both definitions and examples would stay on the screen if all were accessed. A decision was made to always display the first definition, and change the second part of the display to show either a second definition or one of the examples. This method is used whenever second definitions and examples are available throughout the course.

MEANINGS

Implemented as planned.

PRACTICE

Implemented as planned.

If more memory were available, a more complex diagnostic sequence, with a variety of wordings of messages and extra examples and definitions could have been used.

TEST

Learner response to this local structure caused us to add a report of words not mastered in addition to the simple score originally planned for this structure.

3. Presentation

An Apple II offers a choice of hi-resolution screen or low-resolution screen. The low-resolution text screen allows more lines of text, but letters are only available in upper case. The high-resolution screen allows both lower and upper case, but does not allow you to display as many lines of text. Because WORDS relies on textual matter, and the choice bar sometimes expands to two lines, we decided to use the low-resolution text screen. We feel the text is difficult to read, however, and learner feedback may lead to an alternate implementation, losing some mapping information and using high-resolution. Less than forty lines of code would have to be changed to write such an alternate version.

The Elements of CAL

Our standard screen design works well for this course. An adjustment had to be made to accommodate the two line choice bar. Extra spacing was required to compensate for capital letters.

4. Tracking

The memory limitations of this implementation are too great to allow tracking.

Initial learner input indicates, however, that a method of recording which rules have been mastered in each segment would be an advantage. The course currently forgets that the learner was able to provide the correct response to the question about the word *acrobat* the last time she was in the Meanings segment of the course, and asks that same question during subsequent accesses of the segment. Learners who tried the course said they would have preferred to see only the rules they had not mastered in subsequent accesses.

5. Mapping

The map was implemented as designed.

We decided to call each segment a *Lesson* because we felt this term would be more familiar to our target learner.

6. Student Support Structure

The Help support structure was implemented as originally designed. We found that all requests for help could be met with seven generalized messages such as *Select an item from the menu*.

Comment was not implemented due to memory restrictions.

7. Author Support Structures

Registration was not implemented because it was not required by the site. If tracking facilities had been available, registration would have been essential.

Data editing is possible, but is limited to the flexibility of the Apple/PASCAL editor which comes with the system. The instructor will require an understanding of how the course and data structure works in order to edit the data without accidentally creating errors in the program. Care should be taken to always copy files before editing. This editing process is not as easy or as automatic as it possibly should be. Because the database is small, however, it will function.

The following restrictions on the database apply to this implementation. Note that a segment, as defined in the design, is called a Lesson for the learner's view, and called a group by the programmer.

- The database may contain a maximum of twenty-five words.
- The database must contain at least one group (group = segment = lesson) with a maximum of five groups.
- There must be at least one word in each group, with a maximum of five words.
- Each word may have a maximum of twelve characters.
- Each word must have one definition, with a maximum of two definitions.
- Each definition may have a maximum of two hundred characters.
- Each word may have 0-2 examples.
- Each example may have a maximum of two hundred characters.

The data is located in Chapter Fifteen. The group called *Sports* only contains four words. This is to encourage you to immediately personalize WORDS with addition of your own rule and examples. The course will run without this additional word.

FRACTIONS

1. Definitional Layer

The basic concept of FRACTIONS, that of a series of objectives to be learned in a specific order, was threatened by this implementation. In this implementation, since there is no tracking or registration, a learner must move through each segment of the course, even if the segment was mastered in the last access of the course. We decided to leave the objectives as originally designed, in order to show the effect this type of structure has on a learning environment. We do not recommend this as an ideal implementation of this course.

All examples and questions are generated within the program by a function called RAND which essentially returns a random number in a range specified (1-8). The original maximum of 9 was reduced because 9 squares did not fit attractively on the screen.

2. Local Structures

All local structures were implemented as planned.

3. Presentation

We were pleased with the results possible with the Apple II Plus graphics screen. The colors in the displays are a constant declared in the global area of the program. (See Chapter Fourteen for details.) Tests show the course will function quite well in monochrome. In questions, care will have to be taken to alter the prompts to match the color of a monochrome screen, however.

The Elements of CAL

The reduced number of text lines available led us to display only the current segment, rather than full pathways information. We felt this was not a problem, because most of the movement in FRACTIONS is pre-structured and the learner is less likely to need detailed pathway information.

One challenge was to find an attractive and consistent way to display fractions, both as examples provided by the program and as responses from the learner. A decision was made to prompt the learner for the numerator, provide a horizontal line, then prompt for the denominator. This meant a three line prompt area was required in some segments of the course. This prompt method created problems for some of our trial learners. Some learners tried to provide a slash from the keyboard, others did not wait long enough for the second prompt. All learners quickly mastered the system, however, so the decision was made to keep the system and provide a careful explanation in the Help message for such questions.

4. Tracking

Tracking was not implemented due to memory restrictions.

5. Mapping

This course map was implemented as planned, with some reservation as to learner distress at having to repeat segments already mastered if the course was not complete in one session.

As with WORDS, we used the term *Lesson* to identify segments to the learner because we felt the term would be more familiar to our target learner.

6. Student Support Structures

Help was implemented as planned. Because FRACTIONS does not have a sophisticated recognition of anticipated incorrect responses (*one* instead of *1*, for example), numerous detailed Help messages were felt to be essential. In fact, initial learner trials suggest that learners find the main pathway prompts quite clear, and need few accesses to the Help facility. Comment was not implemented due to memory restrictions.

7. Author Support Structures

In order to edit FRACTIONS examples and questions, the instructor would have to alter the parameters of the random number generator in RAND. As explained in Chapter Twelve, the range of 1-9 was selected with the target learner in mind. Eventually, however, it was decided to allow a maximum number of eight parts, because nine created an unattractive display. Changing the parameters is therefore not recommended. It is, however, quite easy to alter RAND to return any number up to and including nine. Since the course is based

13 An Implementation

on accepting single-character input, more extensive changes would have to be made to the program in order to allow input of numbers greater than nine.

The local structures and displays have been designed with the teaching of the rules of counting, regions and parts in mind. Alteration to these rules would be very difficult as they are the foundation for the displays of both questions and examples. If an instructor does want to alter the course, attention must be paid to the screen design. Choice of color for displays can be altered by changing the constant declared in the global area of the program. Remember to change all prompts or messages which refer to the color of the squares to match any changes you make in the displays.

The registration support structure was not implemented due to memory restrictions. This created a inconvenient situation for any instructor who might wish to quickly access specific segment for development purposes. If registration were available, special conditions could apply to the instructor which would eliminate the need to pass sequentially through each lesson. To solve this problem, we allowed any segment to be accessed from any menu. That is, although the menu only lists Counting and Regions and Parts, number 3, for Fractions Drill, will in fact take you into that lesson. This is, of course, completely opposite to the the learner's view of FRACTIONS. No doubt, in time learners will catch on to what appears to be a flaw in course design. Our trial learners did not discover the hidden options, however. Another way around this problem, without registration, would be to create a copy of the course which did not have restrictions placed on the access to lessons. This course could be for instructor use only.

LEARNER GUIDE

We recommend that each learner using Curriculum Four be provided with a simple three point Learner Guide.

- Type H, then the return key if you need HELP.
- Type M, then the return key if you want to see a MENU.
- Type Q, then the return key if you want to QUIT.

14 Curriculum Four: CAL and FRACTIONS

INTRODUCTION

This documentation† is designed with two purposes in mind. All courseware should be documented in each of its implementations. So we have here, in concise form, the regular documentation of two courses, *FRACTIONS* and *WORDS*.

In addition, however, it is assumed that not all of our readers will have worked with PASCAL and indeed some may not be programmers at all. Although we cannot explain PASCAL as a language within one chapter, we have attempted to detail those aspects of PASCAL least likely to be known to readers accustomed to BASIC. The introductory portion of the documentation, therefore, might be slightly longer than usual. As explained in Chapter Thirteen, the code could be somewhat more compact if we were not using it to illustrate a particular implementation in a particular language.

BRIEF INTRODUCTION TO PASCAL
General Structure

PASCAL is designed to exemplify structured programming and all versions draw strongly on the ideas of Wirth, Hoare and Dijkstra. The **goto** statement is permitted but certainly not encouraged and extensive use is made of procedures and functions. In many versions of BASIC, all variables are common to the entire program. Many other languages have global variables which may be accessed anywhere in the program and local variables which are valid only in the

---

†The code for *WORDS* and *FRACTIONS* is available on a single diskette for the Apple II Plus, configured as indicated in Chapter Thirteen. To order, write to the publisher. Pricing (subject to change without notice) is $25.00 per diskette, plus $3.00 for postage and handling. Permission is granted to the reader to key-in a single personal copy of these courses, but not to resell, barter or otherwise distribute. Photocopying of the code and documentation is forbidden under the laws of copyright.

The Elements of CAL

module in which they are declared. PASCAL nests procedures and functions so that variables are valid in the module in which they are declared and in modules "nested" within that module. In this way, one may use the same variable name in different modules as though it were, in effect, a different name.

This concept applies to the names of the modules themselves. For example, in *FRACTIONS* we have a number of functions called *UP* and *QUESTION*. These have the same name because the names express the purpose of the functions, and there is some common code in each, but the specific modules are customized to perform as required at that precise location in the program.

If the PASCAL program is short, one can simply nest the modules and let the structure demonstrate the validity of the different variables. This example shows the structure without being exact about the form of the statements and punctuation in PASCAL.

> *MAIN*.
> Declare *x* and *y*.
> > *TOP_LEVEL*.
> > Declare *z*.
> > > *MID_LEVEL*.
> > > Declare *a* and *b*.
> > > Code for *MID_LEVEL*.
> > > End *MID_LEVEL*.
> >
> > Code for *TOP_LEVEL*.
> > End *TOP_LEVEL*.
>
> Code for *MAIN*.
> End *MAIN*.

Within the code of the *MID_LEVEL* procedures, *x*,*y*,*z*,*a* and *b* would all be known. At the *TOP_LEVEL*, however, *a* and *b* would not be known, only *x*, *y* and *z*. In the code for *MAIN*, only *x* and *y* would be known. In this manner, information can be "hidden". *MAIN* does not really need to know anything about *a* and *b*, therefore we keep that information "hidden" to avoid side-effects.

Include and Use

INCLUDE

When programs become so large that the nesting of procedures begins to make the structure of the program less rather than more visible, it is advisable to use the include process. This permits an ordering of the program in a manner that more clearly reveals the patterns.

Suppose that our example above had four long modules within *MID_LEVEL*: *BOTTOM*, *PYRAMUS*, *THISBE* and *RILE*. The structure would

14 Curriculum Four: CAL and FRACTIONS

be more clearly revealed in this manner:

>MAIN.
>>Declare x and y.
>>TOP_LEVEL.
>>>Declare z.
>>>>MID_LEVEL.
>>>>>Includes BOTTOM, PYRAMUS, THISBE, RILE.
>>>>>Declare a and b.
>>>>>Code for MID_LEVEL.
>>>>End MID_LEVEL.
>>>Code for TOP_LEVEL.
>>End TOP_LEVEL.
>Code for MAIN.
>End MAIN.

Otherwise, several pages might pass by before we saw the code for MAIN.

USE

As we shall see below in the discussion on graphics, functions and procedures that form an extension of the language likely to be used often may be grouped together as segmented modules. They are brought into a specific program through the construct **uses** as demonstrated in INITWORDS in the program WORDS.

Declarations

A further adherence to the tenets of structured programming is shown in the use of declarations. All constants, variables, types and structures used in the program must be declared. This process is well explained in all PASCAL manuals. Although it is true that compilers can perform the function of listing these elements and checking for redundancy, doing it as a formal part of the programming process encourages careful planning of the program and again helps avoid unforeseen side-effects.

CONSTANTS

A constant is a piece of information used by a program, but unchanged as the program progresses. For example, in a calendar program, we may have two constants, *regular_year* and *leap_year*. The first of these would be set to 365 and the second to 366 and those values would remain unchanged throughout the program.

The Elements of CAL

TYPES

A type characterizes a class of objects and the operations that can be performed upon them. PASCAL has the usual fundamental or minimal types: integers, real numbers, characters and boolean truth values. PASCAL is very strict in insisting that a variable may only have values of its specified type and that the only operations allowed on a value are those associated with its type.

In addition to these fundamental types, however, PASCAL has a powerful type extension capability. PASCAL has a number of structured types (some of which are discussed below), and also permits the declaration of user-defined types. *Coin* is often used as an example of a user-defined type:

> **type**
>   *coin* = (
>   *penny*,
>   *nickel*,
>   *dime*,
>   *quarter*,
>   *halfdollar*,
>   *dollar*);

STRUCTURED TYPES

Strings, files, sets and records are all structured types in the language. For example, PASCAL permits the definition of a **record** structure; a **record** is a collection of information pertaining to some real-world entity. The components of a record can be of any type, even other records. In these programs, *passedtype* in program *WORDS* is an example of structured type and *wordtype* is a record.

VARIABLES

As in most other languages, variables in PASCAL are used for pieces of information which change as the program progresses. All variables must be declared before any statements appear.

Procedures and Functions

Procedures and functions are tools which may be used by the program itself or by specific procedures or functions. There are numerous examples in the course. As indicated earlier in the book, a procedure is a function which may not return a value (except with the use of **var**). Functions always return a value. The function can "be" the value. That is, we could have a function *CHECK_FOR_EXISTENCE_OF_LAND*. and a procedure *SAIL_WEST*. An **if** clause of the form

14 Curriculum Four: CAL and FRACTIONS

    if *CHECK_FOR_EXISTENCE_OF_LAND* **then**
       SAIL_WEST;

would eventually bring the sailor to land in the west.

Graphics

The influence of Seymour Papert can be seen in the graphics procedures used in UCSD PASCAL. The reader is referred to Lewis [Lewis] for detailed explanations, but the following comments may be helpful in understanding the use of graphics in *FRACTIONS*.

PIXELS

The Apple screen is normally in *textmode* and is divided into 23 rows and 40 columns. In *grafmode*, however, the screen is divided into 53,760 dots called pixels, based on a division into 192 rows with 280 pixels in each row.

CARTESIAN CO-ORDINATES

The *grafmode* screen has its origin in the lower left-hand corner of the screen at pixel (zero,zero). Other points on the screen can be determined in absolute terms. e.g. the center of the full screen is pixel (96,190).

COLORS

The Apple screen colors are defined using a **type** *screencolor* which defines thirteen possible colors: one of these is *none*, which is used to move the drawing pen from point to point without leaving a trail.

VIEWPORTS

The boundaries of the 192 × 280 pixels are not shown and often the program works within a "virtual box" or *viewport* which is defined using the four integers which define the corners and sides of that rectangle. When a viewport is defined, say the bottom half of the screen, then the statement *FILLSCREEN(orange)* will fill the bottom half of the screen with the color orange.

TURTLEGRAPHICS

All of the above capabilities are added to PASCAL through the module *turtlegraphics* contained in **SYSTEM.LIBRARY**. These functions and procedures are brought into *FRACTIONS* with the statement **uses** *turtlegraphics*.

The Elements of CAL

Strings

In PASCAL, strings are handled as a structured **type**. This **type** is actually a packed **array** of characters. Strings default to a length of 80 characters and it is often useful, as we do in *WORDS*, to select a lower maximum length. PASCAL is somewhat less than ideal in its handling of strings when compared to PLAIN or NATAL, but UCSD PASCAL provides reasonable extensions with its string handling facilities, these are used extensively in *WORDS*.

For further detail on the language, see those texts recommended on page 112.

CAL.TEXT

program CAL;

(* The following is included by the **uses** statement:
*   **procedure** SETCHAIN(tytle:**string**);
*)

uses chainstuff;

var   st   : **string**;

begin
  while true **do**
  begin
  PAGE(output);
  WRITELN;
  WRITELN('welcome to cal ......');
  WRITELN;
  WRITELN;
  WRITELN;
  WRITELN;
  WRITELN;
  WRITELN('what lesson would you like');
  WRITELN;
  WRITELN(' 1 - words');
  WRITELN(' 2 - fractions');
  WRITELN;
  WRITELN('or q to quit');
  WRITELN;
  WRITE(' > ');
  READLN(st);
  if LENGTH(st) > 0 **then**
    case st[1] **of**
    '1','W','w' : SETCHAIN('cal:words');
    '2','F','f' : SETCHAIN('cal:frac');
    'q','Q'   : EXIT(**program**);
    end;
  end;
end.

CAL – This is the small program that links or calls the two parts of this course. *CAL* prompts the student for the course that they want; after completion of the selected course, control returns to this program. Both *WORDS* and *FRAC* can be executed without the presence of *CAL*.

The use of *chaining* is fully explained in *Addendum to the Apple Pascal Language Reference Manual* for Version 1.1.

The Elements of CAL

The FRACTIONS Course Map

FRACTION.TEXT   191
    SYSTUFF.TEXT   192
    CONSTS.TEXT   193
    TYPEVARS.TEXT   194
    RANDWAIT.TEXT   195
    TOLOWER.TEXT   196
    WINDOW.TEXT   197
       WINDOW1.TEXT   198
    HELP.TEXT   199
       HELP1.TEXT   200
       HELP2.TEXT   201
       HELP3.TEXT   202
    PROMPT.TEXT   203
    SHOWBXLN.TEXT   204
    SHOWNUM.TEXT   205
    INITFRAC.TEXT   206
       SETUPWIN.TEXT   207
    MAINFRAC.TEXT   208
       COUNTING.TEXT   209
          COUNT1.TEXT   210
       RPART.TEXT   211
          RPART1.TEXT   212
          RPART2.TEXT   213
       AFRAC.TEXT   214
          AFRAC1.TEXT   215
          AFRAC2.TEXT   216
       BFRAC.TEXT   217
          BFRAC1.TEXT   218
       TESTFRAC.TEXT   219
          TESTF1.TEXT   220
       SHOWMENU.TEXT   221

FRACTION.TEXT

```
(*$S+*)
program FRACTIONS;

(*    FRACTIONS A computer aided learning course
 *    written by p.c. good
 *    copyright 1982 by SOFTWORDS a division of PRESS PORCEPIC
 *)

(*$I systuff.text*)
(*$I consts.text*)
(*$I typevars.text*)
(*$I randwait.text*)

procedure EXITPROGRAM(st:string);
begin
  TEXTMODE;
  PAGE(output);
  WRITE(st);
  SETCHAIN('cal:cal');
  EXIT(program);
end;

(*$I tolower.text*)
(*$I window.text*)

function READY:boolean;    forward;

(*$I help.text*)
(*$I prompt.text*)

function READY;
begin
  READY := (DOPROMPT(clear,'press return to continue : ') = 'm');
end;

(*$I showbxln.text*)
(*$I shownum.text*)
(*$I initfrac.text*)
(*$I mainfrac.text*)

begin  (* main *)
  PAGE(output);
  uname := '';
  helpmesg := helpa;

  INITFRAC;
  MAINFRAC;
end.
```

FRACTIONS —

This program is written in UCSD PASCAL on an Apple II Plus microcomputer. The System Library supplied with the Apple PASCAL is used extensively for access to the Apple high-res graphics screen. Refer to the Apple PASCAL Language Manual for a complete description of these library functions.

EXITPROGRAM — The screen is first cleared then the exit message passed in *st* is displayed. The program is then chained back to *CAL:CAL.CODE*.

READY — Clears the prompt line, then prompts the student with *"press return to continue"*. The character returned is tested for menu, returning *true* if the student wants the menu.

The Elements of CAL   SYSTUFF.TEXT

```
(*  The following are included by the uses statement:
*     function  KEYPRESS: boolean;
*     function  RANDOM: integer;
*     procedure RANDOMIZE;
*
*     procedure SETCHAIN(tytle:string);
*     procedure SETCVAL(val:string);
*     procedure GETCVAL(var val:string);
*
*     type screencolor = (none,white,black,reverse,radar,
*           black1,green,violet,white1,black2,orange,blue,white2);
*
*     procedure INITTURTLE;
*     procedure TURN(angle: integer);
*     procedure TURNTO(angle: integer);
*     procedure MOVE(dist: integer);
*     procedure MOVETO(x,y: integer);
*     procedure PENCOLOR(penmode: screencolor);
*     procedure TEXTMODE;
*     procedure GRAFMODE;
*     procedure FILLSCREEN(fillcolor: screencolor);
*     procedure VIEWPORT(left,right,bottom,top: integer);
*     procedure WCHAR(ch: char);
*     procedure WSTRING(s: string);
*)

uses applestuff, chainstuff, turtlegraphics;
```

CONSTS.TEXT

```
const  minx        =   0;
       maxx        = 279;
       miny        =   0;
       maxy        = 191;

       hchar       =   7;
       vchar       =  10;
       offset      =   4;
       width       =  31;
       woutline    =   5;
       fillcolor       = blue;
       outlinecolor    = orange;
       backgroundcolor = black2;
       colorpen        = white;

       level0      =   1;
       level1      =   2;
       level2      =   3;
       solid1      =   4;
       wname       =   5;
       text0       =  11;
       text1       =   6;
       text2       =   7;
       prompt      =   8;
       choice1     =   9;
       last        =  10;
       numofwindows    =  11;

       count       =   1;
       randpdrill  =   2;
       fracdrill   =   3;
       test        =   4;

       helpa       =   1; (* HELP levels *)
       helpb       =   2; helpc    =   3;
       helpd       =   4; helpe    =   5;
       helpf       =   6; helpg    =   7;
       helph       =   8; helpi    =   9;
       helpj       =  10; helpk    =  11;
       helpl       =  12; helpm    =  13;
       helpn       =  14; helpo    =  15;

       maxstring   = 200;
       shortst     =  12;
       choice      = 'H)elp M)enu Q)uit';
       clear       = true;
       noclear     = false;
```

CONST — The constants are used to hide the numbers that tend to make the reading of code difficult. System constants, such as screen width and machine dependent locations, are found in this **const** area of the program.

The Elements of CAL

TYPEVARS.TEXT

```
type  longstring = string[maxstring];
   xytype   = record
         x  : integer;
         y  : integer;
      end;
   passedtype = (pass,failed,notin);

var  wind       : array[1..numofwindows] of xytype;
   winddiag    : array[1..numofwindows] of xytype;
   vminx,vmaxx  : integer;
   vminy,vmaxy  : integer;
   uname       : string;
   helpmesg    : integer;
   helpflag    : boolean;
   smst1       : string;
   smst2       : string;
   lastrand    : integer;
   numfinshed  : integer;
   passed      : array[count..test] of passedtype;
   promptstring : string;
   lessonname  : array[1..4] of string;
```

TYPE — The **type** area of PASCAL programs is used to declare user defined types.

VAR — The **var** part of the program declaration area declares the variables that can be accessed by all the program.

194

RANDWAIT.TEXT

```
function RAND(low,high:integer):integer;
var   i    : integer;
begin
  i := RANDOM mod (high-low) + low;
  if i = lastrand then
    RAND := RAND(low,high)
  else RAND := i;
  lastrand := i;
end;

procedure WAIT(seconds:integer);
var   i,j   : integer;
begin
  for i := 1 to seconds do
    for j := 1 to 1700 do;
end;
```

RAND — Although a random number can be established directly in PASCAL (using the system function *RANDOM*), there is no assurance that the generated number will be different from the previously generated random number. The function *RAND* establishes a random number (within a specified range) and then checks to make sure that the new number is not the same as *lastrand*.

If it is the same number, the steps are repeated until a different number is generated. This avoids giving the learner exactly the same question twice in a row.

WAIT — This is a loop designed to make the CPU do nothing for a given period. In essence, we are building a little clock to count seconds. Note that the variable *seconds* is passed in to the function so that whenever *WAIT* is called, a variable specific to the calling procedure can establish the exact time limit required.

The second loop, from 1 to 1700, is an "empty" loop. Although nothing is done 1700 times, the CPU is engaged in incrementing a counter.

If your computer has a clock, you could use it to perform this function.

The Elements of CAL

TOLOWER.TEXT

```
function TOLOWER(ch:char):char;
var   ch2   : char;
begin
  if ORD(ch) > 128 then
    ch2 := CHR(ORD(ch) - 128)
  else ch2 := ch;
  if (ORD(ch2) > 64) and
    (ORD(ch2) < 91) then
    ch2 := CHR(ORD(ch2) + 32)
  else ch2 := ch;
  if ORD(ch2) < 32 then
    TOLOWER := CHR(ORD(ch2) + 64)
  else TOLOWER := ch2;
end;

procedure TOLOWST(var st:string);
var   i   : integer;
begin
  for i := 1 to LENGTH(st) do
    st[i] := TOLOWER(st[i]);
end;

procedure REMOVEBLANKS(var st:string);
var   i     : integer;
      temp  : integer;
begin
  temp := LENGTH(st);
  i := 1;
  while i <= temp do begin
    if st[i] = ' ' then begin
      DELETE(st,i,1);
      i := 0;
    end;
    i := i + 1;
    temp := LENGTH(st);
  end;
end;
```

TOLOWER — This procedure takes all uppercase alphabetic characters and changes them to lowercase.

It does so by taking advantage of the fact that all ASCII characters are from a standard table. Capital alphabetics run from 101 to 132 octal. The matching lowercase letters run from 141 to 172 octal. The difference between a capital and its lower case form is therefore 40 octal.

There are two variables in the function, both strings. *ch* is passed in and is thus known here and in the calling procedure. The variable *ch2* is known only in the function and is hidden from the calling module. Within the function, *ch2* is either the converted lowercase form of *ch*, or, if there is no need to change the character, *ch2* is simply made equal to *ch*.

Note that in the last line, the value of the function *TOLOWER* is made equal to *ch2* and that value, as the value of the function, is returned to the calling procedure. *ch2* is not returned.

TOLOWST — This procedure uses the function *TOLOWER* to operate on each element of the given string. It returns a lowercase string in the **var** string *st*.

REMOVEBLANKS — This procedure passes in a string which may contain blanks, removes the blanks, and sends back the shortened string. Note that the length of the **string** must be reevaluated during each pass of the loop.

WINDOW.TEXT

```
procedure MOVEWIND(window:integer);
var    i    : integer;
begin
 VIEWPORT(wind  [window].x, winddiag[window].x,
     winddiag[window].y, wind   [window].y);
 FILLSCREEN(backgroundcolor);
 MOVETO( wind  [window].x, wind  [window].y);
end;

procedure WRITEWIND(doclear:boolean;window:integer;st:longstring);
(*$I window1.text*)
begin
 if LENGTH(st) > 0 then begin
   CHECKFORLONGLINES;
   WRITEOUTLONGSTRING;
   end;
end;
```

MOVEWIND — This procedure uses *VIEWPORT, FILLSCREEN* and *MOVETO*. It establishes a box on the screen, based on a pair of x and y coordinates, found in the **arrays** *wind* and *winddiag*, then fills that box with the established background color, and then repositions the cursor. This, in effect, clears the window.

WRITEWIND — If the length of the string is not zero, then the string is first checked for right word justification then written out. This procedure includes and uses the following two procedures, *CHECKFORLONGLINES* and *WRITEOUTLONGSTRING*. Note however that all the arguments passed to *WRITEWIND* when it is called are available within the procedure *WRITEWIND* and its nested procedures, *CHECKFORLONGLINES* and *WRITEOUTLONGSTRING*.

The actual code within the procedure *WRITEWIND* consists only of an **if** clause. A test is made to see if the string is longer than zero.

If it is, then the two procedures *CHECKFORLONGLINES* and *WRITEOUTLONGSTRING* are called.

```
procedure CHECKFORLONGLINES;
var i, chcount     : integer;
begin
  i    := 1; chcount := 0;
  while i <= LENGTH(st) do begin
    if chcount >=
    (winddiag[window].x - wind[window].x) div hchar then
      begin
        while (st[i] <> ' ') and (i <> 1) do
          i := i -1;
        if i <> 1 then st[i] := '$';
        chcount := -1;
      end;
    if st[i] = '$' then chcount := -1;
    i := i + 1;
    chcount := chcount + 1;
  end;
end;

procedure WRITEOUTLONGSTRING;
var    i, linecount     : integer;
begin
  linecount := 1;
  if doclear then MOVEWIND(window);
  MOVETO(wind[window].x, wind[window].y - vchar);
  PENCOLOR(colorpen);
  for i := 1 to LENGTH(st) do
    if st[i] = '$' then begin
      PENCOLOR(none);
      linecount := linecount + 1;
      if linecount >
      ((wind   [window].y -
        winddiag[window].y) div vchar) then
        EXIT(WRITEOUTLONGSTRING);
      MOVETO(wind[window].x,
          wind[window].y - (linecount*vchar));
      PENCOLOR(colorpen);
    end
    else WCHAR(st[i]);
  PENCOLOR(none);
end;
```

CHECKFORLONGLINES — Here we check for words that would fall beyon the right edge of the screen. If the word crosses the edge of the screen, we back up to the beginning of the word and insert the character "$", to denote a new line. As can be seen throughout the program, a new line can be created by putting in the character "$" in the **string** that is given to *WRITEWIND*.

WRITEOUTLONGSTRING — If the **boolean** *doclear* is *true*, then window is first cleared. We write the strings out to the screen, going to a new line whenever we find the character "$" in the line.

HELP.TEXT

```
function HELP:char;
(*$I help1.text*)
(*$I help2.text*)
(*$I help3.text*)

begin (* HELP *)
 MOVEWIND(prompt);
 MOVEWIND(choice1);
 case helpmesg of
  helpa : HA;
  helpb : HB;
  helpc : HC;
  helpd : HD;
  helpe : HE;
  helpf : HF;
  helpg : HG;
  helph : HH;
  helpi : HI;
  helpj : HJ;
  helpk : HK;
  helpl : HL;
  helpm : HM;
  helpn : HN;
  helpo : HO;
 end;
 if READY then;
  MOVEWIND(text0);
  WRITEWIND(clear,choice1,choice);
  helpflag := true;
  HELP := '$';
end; (* HELP *)
```

HELP — This portion of the code is likely to be edited by instructors a good deal as they personalize the course.

All messages initiated by a learner requesting assistance are stored here. When "h" or "help" is given, the response control passes to this function. All of the fifteen procedures (*HA* to *HO*) are organized within the case statement. The location of the student requesting help is indicated by *helpmesg* which acts as the selector or flag and initiates the specified *HELP* response.

As long as the structure of the course remains unchanged, it is a simple matter to edit any help message. Change the required words (within length restrictions) and recompile the course.

To add help messages for a new module, you must: add a constant to the constant table in **const**, add a line to the case statement and add a new procedure containing the messages.

```
procedure HA;
begin
 WRITEWIND(clear,text0,CONCAT(
 'Hit return to see the first lesson.$$',
 'M will always show you a menu.$$',
 'Q for quit will stop the course.$$Have fun!'));
end;

procedure HB;
begin
 WRITEWIND(clear,text0,CONCAT(
 'This is a lesson about counting boxes.$$',
 'Answer each question.'));
end;

procedure HC;
begin
 WRITEWIND(clear,text0,CONCAT(
 'When you see:$$',
 '    How many boxes?$',
 'Count the boxes.$Then, type the number.$$',
 'I will tell you if your answer is right or wrong.'));
end;

procedure HD;
begin
 WRITEWIND(clear,text0,CONCAT(
 'Now you can review or start a new lesson.$$',
 'Hit return to see the menu.'));
end;

procedure HE;
begin
 WRITEWIND(clear,text0,CONCAT(
 'Select an item from the menu.$$'));
end;

procedure HF;
begin
 WRITEWIND(clear,text0,CONCAT(
 'Hit return to find out about regions and parts.'));
end;
```

HELP2.TEXT   **14 Curriculum Four: CAL and FRACTIONS**

```
procedure HG;
begin
 WRITEWIND(clear,text0,CONCAT(
 'When you see this:$',
 'How many regions?$',
 'Type in the right number.$$',
 'When you see this$',
 'How many parts?$',
 'Type in the right number'));
end;

procedure HH;
begin
 WRITEWIND(clear,text0,CONCAT(
 'This is the most important lesson.$',
 'Read carefully and answer each question$',
 'Hit return to find out about fractions'));
end;

procedure HI;
begin
 WRITEWIND(clear,text1,CONCAT(
 'A fraction looks like this   1$',
 '                ---$',
 '                 2$'));
 WRITEWIND(clear,text2,CONCAT(
 'You must first type in the number of ',
 'parts that are blue$',
 'Then the number of parts altogether'));
end;

procedure HJ;
begin
 WRITEWIND(clear,text0,CONCAT(
 'Hit return to see some questions about fractions.'));
end;

procedure HK;
begin
 WRITEWIND(clear,text0,CONCAT(
 'When you see:$$',
 'What is the fraction?$',
 'First type the number of parts that are blue.$',
 'Then type the number of parts there are altogether.'));
end;
```

```
procedure HL;
begin
 WRITEWIND(clear,text0,CONCAT(
 'This is a test.$$',
 'If you do not want to test right now,',
 'hit return then$',
 'm for menu'));
end;

procedure HM;
begin
 WRITEWIND(clear,text0,CONCAT(
 'You did not pass the counting lesson.$$',
 'You can start again, if you want.'));
end;

procedure HN;
begin
 WRITEWIND(clear,text0,CONCAT(
 'Now you can review or start the lesson again$$',
 'Hit return to see the menu.'));
end;

procedure HO;
begin
 WRITEWIND(clear,text0,CONCAT(
 'Now you can review or leave fractions.$$',
 'Hit return to see the menu.'));
end;
```

PROMPT.TEXT

```
function DOLNPROMPT(doclear:boolean; pst:string;
         var retst:string):boolean;
var  st    : string;
     pa    : packed array[1..1] of char;
     ch    : char;
     stst  : string[1];
begin
 DOLNPROMPT := false; helpflag := false;
 if LENGTH(pst) = 0 then
     WRITEWIND(doclear,prompt,'Choose One : ')
 else WRITEWIND(doclear,prompt,pst);
 st := '';
 UNITREAD(2,pa[1],1,,12);
 while (pa[1] <> CHR(13)) and
      (pa[1] <> CHR(13+128)) do begin
    if pa[1] = CHR(8) then begin
       if LENGTH(st) > 1 then
          DELETE(st,LENGTH(st)-1,1)
       else st := '';
       TURNTO(180);
       MOVE(hchar);
       TURNTO(0);
    end
    else begin
       ch := TOLOWER(pa[1]);
       WCHAR(ch);
       stst := ' ';
       stst[1] := ch;
       st := CONCAT(st,stst);
     end;
    UNITREAD(2,pa[1],1,,12);
  end;
 TOLOWST(st);
 REMOVEBLANKS(st);
 if LENGTH(st) = 0 then
    st := ' ';
 if LENGTH(st) = 1 then begin
    if st[1] = 'q' then EXITPROGRAM('');
    DOLNPROMPT := (st[1] = 'm');
    if st[1] = 'h' then st[1] := HELP;
    end;
 if POS('help',st) = 1 then st[1] := HELP;
 retst := st; (* cannot return a null string*)
 if doclear then MOVEWIND(prompt);
end;

function DOPROMPT(doclear:boolean;pst:string):char;
var  st    : string;
begin
  if DOLNPROMPT(doclear,pst,st) then;
  DOPROMPT := st[1];
end;
```

DOLNPROMPT — This is an important function designed to handle all input from the keyboard in a consistent manner throughout the course and to handle some of the standard I/O problems.

The variable *pst* is the *prompt* string which is established before calls to this function.

There are a number of steps in the process, designed to insure that input of various kinds (numbers, characters, words) is handled correctly. The steps are done until the *return key* is pressed:

- Read the first character.
- If null, do prompting again.
- If character, change to lower case.
- If only one character, then do the following sequence:
- If the input is ''q'' then exit (*EXITPROGRAM*).
- If the input is ''m'' then get ready to go up a level by setting *DOLNPROMPT* to a true value.
- If the input is ''h'' then call for help (*HELP*).

DOPROMPT — Using *DOLNPROMPT*, we return the first character of the response.

203

The Elements of CAL   SHOWBXLN.TEXT

```
procedure SHOWBOX(num:integer);
var  i   : integer;
begin
 VIEWPORT(vminx,vmaxx,vminy,vmaxy);
 FILLSCREEN(backgroundcolor);
 for i := 1 to num do
   begin
   VIEWPORT(vminx + (i-1)*width + offset,
       vminx + i*width-offset,
       vminy,vmaxy);
   FILLSCREEN(outlinecolor);
   end;
 PENCOLOR(none);
end;

procedure SHOWOUTLINE(num:integer);
var  i   : integer;
begin
 VIEWPORT(vminx,vmaxx,vminy,vmaxy);
 MOVETO(vminx,vminy);
 TURNTO(0);
 PENCOLOR(outlinecolor);
 MOVETO(vminx + num*width,
     vminy);
 MOVETO(vminx + num*width,
     vmaxy);
 MOVETO(vminx,vmaxy);
 MOVETO(vminx,vminy);
 PENCOLOR(none);

 for i := 1 to num do
   begin
   MOVETO(vminx + i*width,vmaxy);
   PENCOLOR(outlinecolor);
   MOVETO(vminx + i*width,vminy);
   PENCOLOR(none);
   end;
  VIEWPORT(minx,maxx,miny,maxy);
end;
```

SHOWBOX — Puts boxes in the window *text2*. Used by *COUNTINGTEST*. One rectangle of outline color is displayed.

SHOWOUTLINE — Puts a line around each box up to *num*. The line is in the outline color, and then *pencolor* is set back to *none*.

SHOWNUM.TEXT

```
procedure FILLPARTS(num:integer);
begin
    VIEWPORT(vminx,
        vminx + num*width,
        vminy,vmaxy);
    FILLSCREEN(fillcolor);
end;
```

FILLPARTS — Fills boxes with the *fillcolor* to the number of boxes specified by *num*.

```
procedure SHOWTOPNUM(line:integer;i:integer);
begin
    VIEWPORT(wind  [text2 ].x,
        winddiag[text2 ].x,
        winddiag[prompt].y,
        wind  [text2 ].y);
    MOVETO(wind[text2].x + 18 * hchar,
        wind[text2].y - line * vchar);
    WCHAR(CHR(i + 48));
end;
```

SHOWTOPNUM — This bypasses the use of windows: here we place the **integer** *i* into the 18th character position of the text window *text2*, at *line i* number of spaces from the top of the window.

```
procedure PLACELINE(line:integer);
begin
    VIEWPORT(wind  [text2 ].x,
        winddiag[text2 ].x,
        winddiag[prompt].y,
        wind  [text2 ].y);
    MOVETO(wind[text2].x + 18 * hchar -1,
        wind[text2].y - line * vchar - 1);
    PENCOLOR(colorpen);
    TURNTO(0);
    MOVE(hchar + 3);
    PENCOLOR(backgroundcolor);
end;
```

PLACELINE — Here again we output some information to the screen, without the use of WRITEWIND.

```
procedure SHOWBOTNUM(line:integer;i:integer);
begin
    VIEWPORT(wind  [text2 ].x,
        winddiag[text2 ].x,
        winddiag[prompt].y,
        wind  [text2 ].y);
    MOVETO(wind[text2].x + 18 * hchar,
        wind[text2].y - (line + 1) * vchar);
    WCHAR(CHR(i + 48));
end;
```

SHOWBOTNUM — Much like SHOWTOPNUM, but the **integer** is placed one line lower.

The Elements of CAL   INITFRAC.TEXT

procedure *INITFRAC*;
var *st*   : **string**;
   ch : **char**;
   i   : **integer**;

(*$I setupwin.text*)

begin (* *INITFRAC* *)
 RANDOMIZE;
 INITTURTLE;
 GRAFMODE;
 VIEWPORT(*minx,maxx,miny,maxy*);
 SETUPWIND;

 PENCOLOR(*none*);
 TURNTO(0);
 MOVETO(*wind [solid1].x,
    winddiag[solid1].y* + 5);
 PENCOLOR(*colorpen*);
 MOVE (*winddiag[solid1].x*);

 PENCOLOR(*none*);
 TURNTO(0);
 MOVETO(*wind [choice1].x,
    wind [choice1].y* + 5);
 PENCOLOR(*colorpen*);
 MOVE (*winddiag[choice1].x*);
 PENCOLOR(*none*);

 WRITEWIND(*clear,level0,*'Curriculum Four');
 VIEWPORT(*wind [solid1].x,
     winddiag[solid1].x,
     winddiag[solid1].y,
     wind [solid1].y*);
 RANDOMIZE;

 MOVEWIND(*level1*);
 MOVEWIND(*level2*);
 WRITEWIND(*clear,text0,*'Fractions$$A Course with Four Lessons');
 WRITEWIND(*clear,choice1,choice*);
 if *READY* **then**;
 MOVEWIND(*text0*);
end;   (* *INITFRAC* *)

INITFRAC — This procedure sets up the screen so that *MAINFRAC* can begin, by calling *RANDOMIZE* *INITTURTLE* and *GRAFMODE*. This **procedure** is called by *FRAC* and does all the initialization of all the global **var**iables and **arrays** by calling *SETUPWIND*, *RANDOMIZE*, *INITTURTLE* and *GRAFMODE*.

SETUPWIN.TEXT   **14 Curriculum Four: CAL and FRACTIONS**

```
procedure SETUPWIND;
var  i  : integer;
begin
  wind  [level0 ].y := 191;
  wind  [level1 ].y := 181;
  wind  [level2 ].y := 171;
  wind  [solid1 ].y := 161;
  wind  [wname ].y := 191;
  wind  [text0  ].y := 140;
  wind  [text1  ].y := 140;
  wind  [text2  ].y :=  90;
  wind  [prompt ].y :=  50;
  wind  [choice1].y :=  10;
  wind  [last   ].y :=   0;

  winddiag[level0 ].y := 181;
  winddiag[level1 ].y := 171;
  winddiag[level2 ].y := 161;
  winddiag[solid1 ].y := 151;
  winddiag[wname  ].y := 181;
  winddiag[text0  ].y :=  60;
  winddiag[text1  ].y := 100;
  winddiag[text2  ].y :=  60;
  winddiag[prompt ].y :=  20;
  winddiag[choice1].y :=   0;
  winddiag[last   ].y :=   0;

  for i := level0 to last do begin
    wind    [i].x := minx;
    winddiag[i].x := maxx;
    end;
  wind    [wname ].x := 150;
  winddiag[level0].x := 150;

  vminx  := wind    [text1].x;
  vmaxx  := winddiag[text1].x;
  vminy  := winddiag[text1].y;
  vmaxy  := wind    [text1].y;

  lessonname[count]     := ' Counting ';
  lessonname[randpdrill] := ' Region and Parts ';
  lessonname[fracdrill]  := ' Fractions ';
  lessonname[test]       := ' Test ';

  promptstring  := '';
  for i := count to test do
    passed[i] := notin;
  numfinshed := 0;

end; (* SETUPWIND *)
```

SETUPWIND — Its purpose is to update the **arrays** that contain the window information.

The Elements of CAL   *MAINFRAC.TEXT*

```
procedure MAINFRAC;
var   exitflag, comflag, upflag : boolean;
      dofpnum      : integer;

function DOFPROMPT(doclear:boolean;int:integer;st:string):boolean;
var   tempst : string;
begin
  if DOLNPROMPT(doclear,st,tempst) then
     upflag := true;
  dofpnum := ORD(tempst[1]) - 48;
  if LENGTH(tempst) > 1 then dofpnum := -16;
  if CHR(dofpnum+48) = ' ' then dofpnum := 40;
  DOFPROMPT := (dofpnum = int);
end; (* DOFPROMPT *)

(*$I counting.text*)
(*$I rpart.text*)
(*$I afrac.text*)
(*$I bfrac.text*)
(*$I testfrac.text*)
(*$I showmenu.text*)

begin  (* MAINFRAC *)
  WRITEWIND(clear,level1,'Fractions');
  exitflag := false; comflag := false;
  upflag  := false; helpflag := false;
  if COUNTINGTEST then
     numfinshed := 1
  else numfinshed := 0;
  while true do begin
    MOVEWIND(level2);
    SHOWMENU;
    case DOPROMPT(clear,'') of
    '1','c' : if COUNTINGTEST then
                numfinshed := 1
              else numfinshed := 0;
    '2','r' : if RPARTSDRILL then
                numfinshed := 2
              else numfinshed := 1;
    '3','f' : if AFRACTIONSDRILL then
                 if BFRACTIONSDRILL then
                   numfinshed := 3
                 else numfinshed := 2
              else numfinshed := 2;
    '4','t' : if TESTFRACTIONS then
                numfinshed := 4
              else numfinshed := 3;
    'm'     : EXIT(MAINFRAC);
    end; (* case *)
  end; (* while *)
end; (* MAINFRAC *)
```

MAINFRAC — All the **procedures** and **functions** preceding *MAINFRAC* are considered supporting and are totally concerned with the maintenance of the screen and learner input. There are four main **functions** in this **procedure**: *COUNTINGTEST, RPARTSDRILL, AFRACTIONSDRILL* and *TESTFRACTIONS*. The internal structure of all these **functions** is similar, all exit via a **procedure** called *UP* and all have a **function** called *QUESTION* that checks the response and looks after the help and menu commands. The **array** *passed* keeps track of the lessons that have been *passed* and *failed*. The **variable** *numfinshed* is used by *SHOWMENU* to prompt the student with the correct menu.

DOFPROMPT — Here we do the comparison between the **characters** returned by calling *DOLNPROMPT* and the **integer** that is the correct response. We cannot do a comparison on a **character** and a **integer**, so we put the **character** into the **var** *dofpnum*, do some conversions and test on the resulting **integer**. If the learner answers the question correctly, we return *true*.

COUNTING.TEXT

```
function COUNTINGTEST:boolean;
var   i, k, int, numcorrect, numanswered : integer;

(*$I count1.text*)

begin  (* COUNTINGTEST *)
 helpmesg   := helpb;
 WRITEWIND(clear,level2,'Counting Lesson');
 numcorrect  := 0;
 numanswered := 0;

 WRITEWIND(clear,text0,'This is a counting lesson.');
 if READY then UP;
 while (numcorrect < 5) and
       (numanswered < 10) do begin
   MOVEWIND(text2);
   i := RAND(2,9);
   STR(i,smst1);
   if QUESTION then begin
     numcorrect := numcorrect + 1;
     WRITEWIND(clear,text2,CONCAT(
       'Right There are ',smst1,' boxes.'));
     end
   else begin
     WRITEWIND(clear,text2,CONCAT(
       'No There are ',smst1,' boxes.'));
     numcorrect := 0;
     end;
   numanswered := numanswered + 1;
   if READY then UP;
   end; (* while *)
 if numcorrect = 5 then begin
   helpmesg   := helpd;
   COUNTINGTEST := true;
   passed[count] := pass;
   WRITEWIND(clear,text0,'Terrific!$You have completed 1 of 4 lessons.');
   end
 else begin
   helpmesg   := helpm;
   WRITEWIND(clear,text0,CONCAT(
       'You are having trouble counting.$$',
       'Start again.$$Or, hit return, then ',
       'M to choose another course.'));
   COUNTINGTEST := false;
   passed[count] := failed;
   end;
 if READY then UP;
 helpmesg   := helpe;
 MOVEWIND(level2);
 end;  (* COUNTINGTEST *)
```

COUNTINGTEST – In this lesson, we put a random number of rectangles on the screen and ask the student to count them. Positive and negative feedback is given. If the student answers five correctly, in a row we return to *MAINFRAC* for the next lesson. If ten questions are asked and the student is still having trouble, then it is suggested that she start all over.

209

The Elements of CAL   COUNT1.TEXT

```
procedure UP;
begin
  MOVEWIND(level2);
  passed[count]    := failed;
  COUNTINGTEST     := false;
  helpmesg         := helpe;
  EXIT(COUNTINGTEST);
end; (* UP *)

function QUESTION:boolean;
begin
  helpmesg         := helpc;
  MOVEWIND(text2);
  SHOWBOX(i);
  QUESTION := DOFPROMPT(clear,i,'How many boxes? ');
  if upflag then UP;
  if helpflag then
    QUESTION := QUESTION;
end; (* QUESTION *)
```

UP – (in *COUNTINGTEST*) Do the clean up and exit *COUNTINGTEST*.

QUESTION – (in *COUNTINGTEST*) Here we pose the question by displaying the boxes on the screen and also check for requests for help and menuing out.

RPART.TEXT   14 Curriculum Four: CAL and FRACTIONS

```
function RPARTSDRILL:boolean;
var     i, numcorrect, numincorrect : integer;

(*$I rpart1.text*)

begin  (* RPARTSDRILL *)
  helpmesg   := helpf;
  WRITEWIND(clear,level2,'Region and Parts Drill');
  numcorrect := 0; numincorrect := 0;
  WRITEWIND(clear,text0,'This is a lesson on Regions and Parts.');
  if READY then UP;
  MOVEWIND(text1); FILLPARTS(2);
  helpmesg   := helpg;
  WRITEWIND(clear,text2,'This is a region.');
  WAIT(3); SHOWOUTLINE(2);
  WRITEWIND(clear,text2,'This region has 2 parts.');
  if READY then UP;

(*$I rpart2.text*)

  if numcorrect = 3 then begin
    helpmesg   := helpd;
    WRITEWIND(clear,text0,'Great!$You have completed 2 of 4 lessons.');
    RPARTSDRILL := true;
    passed[randpdrill] := pass;
    end
  else begin
    helpmesg   := helpn;
    WRITEWIND(clear,text0,CONCAT(
        'You do not understand regions and parts.$$',
        'Maybe you should take a rest.'));
    RPARTSDRILL := false;
    passed[randpdrill] := failed;
    end;
  if READY then UP;
  helpmesg   := helpe;
  MOVEWIND(level2);
  end;   (* RPARTSDRILL *)
```

RPARTSDRILL – In this segment, we first show the student a region and then divide it into a random number of parts. The **function** *QUESTION* is called to setup the question and get the student's response. If the student gets three correct in a row, then she has completed the lesson and is given reinforcement before exiting this **function**. When the student gets three incorrect, a message is displayed and we exit from the **function** *RPARTSDRILL* after setting the **array** *passed* to *failed*.

211

The Elements of CAL RPART1.TEXT

```
procedure UP;
begin
  MOVEWIND(level2);
  helpmesg      := helpe;
  passed[randpdrill] := failed;
  RPARTSDRILL   := false;
  EXIT(RPARTSDRILL );
end; (* UP *)

function QUESTION:boolean;
begin
  MOVEWIND(text0);
  FILLPARTS(i);
  if DOFPROMPT(clear,1,'How many Regions > ') then
    begin
    if upflag then UP;
    SHOWOUTLINE(i);
    if helpflag then
      QUESTION := QUESTION
    else if DOFPROMPT(clear,i,'How many Parts  > ') then
      QUESTION := true
    else QUESTION := false;
    end;
  if upflag then UP;
  if helpflag then
    QUESTION := QUESTION;
end; (* QUESTION *)
```

UP – (in *RPARTSDRILL*) The global variables are updated and the **array** *passed* is marked as *failed* for this lesson.

QUESTION – (in *RPARTSDRILL*) This **function** asks the question for *RPARTSDRILL* and returns *true* if the correct response is received or *false* if the answer is incorrect.

RPART2.TEXT

```
while (numcorrect < 3) and (numincorrect < 3) do begin
  i := RAND(2,9);
  STR(i,smst1);
  if QUESTION then begin
    numcorrect := numcorrect + 1;
    WRITEWIND(clear,text2,CONCAT('Right! 1 region$     ',
        smst1,' parts.'));
    end
  else begin
    numincorrect := numincorrect + 1;
    numcorrect := 0;
    WRITEWIND(clear,text2,CONCAT('Hum. Having problems?$$',
        'There is always 1 region.'));
    MOVEWIND(text1); FILLPARTS(i);
    if READY then UP;
    WRITEWIND(clear,text2,CONCAT('This region is divided into ',
        smst1,' parts$$COUNT THEM!'));
    SHOWOUTLINE(i);
    end;
  if READY then UP;
  end; (* while *)
```

The Elements of CAL   AFRAC.TEXT

function *AFRACTIONSDRILL* :**boolean**;
var   *i,k, numcorrect, numincorrect* : **integer**;

(*$I afrac1.text*)

begin (* *AFRACTIONSDRILL* *)
  helpmesg := *helph*;
  WRITEWIND(*clear,level2*,'Fractions Drill');
  numcorrect := 0; *numincorrect* := 0;
  WRITEWIND
    (*clear,text0*,'This is a lesson on how Regions and Parts make fractions.$$Have fun');
  if *READY* **then** *UP*;

(*$I afrac2.text*)

  if *numcorrect* = 3 **then** *AFRACTIONSDRILL* := *true*
  else begin
    helpmesg   := *helpn*;
    WRITEWIND(*clear,text0,CONCAT*(
      'You are having problems with Fractions.$$',
      'Review or take a rest'));
    AFRACTIONSDRILL := *false*;
    passed[*fracdrill*] := *failed*;
    if *READY* **then**;
    end; (* **else** *)
end; (* *AFRACTIONSDRILL* *)

AFRACTIONSDRILL – This is the first of two related lessons; both ask the same basic question, but have different prompting and response messages. In this **function**, we introduce fractions by using a colored area of a region divided into many parts. There is a long feedback in the event of an incorrect response. Note the use of *WAIT* to slow down the speed of the screen output. When the student gets three correct in a row, she is sent into *BFRACTIONSDRILL* via *MAINFRAC*. If she makes three incorrect responses in a row, then she will exit *AFRACTIONSDRILL* and return to the menu after updating the globals. That means there is no upper limit to the number of times the student goes through the **while** loop. The student must get three correct or incorrect in a row before the program will take her out.

AFRAC1.TEXT   **14 Curriculum Four: CAL and FRACTIONS**

```
procedure UP;
begin
  MOVEWIND(level2);
  helpmesg   := helpn;
  passed[fracdrill] := failed;
  AFRACTIONSDRILL := false;
  EXIT(AFRACTIONSDRILL);
end; (* UP *)

function QUESTION:boolean;
begin
  helpmesg := helpi;
  MOVEWIND(prompt);
  MOVEWIND(text1);
  SHOWOUTLINE(i);
  if i <> 1 then
     WRITEWIND(clear,text2,CONCAT('$In this region there are ',
              smst1,' parts'))
  else WRITEWIND(clear,text2,CONCAT('$In this region there is only ',
              smst1,' part'));
  WAIT(3);
  FILLPARTS(k);
  SHOWOUTLINE(k);
  if k <> 1 then
     WRITEWIND(clear,text2,'         parts are blue')
  else WRITEWIND(clear,text2,'         part is blue');
  SHOWTOPNUM(1,k);
  WAIT(3);
  WRITEWIND(clear,text2,'The fraction is ');
  SHOWTOPNUM(1,k);
  PLACELINE(1);
  SHOWBOTNUM(1,i);
  WAIT(3);
  QUESTION := DOFPROMPT(noclear,k,'Now you type the fraction > ');
  MOVEWIND(prompt);
  if upflag then UP;
  if helpflag then
    QUESTION := QUESTION;
  PLACELINE(5);
  SHOWTOPNUM(5,dofpnum);
  if not DOFPROMPT(noclear,i,'$ Now the bottom > ') then
    QUESTION := false;
  if upflag then UP;
  if helpflag then
    QUESTION := QUESTION;
end; (* QUESTION *)
```

UP — (in *AFRACTIONSDRILL*) Again here we clean up and update the globals before returning to *MAINFRAC*.

QUESTION — (in *AFRACTIONSDRILL*) This is where the question is put to the student; random number of squares are placed on the screen and the student is prompted to enter the correct number. Both question must be answered before any corrective action is taken.

215

```
while (numcorrect < 3) and (numincorrect < 3) do begin
  i := RAND(2,9); STR(i,smst1);
  k := RAND(1,i); STR(k,smst2);
  if QUESTION then begin
    numincorrect := 0; numcorrect := numcorrect + 1;
    WRITEWIND(clear,text2,'right!$ The fraction is ');
    SHOWTOPNUM(1,k);
    PLACELINE(1);
    SHOWBOTNUM(1,i);
    end
  else begin
    numcorrect := 0; numincorrect := numincorrect + 1;
    MOVEWIND(text1);
    MOVEWIND(prompt);
    SHOWOUTLINE(i);
    if i <> 1 then WRITEWIND(clear,text2,CONCAT(
          'Count carefully!$   There are ',
          smst1,' parts altogether'))
    else WRITEWIND(clear,text2,CONCAT(
          'Count carefully!$   There is only ',
          smst1,' part'));
    WAIT(3);
    MOVEWIND(text2);
    FILLPARTS(k);
    SHOWOUTLINE(k);
    if k <> 1 then WRITEWIND(noclear,text2,
        'Count carefully!   parts are blue')
    else WRITEWIND(noclear,text2,
        'Count carefully!   part is blue');
    SHOWTOPNUM(1,k);
    PLACELINE(1);
    SHOWBOTNUM(1,i);
    WAIT(3);
    WRITEWIND(clear,text2,'  The fraction is ');
    SHOWTOPNUM(1,k);
    PLACELINE(1);
    SHOWBOTNUM(1,i);
    end; (* else *)
  if READY then UP;
  WRITEWIND(clear,text2,'');
  end; (* while *)
```

BFRAC.TEXT

```
function BFRACTIONSDRILL:boolean;
var    i, k, numcorrect, numincorrect : integer;

(*$I bfrac1.text*)

begin (* BFRACTIONSDRILL *)
 helpmesg  := helpj;
 numcorrect  := 0;
 numincorrect := 0;
 WRITEWIND(clear,text0,'Terrific! Now practice doing FRACTIONS.');
 if READY then UP;
 while (numcorrect < 3) and (numincorrect < 3) do begin
    i := RAND(2,9); STR(i,smst1);
    k := RAND(1,i); STR(k,smst2);
    if QUESTION then begin
       WRITEWIND(clear,text2,'right!');
       numincorrect := 0;
       numcorrect  := numcorrect + 1;
       if READY then UP;
       end
    else begin
       WRITEWIND(clear,text2,'Sorry.$The fraction is ');
       SHOWTOPNUM(1,k);
       PLACELINE(1);
       SHOWBOTNUM(1,i);
       numincorrect := numincorrect + 1;
       numcorrect  := 0;
       if READY then UP;
       end;
    end; (* while *)
 if numcorrect = 3 then begin
    helpmesg   := helpd;
    BFRACTIONSDRILL  := true;
    passed[fracdrill] := pass;
    WRITEWIND(clear,text0,
       'GOOD WORK$You have now completed 3 of 4 lessons!');
    if READY then UP;
    end
 else begin
    helpmesg   := helph;
    BFRACTIONSDRILL := false;
    WRITEWIND(clear,text0,'You are having problems. Lets start over.');
    passed[fracdrill] := failed;
    if not READY then
       BFRACTIONSDRILL := AFRACTIONSDRILL;
    UP;
    end;
 helpmesg   := helpe;
 MOVEWIND(level2);
end;  (* BFRACTIONSDRILL *)
```

BFRACTIONSDRILL — This **function** is much like *AFRACTIONSDRILL*, but without a extensive feedback for incorrect answers. If three incorrect responses are received, then the student is sent back to *AFRACTIONSDRILL*.

```
procedure UP;
begin
  MOVEWIND(level2);
  helpmesg    := helpe;
  passed[fracdrill] := failed;
  BFRACTIONSDRILL  := false;
  EXIT(BFRACTIONSDRILL);
end; (* UP *)

function QUESTION:boolean;
begin
  helpmesg := helpk;
  QUESTION := false;
  MOVEWIND(text0);
  FILLPARTS(k);
  SHOWOUTLINE(i);
  QUESTION := false;
  if DOFPROMPT(clear,k,'What is the fraction? ') then
     QUESTION := true
  else QUESTION := false;
  if upflag then UP;
  if helpflag then
     QUESTION := QUESTION
  else begin
    MOVEWIND(prompt);
    PLACELINE(5);
    SHOWTOPNUM(5,dofpnum);
    if not DOFPROMPT(noclear,i,'$The second part > ') then
       QUESTION := false;
    if upflag then UP;
    if helpflag then
       QUESTION := QUESTION;
    end;
end; (* QUESTION *)
```

UP — (in *BFRACTIONSDRILL*) Clean up and exit to *MAINFRAC*.

QUESTION — (in *BFRACTIONSDRILL*) Most of this **function** is involved with support actions such as the menuing and help. The question only requires, about six lines.

TESTFRAC.TEXT   14 Curriculum Four: CAL and FRACTIONS

```
function TESTFRACTIONS:boolean;
var    i, k, numcorrect, numanswered : integer;

(*$I testf1.text*)

begin  (* TESTFRACTIONS *)
  helpmesg  := helpI;
  WRITEWIND(clear,level2,'Test Fractions');
  WRITEWIND(clear,text0,'This is a test on Fractions');
  numcorrect  := 0;
  numanswered := 1;
  if READY then UP;
  MOVEWIND(text0);
  for numanswered := 1 to 6 do begin
    i := RAND(2,9); STR(i,smst1);
    k := RAND(1,i); STR(k,smst2);
    if QUESTION then begin
      numcorrect := numcorrect + 1;
      WRITEWIND(clear,text2,'Right!');
      end
    else WRITEWIND(clear,text2,'Sorry, that is wrong.');
    WAIT(2);
    end;
  STR(numcorrect,smst1);
  STR(numanswered-1,smst2);
  WRITEWIND(clear,text0,CONCAT(
    'GOOD FOR YOU$You finished the test$your score: ',
    smst1,' out of ',smst2));
  if numcorrect = 6 then begin
    helpmesg  := helpo;
    promptstring := 'Well Done!$You have finished Fractions.$';
    TESTFRACTIONS := true;
    passed[test] := pass;
    end
  else begin
    promptstring := 'You should do some Fractions review.$';
    TESTFRACTIONS := false;
    passed[test] := pass;
    end;
  helpmesg  := helpe;
  if READY then;
  MOVEWIND(level2);
  end;  (* TESTFRACTIONS *)
```

TESTFRACTIONS — The last of the lessons is a test; the student must have been in all the other lessons before getting here. There is very little feed back to the student. This is the simplest of the lessons. A total of six questions are asked and the student must get all six correct before the lesson is considered *passed*.

219

The Elements of CAL — TESTF1.TEXT

```
procedure UP;
begin
 STR(numcorrect,smst1);
 STR(numanswered-1,smst2);
 WRITEWIND(clear,text0,CONCAT(
   'You did not finish the test$$',
   'your score: ',smst1,' out of ',smst2));
 promptstring := 'You should do some Fractions review.$';
 MOVEWIND(level2);
 helpmesg  := helpe;
 passed[test] := failed;
 TESTFRACTIONS := false;
 if READY then;
 EXIT(TESTFRACTIONS);
end; (* UP *)
```

UP — (in *TESTFRACTIONS*) Clean up the globals and display the score that the student obtained before exiting. Also, the **string** *promptstring* is setup with a new message: this is used by *SHOWMENU* when asking the student for a lesson.

```
function QUESTION:boolean;
begin
 MOVEWIND(text0);
 FILLPARTS(k);
 SHOWOUTLINE(i);
 QUESTION := DOFPROMPT(clear,k,'What is the fraction? > ');
 if helpflag then begin
   QUESTION := QUESTION;
   if upflag then UP;
   end
 else begin
   if upflag then UP;
   MOVEWIND(prompt);
   PLACELINE(5);
   SHOWTOPNUM(5,dofpnum);
   if DOFPROMPT(noclear,i,'$The second part > ') then
     QUESTION := true;
   end;
 if upflag then UP;
end; (* QUESTION *)
```

QUESTION — (in *TESTFRACTIONS*) Like the question in *BFRACTIONSDRILL*, a simple **function** with a good deal of overhead concerned global variables.

```
procedure SHOWMENU;
var   i    : integer;
      st   : longstring;

begin
  st := promptstring;
  for i := 1 to numfinshed do
    begin
    STR(i,smst1);
    if passed[i] = pass then
       st := CONCAT(st,'$ ',smst1,lessonname[i],'review')
    else st := CONCAT(st,'$ ',smst1,lessonname[i]);
    end;
  if i <= test then
    begin
    STR(i,smst1);
    if (passed[i] = pass) or
       (passed[i] = failed) then
       st := CONCAT(st,'$ ',smst1,lessonname[i])
    else st := CONCAT(st,'$ ',smst1,' next lesson');
    end;
  WRITEWIND(clear,text0,st);
  promptstring := '';
  upflag    := false;
end; (* SHOWMENU *)
```

SHOWMENU — Using *numfinshed* and *passed*, we set up and display the menu. If the lesson has been *passed*, then "review" is appended to the line. If the lesson was *failed*, then we just show the name of the lesson. When the learner has not seen the lesson, she is prompted with "next lesson".

15 Curriculum Four: WORDS

The WORDS Course Map

WORDS.TEXT   224
   SYSTUFF.TEXT   225
   CONSTS.TEXT   226
   TYPEVARS.TEXT   227
   INITWORDS.TEXT   228
      SETUPWIN.TEXT   229
      INIT0.TEXT   230
      INIT1.TEXT   231
      INIT2.TEXT   232
   WINDOW.TEXT   233
   TOLOWER.TEXT   234
   HELP.TEXT   235
      HELP0.TEXT   236
      HELP1.TEXT   237
      HELP2.TEXT   238
   PROMPT.TEXT   239
   MAINWORDS.TEXT   240
      DISPLAY.TEXT   241
         DISPLAY1.TEXT   242
         DISPLAY2.TEXT   243
      DICTION.TEXT   244
         DICTION1.TEXT   245
      LESSON.TEXT   246
         CHOOSEM.TEXT   247
            CHECKQUE.TEXT   248
            TESTS.TEXT   249
               UPTESTS.TEXT   250
            MEANINGS.TEXT   251
            PRACTICE.TEXT   252
               UPPRAC.TEXT   253
               ERRCHK.TEXT   254

The Elements of CAL

```
(*$S+*)
program WORDS;
(*      WORDS A computer aided learning course
 *      written by p.c. good
 *      copyright 1982 by SOFTWORDS a division of PRESS PORCEPIC
 *)

(*$I systuff.text*)
(*$I consts.text*)
(*$I typevars.text*)

function TOLOWER(ch:char):char; forward;
procedure TOLOWST(var st:string); forward;
procedure REMOVEBLANKS(var st:string); forward;

(*$I initwords.text*)
(*$I window.text*)

procedure EXITPROGRAM(st:string);
begin
  PAGE(output);
  MOVEWIND(text1);
  WRITE(st);
  SETCHAIN('cal:cal');
  EXIT(program);
end;

(*$I tolower.text*)
(*$I help.text*)
(*$I prompt.text*)
(*$I mainwords.text*)

begin   (* MAIN *)
  PAGE(output); WRITELN('curriculum four');
  WRITELN; WRITELN;
  WRITELN; WRITELN;
  WRITELN; WRITELN(' welcome to words ');
  WRITELN; WRITELN;
  WRITELN('reading data');
  WRITELN; WRITE ('please wait ');

  INITWORDS;
  if READY then;
  PAGE(output); WRITELN('curriculum four');
  MOVEWIND(solid1);
  WRITELN('--------------------------------------');
  MOVEWIND(text0);
  WRITEWIND(choice2,choice);
  helpmesg := hmain;
  MAINWORDS;
end.
```

WORDS – This program is written in UCSD PASCAL on an Apple II Plus micro-computer. We have used the System Library supplied with Apple PASCAL. Refer to the Apple PASCAL Language Manual for a complete description of these library functions.

TOLOWER TOLOWST REMOVEBLANKS – These **procedures** and **functions** must be forwarded because they are used in the **segmented procedure**, *INITWORDS*. Their code, as the name expresses, is "ahead of" *INITWORDS*.

EXITPROGRAM – Here we do some cleaning up before chaining back to the program *CAL:CAL.TEXT*. The program always exits via this **procedure**.

SYSTUFF.TEXT

```
(*  The following are included by the uses statement:
 *      function  KEYPRESS: boolean;
 *      function  RANDOM: integer;
 *      procedure RANDOMIZE;
 *
 *      procedure SETCHAIN(tytle:string);
 *      procedure SETCVAL(val:string);
 *      procedure GETCVAL(var val:string);
 *)

uses applestuff, chainstuff;
```

The Elements of CAL — CONSTS.TEXT

```
const
    screenw   = 39;
    screenl   = 23;
    clearln   = 29;

    level0    = 1;
    level1    = 2;
    level2    = 3;
    level3    = 4;
    level4    = 5;
    solid1    = 6;
    text0     = 9;
    text1     = 7;
    text2     = 8;
    prompt    = 10;
    choice1   = 11;
    choice2   = 12;
    last      = 13;

    numofwindows = 13;

    hmain     = 1; (* HELP levels *)
    hwords    = 2;
    hdictionary = 3;
    hdisplay  = 4;
    hlearn    = 6;
    hlesson   = 7;
    hchoosemethod = 8;
    htest     = 9;
    hmeaning  = 10;
    hprac1    = 11;
    hprac2    = 12;
    hinit     = 13;

    maxsegm   = 5;
    maxword   = 5;
    maxdef    = 2;
    maxex     = 2;
    maxstring = 200;
    shortst   = 12;
    choice    = ' h)elp  m)enu  q)uit';
```

CONST – The constants are used to hide the numbers that tend to make the reading of code difficult. System constants, such as screen width and machine dependent locations, are found in this **const** area of the program.

TYPEVARS.TEXT

```
type  longstring = string[maxstring];
      wordtype  = record
              segm : string[shortst];
              word : string[shortst];
              def  : array[1..maxdef] of longstring;
              exam : array[1..maxex] of longstring;
           end;
      xytype   = record
              x : integer;
              y : integer;
           end;
      passedtype = (pass,failed,notin);

var   wind     : array[1..numofwindows] of xytype;
      winddiag : array[1..numofwindows] of xytype;
      uname    : string;
      helpmesg : integer;
      wordarr  : packed array[1..maxsegm,1..maxword] of wordtype;
      segmmax  : integer;
      wordmax  : array[1..maxsegm] of integer;
```

TYPE – This area of the program is used to define these types for later use.

VAR – The **var** part of the program declaration area declares those variables that can be accessed anywhere in the program.

The Elements of CAL   INITWORDS.TEXT

```
segment procedure INITWORDS;
var   segmnum, wordnum, defnum, exnum  : integer;
    oldtype, ch  : char;
    st      : string;
    worddata : text;
    i      : integer;
(*$I setupwin.text*)
(*$I init0.text*)
(*$I init1.text*)
(*$I init2.text*)

begin (* INITWORDS *)
 helpmesg : = hinit;
 SETUPWIND;
 segmnum  : = 0; wordnum  : = 0;
 defnum   : = 0; exnum    : = 0;
 oldtype  : = 'd';
 for i : = 1 to maxsegm do wordmax[i] : = 0;
 RANDOMIZE;
(*$I-*)
 RESET(worddata,'cal:wordsdata.text');
 if ioresult <> 0 then
   begin
   WRITELN;
   WRITELN('Cannot find cal:wordsdata.text');
   EXIT(program);
   end; (*$I+*)
 SETUPWORDARR;
 while not EOF(worddata) do
   begin
   READLN(worddata,st);
   TOLOWST(st);
   if LENGTH(st) > 0 then
     if st[2] = ':' then
       case st[1] of
       'g' : segmnum : = NEXTSEGM(segmnum);
       'w' : wordnum : = NEXTWORD (wordnum );
       'd' : defnum  : = NEXTDEF (defnum );
       'e' : exnum   : = NEXTEX  (exnum );
       end
     else case oldtype of
       'd' : ADDTODEF (defnum);
       'e' : ADDTOEX  (exnum );
       end;
   end; (* while *)
 segmmax : = segmnum;
 wordmax[segmmax] : = wordnum;
 CLOSE(worddata);
end;   (* INITWORDS *)
```

INITWORDS — This procedure performs the initialization of all the global variables and reads in the words, definitions and examples for the dictionary. The data must be in a file called *CAL:WORDSDATA.TEXT*.

The variable *helpmesg* is initialized along with all the other global variables. *SETUPWORDARR* is called to set all strings in the array *wordarr* to null. *SETUPWIND* is called to initialize the windows.

228

SETUPWIN.TEXT

```
procedure SETUPWIND;
var   i      : integer;
begin
  wind  [level0 ].y := 0;
  wind  [level1 ].y := 1;
  wind  [level2 ].y := 2;
  wind  [level3 ].y := 3;
  wind  [level4 ].y := 4;
  wind  [solid1 ].y := 5;
  wind  [text0  ].y := 7;
  wind  [text1  ].y := 7;
  wind  [text2  ].y := 13;
  wind  [prompt ].y := 19;
  wind  [choice1].y := 21;
  wind  [choice2].y := 22;
  wind  [last   ].y := 23;

  winddiag[level0 ].y := 0;
  winddiag[level1 ].y := 1;
  winddiag[level2 ].y := 2;
  winddiag[level3 ].y := 3;
  winddiag[level4 ].y := 4;
  winddiag[solid1 ].y := 5;
  winddiag[text0  ].y := 17;
  winddiag[text1  ].y := 12;
  winddiag[text2  ].y := 17;
  winddiag[prompt ].y := 19;
  winddiag[choice1].y := 21;
  winddiag[choice2].y := 22;
  winddiag[last   ].y := 23;

  for i := level0 to last do
    begin
      wind     [i].x := 0;
      winddiag[i].x := 40;
    end;
end;
```

SETUPWIND — This **procedure** sets up the **arrays** *wind* and *winddiag* with the position of the windows used in this program. If the windows are to be moved, then this is where such changes should be made.

```
procedure SETUPWORDARR;
var   i,j   : integer;
begin
 for i := 1 to maxsegm do
   for j := 1 to maxword do
     begin
     wordarr[i,j].segm   := '';
     wordarr[i,j].word   := '';
     wordarr[i,j].def[1] := '';
     wordarr[i,j].def[2] := '';
     wordarr[i,j].exam[1] := '';
     wordarr[i,j].exam[2] := '';
     end;
end;

procedure SHOWERROR(st:string);
var   ch    : char;
begin
 WRITELN('segm = ',wordarr[segmnum,wordnum].segm);
 WRITELN('word = ',wordarr[segmnum,wordnum].word);
end;
```

SETUPWORDARR — Before reading in the data, the **array** *wordarr* is first initialized to null strings. This step is required in Apple PASCAL because variables are not always left in a zero or null state. This is a normal procedure to follow, no matter whose compiler you are using.

SHOWERROR — If we find a error when reading a file, this **procedure** is called to write out the segment and word. Also the **var** *st* is written, giving some feedback on where in the file the error occurred. This will help the instructor to find errors in the format of the data file when modifying it. The field that is in question is still added to the appropriate field in *wordarr*. Note that this may lead to invalid fields.

INIT1.TEXT   *15 Curriculum Four: WORDS*

```
function NEXTSEGM(segmnum:integer):integer;
var  i   : integer;
begin
 if segmnum <> 0 then
   wordmax[segmnum] := wordnum;
 wordnum := 0;
 segmnum := segmnum + 1;
 if segmnum > maxsegm then
   WRITELN('too many segms in data file');
 REMOVEBLANKS(st);
 for i := 1 to maxword do
   if LENGTH(st) > shortst + 2 then
      wordarr[segmnum,i].segm := COPY(st,3,shortst + 2-2)
   else wordarr[segmnum,i].segm := COPY(st,3,LENGTH(st)-2);
 NEXTSEGM := segmnum;
end;

function NEXTWORD (wordnum :integer):integer;
var  i   : integer;
begin
 defnum := 0;
 exnum  := 0;
 wordnum := wordnum + 1;
 if wordnum > maxword then
   begin
   WRITELN('too many words in data file');
   WRITELN('segm = ',wordarr[segmnum,1].segm);
   end;
 REMOVEBLANKS(st);
 if LENGTH(st) > shortst + 2 then
    wordarr[segmnum,wordnum].word := COPY(st,3,shortst + 2-2)
 else wordarr[segmnum,wordnum].word := COPY(st,3,LENGTH(st)-2);
 NEXTWORD := wordnum;
end;
```

NEXTSEGM — This **function** cleans up the segment name; any blanks found in the segment name are removed. If the segment name is too long, then it is shortened to 12 characters. This name is then placed in the nextsegment field in the **array** *wordarr* and the variables *segmnum* and *wordnum* are set up.

NEXTWORD — This **function** cleans up the word name. Any blanks found in the word are removed. If the word is too long, then it is shortened to 12 characters. This name is then put in the nextword field in the **array** *wordarr* and the variables *defnum* and *exnum* are set up.

231

The Elements of CAL　　　　　　　　　　　　　　　INIT2.TEXT

```
function NEXTDEF (defnum :integer):integer;
begin
 defnum := defnum + 1;
 if defnum > maxdef then
  SHOWERROR('too many definitions in data file');
 wordarr[segmnum,wordnum].def[defnum]
  := COPY(st,3,LENGTH(st)-2);
 NEXTDEF := defnum;
end;

function NEXTEX (exnum :integer):integer;
begin
 exnum := exnum + 1;
 if exnum > maxex then
  SHOWERROR('too many examples in data file');
 wordarr[segmnum,wordnum].exam[exnum]
  := COPY(st,3,LENGTH(st)-2);
 NEXTEX := exnum;
end;

procedure ADDTODEF(defnum:integer);
begin
 if (segmnum = 0) or (segmnum > maxsegm) then
  SHOWERROR('segm must come first');
 if (wordnum = 0) or (wordnum > maxword ) then
  SHOWERROR('word must come first');
 if (defnum = 0) or (defnum > maxdef ) then
  SHOWERROR('definition out of range');

 if (LENGTH(st) + LENGTH(wordarr[segmnum,wordnum].def[defnum])) <=
  maxstring then
  wordarr[segmnum,wordnum].def[defnum] :=
   CONCAT(wordarr[segmnum,wordnum].def[defnum],st)
 else SHOWERROR('length of definition too long');
end;

procedure ADDTOEX(exnum:integer);
begin
 if (segmnum = 0) or (segmnum > maxsegm) then
  SHOWERROR('segm must come first');
 if (wordnum = 0) or (wordnum > maxword ) then
  SHOWERROR('word must come first');
 if (exnum = 0) or (exnum > maxex ) then
  SHOWERROR('example out of range');

 if (LENGTH(st) + LENGTH(wordarr[segmnum,wordnum].exam[exnum])) <=
  maxstring then
  wordarr[segmnum,wordnum].exam[exnum] :=
   CONCAT(wordarr[segmnum,wordnum].exam[exnum],st)
 else SHOWERROR('length of example too long');
end;
```

NEXTDEF — Check to make sure that there are not too many definitions. If there are, the current word will then put the current string into the field wordarr[ ].def.

ADDTODEF — If a definition is too long to fit on one line, it may be continued on the next line (as shown in FILE FORMAT). This **procedure** appends the second line on to the first line now saved in the **array** wordarr.

WINDOW.TEXT

```
procedure MOVEWIND(window:integer);
var   i   : integer;
begin
  for i := wind[window].y to winddiag[window].y do
  begin
    GOTOXY(wind[window].x,i);
    WRITE(CHR(clearln));
  end;
  GOTOXY(wind[window].x,wind[window].y);
end;

procedure WRITEWIND(window:integer;st:longstring);
  procedure CHECKFORLONGLINES;
  var i, chcount : integer;
  begin
    chcount := 0;
    i    := 1;
    while i <= LENGTH(st) do begin
      if chcount = screenw then begin
        while (st[i] <> ' ') and (i <> 1 ) do
          i := i -1;
        if i <> 1 then
          st[i] := '$';
        chcount := -1;
      end;
      if st[i] = '$' then
        chcount := -1;
      i := i + 1;
      chcount := chcount + 1;
    end;
  end; (* CHECKFORLONGLINES *)

  procedure WRITEOUTLONGSTRING;
  var i    : integer;
  begin
    for i := 1 to LENGTH(st) do
      if st[i] = '$' then
        WRITELN
      else WRITE(st[i]);
  end;

begin (* WRITEWIND *)
  MOVEWIND(window);
  if LENGTH(st) > 0 then begin
    CHECKFORLONGLINES;
    WRITEOUTLONGSTRING;
  end;
end;
```

MOVEWIND – Uses a predeclared window on the screen, based on a pair of x and y coordinates (found in *wind* and *winddiag*); clears all the lines in this window; then repositions the cursor at the first space of the first line. In effect, this **procedure** clears the box.

WRITEWIND – Almost all the text shown on the screen is formatted and displayed via this **procedure**. This procedure includes and uses the following two procedures: CHECKFORLONGLINES and WRITEOUTLONGSTRING. The window is first cleared. Then if the string has something in it, we first format it for the window and then display the string.

CHECKFORLONGLINES Takes the input string and then breaks the string for the screen size by putting in the character '$' to denote a new line. If the edge of the screen divides a word then we back up so that words are not split over on two lines.

WRITEOUTLONGSTRING – Writes the strings out to the screen, character by character, putting in new lines (going to the next line) whenever the character '$' is found.

```
function TOLOWER;
        (*ch:char):char;*)
var   ch2    : char;
begin
 if ORD(ch) > 128 then
   ch2 := CHR(ORD(ch) - 128)
 else ch2 := ch;
 if (ORD(ch2) > 64) and
   (ORD(ch2) < 91) then
   ch2 := CHR(ORD(ch2) + 32)
 else ch2 := ch;
 if ORD(ch2) < 32 then
   TOLOWER := CHR(ORD(ch2) + 64)
 else TOLOWER := ch2;
end;

procedure TOLOWST;
        (*var st:string);*)
var   i    : integer;
begin
 for i := 1 to LENGTH(st) do
   st[i] := TOLOWER(st[i]);
end;

procedure REMOVEBLANKS;
        (*var st:string);*)
var   i    : integer;
   temp   : integer;
begin
 temp := LENGTH(st);
 i := 1;
 while i <= temp do begin
   if st[i] = ' ' then
     DELETE(st,i,1);
   i := i + 1;
   temp := LENGTH(st);
(*force the reevaluation of the length of st*)
 end;
end;
```

TOLOWST — This procedure uses the function **TOLOWER** to operate on each element of the given string. The **for** loop is as long as the string that is passed in. It returns a lowercase string in st. Note that st is passed in as a **var**, thus allowing the **procedure** to change the string. This is not unusual, as ordinarily you cannot change the string.

TOLOWER — This procedure takes all uppercase alphabetic characters and changes them to lowercase.

It does so by taking advantage of the fact that all ASCII characters are from a standard table. Capital alphabetics run from 101 to 132 octal. The matching lower case letters run from 141 to 172 octal. The difference between a capital and its lower case form is therefore 40 octal. The control characters and special characters are similarly mapped into the lowercase set.

There are two variables in the function, both strings. *ch* is passed in and is thus known here and in the calling procedure. The variable *ch2* is known only in the function and is hidden from the calling module within the function. *ch2* is either the converted lowercase form of *ch*, or, if there is no need to change the character, *ch2* is simply made equal to *ch*.

Note that in the last line, the value of the function TOLOWER is made equal to *ch2* and that value, as the value of the function, is returned to the calling procedure. *ch2* is not returned.

REMOVEBLANKS — This procedure passes in a string (which may contain blanks), removes any blanks, and sends back the shortened string. The variable *temp* is used to force the reevaluation of the length of the string.

HELP.TEXT

```
function HELP:char;
type   inttype = record
          case boolean of
             true : (it :integer);
             false : (pt : ^integer);
          end;
var  mem     : inttype;
     int     : integer;
     linecount : integer;
     i       : integer;
     st      : string;

(*$I help0.text*)
(*$I help1.text*)
(*$I help2.text*)

begin (* HELP *)
 GOTONEXTPAGE;
 linecount := 1;
 for i := 0 to screenl do
   begin
    GOTOXY(40,i);
    WRITE(CHR(clearln));
   end;
 case helpmesg of
   hinit,
   hmain,
   hwords     : WORDS;
   hmeaning,
   hdictionary : DICTIONARY;
   hdisplay   : DISPLAY;
   hlesson,
   hlearn     : LEARN;
   hchoosemethod : CHOOSEMETHOD;
   htest,
   hprac1     : TEST;
   hprac2     : PRAC2;
   end; (* case *)
 READLN(st);
 if LENGTH(st) = 0 then
    HELP := ' '
 else HELP := TOLOWER(st[1]);
 GOTOFIRSTPAGE;
end; (* HELP *)
```

15 Curriculum Four: WORDS

HELP — This portion of the code is likely to be edited by instructors a good deal as they personalize the course.

All messages initiated by a learner requesting assistance are stored here. When *h* is given as the response, control passes to this function. The location of the student requesting help is indicated by the global *helpmesg* which acts as the selector or flag and initiates the specified *HELP* response.

As long as the structure of the course remains unchanged, it is a simple matter to edit any help message. Change the required words (within length restrictions) and recompile the course.

To add help messages for a new module, you must: add a constant to the constant table in **const**, add a line to the case statement and add a new procedure containing the messages.

The Elements of CAL   HELP0.TEXT

```
procedure WRITEST(st:string);
begin
 GOTOXY(40,linecount);
 WRITE(st);
 linecount := linecount + 1;
end;

procedure GOTONEXTPAGE;
begin
 mem.it := -16299;
 int   := mem.pt^;
end;

procedure GOTOFIRSTPAGE;
begin
 mem.it := -16300;
 int   := mem.pt^;
end;

procedure SHOWPROMPT;
begin
 GOTOXY(wind[choice2].x + screenw + 1,wind[choice1].y);
 WRITE(' m)enu  q)uit ');
 GOTOXY(wind[prompt ].x + screenw + 1,wind[prompt ].y-1);
 WRITE('press return to continue ');
end;
```

The **procedures** *GOTONEXTPAGE* and *GOTOFIRSTPAGE* poke the location of the second page of the Apple's second page of text. This page is used for displaying the help messages. On other machines that do not have a second text screen, the help messages can be displayed in the same windows as the rest of the text.

Note: a new prompt is used that does not contain the prompt for help itself.

HELP1.TEXT

procedure *WORDS*;
begin
 WRITEST(' welcome to words');
 WRITEST('');
 WRITEST('');
 WRITEST('dictionary lets you look up the');
 WRITEST(' meaning of a word.');
 WRITEST('');
 WRITEST('');
 WRITEST('learn will teach you some');
 WRITEST(' new words.');
 SHOWPROMPT;
end;

procedure *DICTIONARY*;
begin
 WRITEST('when you see this:');
 WRITEST('');
 WRITEST(' which word?');
 WRITEST('');
 WRITEST('');
 WRITEST('type in the word you want to see.');
 SHOWPROMPT;
end;

procedure *DISPLAY*;
begin
 WRITEST('e - will show you an example');
 WRITEST('');
 WRITEST('');
 WRITEST('d - will show you another definition');
 WRITEST('');
 WRITEST('');
 WRITEST('x - will let you choose a new word');
 SHOWPROMPT;
end;

procedure *LEARN*;
begin
 WRITEST('you must choose one of the lessons.');
 WRITEST('');
 WRITEST('choose a number, then hit return.');
 WRITEST('');
 WRITEST('');
 WRITEST('if you do not want any of the lessons');
 WRITEST('');
 WRITEST('type m to go back to the dictionary');
 WRITEST('or q to quit words');
 SHOWPROMPT;
end;

```
procedure CHOOSEMETHOD;
begin
  WRITEST('test    will give you a test');
  WRITEST('       on the words');
  WRITEST('');
  WRITEST('');
  WRITEST('practice will let you practice');
  WRITEST('        answering questions.');
  WRITEST('');
  WRITEST('');
  WRITEST('meanings will tell you what the');
  WRITEST('        words mean');
  WRITEST('');
  WRITEST('');
  WRITEST('if you want to choose a new lesson');
  WRITEST('select m for menu');
  SHOWPROMPT;
end;

procedure TEST;
begin
  WRITEST('when the meaning appears, you must');
  WRITEST('type in the word.');
  WRITEST('');
  WRITEST('');
  WRITEST('you must spell the word correctly');
  SHOWPROMPT;
end;

procedure PRAC2;
begin
  WRITEST('no   will get help for you');
  WRITEST('');
  WRITEST('');
  WRITEST('yes will give you a new word');
  SHOWPROMPT;
end;
```

PROMPT.TEXT

```
function DOLNPROMPT(pst:string; var retst:string):boolean;
var  st    : longstring;
begin
 DOLNPROMPT := false;
 if LENGTH(pst) = 0 then
    WRITEWIND(prompt,'choose one : ')
 else WRITEWIND(prompt,pst);
 READLN(st);
 if LENGTH(st) > 80 then
    DELETE(st,80,LENGTH(st)-80);
 REMOVEBLANKS(st);
 if LENGTH(st) = 0 then
    st := '';
 TOLOWST(st);
 if POS('help',st) = 1 then begin
    st := '';
    st[1] := HELP;
    DOLNPROMPT := DOLNPROMPT(pst,st);
    end;
 if LENGTH(st) = 1 then begin
    if st[1] = 'h' then begin
       st := '';
       st[1] := HELP;
       DOLNPROMPT := DOLNPROMPT(pst,st);
       end;
    if st[1] = 'q' then
       EXITPROGRAM('');
    DOLNPROMPT := (st[1] = 'm');
    end;
 retst := st;
 MOVEWIND(prompt);
end;

function DOPROMPT(pst:string):char;
var  st    : string;
begin
 if DOLNPROMPT(pst,st) then;
 DOPROMPT := st[1];
end;

function READY:boolean;
var  dumbst : string;
begin
 READY := DOLNPROMPT('press return to continue : ',dumbst);
end;
```

DOLNPROMPT — This is an important function designed to handle input from the keyboard in a consistent manner throughout the course and to handle some of the standard I/O problems. All input is via this **function**.

The variable *pst* is the *prompt* string which is established before calls to this function.

There are a number of steps in the process, designed to insure that input of various kinds (numbers, characters, words) is handled correctly.

- If character, change to lower case.
- If only one character, then do the following sequence:
- If the input is "h" then call for help (*HELP*).
- If the input is "q" then exit (*EXITPROGRAM*).
- If the input is "m" then get ready to go up a level by setting *DOLPROMPT* to a true value.

DOPROMPT — Calls *DOLNPROMPT*, returning the first non-blank character typed in by the student

READY — Clears the prompt line, then prompts the student with *"press return to continue"*. The character returned is tested for menu, returning *true* if the student wants the menu.

The Elements of CAL — MAINWORDS.TEXT

```
procedure MAINWORDS;

(*$I display.text*)

function SEARCHFORMATCH(inword:string;segmnum:integer):integer;
 var    wordnum :integer;
 begin
  for wordnum := 1 to wordmax[segmnum] do
   if (POS(inword,wordarr[segmnum,wordnum].word) = 1) and
      (LENGTH(inword) = LENGTH(wordarr[segmnum,wordnum].word)) then
    begin
    helpmesg := hdisplay;
    if DISPLAY(segmnum,wordnum,false,'','') then
      begin
      SEARCHFORMATCH := -1;
      EXIT(SEARCHFORMATCH);
      end;
    SEARCHFORMATCH := wordnum;
    EXIT(SEARCHFORMATCH);
    end;
 SEARCHFORMATCH := 0;
end; (* SEARCHFORMATCH *)

(*$I diction.text*)
(*$I lesson.text*)

begin  (* MAINWORDS *)
uname := '';
GETCVAL(uname);
GOTOXY(20,0);
WRITE(uname);
WRITEWIND(level1,'words');
while true do
  begin
  helpmesg := hwords;
  WRITEWIND(text0,'words$$ 1 - dictionary$ 2 - learn');
  case DOPROMPT('') of
   'm'   : EXIT(MAINWORDS);
   'd','1': DICTIONARY;
   'l','2': LESSON;
  end; (* case *)
  end;
end;   (* MAINWORDS *)
```

MAINWORDS — The top level of *WORDS* called after the initialization is done. It sets up the menu for *DICTIONARY* and *LESSON*.

SEARCHFORMATCH — Searches all the available words in the current segment of the dictionary for a exact match to *inword*. If a match is found, then *DISPLAY* is called to display the word and its definition.

DISPLAY.TEXT

```
function DISPLAY(segmnum,wordnum:integer;
         prompt:boolean;st1,st2:longstring):boolean;
var exampnum : integer;
    defnum   : integer;
    window   : integer;

  procedure UPDISPLAY(how:boolean);
  begin
    MOVEWIND(text0 );
    MOVEWIND(level3 );
    MOVEWIND(choice1);
    DISPLAY := how;
    EXIT(DISPLAY);
  end; (* UPDISPLAY *)

(*$I display1.text*)
(*$I display2.text*)

begin (*-------- DISPLAY -------------*)
  exampnum := 0;
  if prompt then
    defnum := 0
  else defnum := 1;
  if not prompt then
    WRITEWIND(text1,CONCAT(wordarr[segmnum,wordnum].word,' : ',
         wordarr[segmnum,wordnum].def[1]));
  while true do
    begin
    window := text2;
    if prompt then
      begin
        WRITEWIND(text1,st1);
        WRITEWIND(text2,st2);
        window := text0;
      end
    else WRITEWIND(choice1,'e)xample d)efinition x) new word ');
    case DOPROMPT('? ') of
      'm' :   UPDISPLAY(true );
      'x' :   UPDISPLAY(false);
      'e' : if EXAMPLE(segmnum,wordnum,prompt,window) then
              UPDISPLAY(false);
      'd' : if DEFINITION(segmnum,wordnum,prompt,window) then
              UPDISPLAY(false);
      'a' : if ADDITIONAL then
              UPDISPLAY(false);
    end;
  end; (* while *)
end; (* DISPLAY *)
```

DISPLAY — Shows the first definition of the word, then prompts the learner to ask for another definition or example. When called by *PRACTICE*, the first definition is not displayed and the two strings that are passed in are used to prompt the learner. *ADDITIONAL* is used for additional information when called by *PRACTICE*.

UPDISPLAY — Used to exit from *DISPLAY*. The windows are cleared before leaving. The variable *how* is passed back; this is used to move up to the next menu.

```
function EXAMPLE(segmnum,wordnum:integer;
        wait:boolean;window:integer):boolean;
var    i,j   : integer;
begin
 WRITEWIND(level4,'example');
 case exampnum of

  0 : if LENGTH(wordarr[segmnum,wordnum].exam[1]) <> 0 then
        WRITEWIND(window,wordarr[segmnum,wordnum].exam[1])
      else begin
        WRITEWIND(window,'sorry, there are no examples');
        exampnum := -1;
      end;
  1 : if LENGTH(wordarr[segmnum,wordnum].exam[2]) <> 0 then
        WRITEWIND(window,wordarr[segmnum,wordnum].exam[2])
      else begin
        WRITEWIND(window,'sorry, only one example');
        exampnum := -1;
      end;
  2 : begin
        WRITEWIND(window,'sorry, only two examples');
        exampnum := -1;
      end;
 end; (* case *)
 exampnum := exampnum + 1;
 if wait then
   begin
    WRITEWIND(text2,'1 - yes$2 - no');
    case DOPROMPT('do you understand now? ') of
     '1','y' : EXAMPLE := true;
    end;
   end
 else EXAMPLE := false;
 MOVEWIND(level4);
end; (* EXAMPLE *)

function ADDITIONAL:boolean;
begin
 ADDITIONAL := false;
 WRITEWIND(text1,CONCAT(
  'when the meaning appears, you must type in the word.$$',
  'you must spell the word correctly'));
 WRITEWIND(text2,'1 - yes$2 - no');
 WRITEWIND(choice2,' u)p   q)uit ');
 case DOPROMPT(' do you understand now? ') of
  '1', 'y' : ADDITIONAL := true;
 end;
end; (* ADDITIONAL *)
```

EXAMPLE — Displays the next example for the current word. The variable *exampnum* keeps track of the next example to be used. If there are no more examples, then a suitable error message is displayed.

ADDITIONAL — Gives additional help when requested in *DISPLAY*. Only used when *DISPLAY* is called by *PRACTICE*.

DISPLAY2.TEXT

```
function DEFINITION(segmnum,wordnum:integer;
           wait:boolean;window:integer):boolean;
var    i,j  : integer;
begin
  WRITEWIND(level4,'definition');
  case defnum of

  0 : if LENGTH(wordarr[segmnum,wordnum].def[1]) <> 0 then
        WRITEWIND(window,wordarr[segmnum,wordnum].def[1])
      else WRITEWIND(window,'sorry, there are no definitions');
  1 : if LENGTH(wordarr[segmnum,wordnum].def[2]) <> 0 then
        WRITEWIND(window,wordarr[segmnum,wordnum].def[2])
      else begin
        WRITEWIND(window,'sorry, only one definition');
        defnum := -1;
      end;
  2 : begin
        WRITEWIND(window,'sorry, only two definitions');
        defnum := -1;
      end;
  end; (* case *)
  defnum := defnum + 1;
  if wait then
    begin
    DEFINITION := false;
    WRITEWIND(text2,'1 - yes$2 - no');
    case DOPROMPT('do you understand now? ') of
    '1','y' : DEFINITION := true;
     end;
    end
  else begin
    DEFINITION := false;
    if defnum = 0 then
      defnum := 1;
    end;
  MOVEWIND(level4);
end; (* DEFINITION *)
```

DEFINITION – Like *EXAMPLE*, this procedure displays the next definition for the current word. If all the definitions have been seen, then an error message is displayed.

The Elements of CAL — DICTION.TEXT

```
procedure DICTIONARY;
var   wordid : integer;
      inword : string;
      segmnum : integer;
      wordnum : integer;
      i       : integer;

(*$I diction1.text*)

begin   (*----------- DICTIONARY -------------*)
 wordid := 0;
 MOVEWIND(text1);
 WRITEWIND(level2,'dictionary     ');
 while true do
  begin
   helpmesg := hdictionary;
   if DOLNPROMPT('which word? ',inword) then
      begin
       MOVEWIND(level0);
       MOVEWIND(text2 );
       EXIT(DICTIONARY);
      end;
   MOVEWIND(text0);
   segmnum := 0;
   for i := 1 to segmmax do
     begin
      wordid := SEARCHFORMATCH(inword,i);
      if wordid = -1 then
        EXIT(DICTIONARY);
      if wordid <> 0 then
        begin
         segmnum := i;
         i := segmmax;
        end;
     end;
   if segmnum = 0 then
     if not DISPLAYCHOICE then
       SHOWALLWORDS;
  end; (* while *)
end;    (* DICTIONARY *)
```

DICTIONARY – First prompt the student for a word that they want to look up. The **function** SEARCHFORMATCH is then called to see if there is an exact match in the dictionary. If found, SEARCHFORMATCH looks after the display of the word. If no exact match is found, then *DISPLAYCHOICE* is called to try and find words that match the first letter of the student's request. If no close match is found, then all the words in the dictionary are displayed by *SHOWALLWORDS*.

DICTION1.TEXT

```
function DISPLAYCHOICE:boolean;
var i,j    : integer;
    st     : longstring;
begin
  if LENGTH(inword) = 0 then
    begin
      DISPLAYCHOICE := false;
      EXIT(DISPLAYCHOICE);
    end;
  st := 'these are the words i can find $';
  for i := 1 to segmmax do
    for j := 1 to wordmax[i] do
      if TOLOWER(wordarr[i,j].word[1]) = TOLOWER(inword[1]) then
        st := CONCAT(st,' ',wordarr[i,j].word);
  if LENGTH(st) > 33 then
    begin
      WRITEWIND(text0,st);
      DISPLAYCHOICE := true;
    end
  else DISPLAYCHOICE := false;
end; (*DISPLAYCHOICE *)

procedure SHOWALLWORDS;
var i,j,k,l  : integer;
begin
  WRITEWIND(text1,'these are the words available$$');
  k := 1;
  for i := 1 to segmmax do
    for j := 1 to wordmax[segmmax] do
      begin
        if LENGTH(wordarr[i,j].word) <> 0 then
          if k >= 3 then
            begin
              WRITELN(wordarr[i,j].word);
              k := 0;
            end
          else begin
            WRITE(wordarr[i,j].word);
            for l := 1 to (14 - LENGTH(wordarr[i,j].word)) do
              WRITE(' ');
            k := k + 1;
          end;
      end;
end; (* SHOWALLWORDS *)
```

DISPLAYCHOICE — This **function** searches all of the dictionary for words that match the first character of *inword*; if any are found then they are displayed as possible words.

SHOWALLWORDS — Displays all the words in the dictionary. Formatted to show three words per line.

The Elements of CAL — LESSON.TEXT

```
procedure LESSON;
var   i    : integer;
   passed  : array[1..maxword] of passedtype;

(*$I choosem.text*)

begin  (* LESSON *)
  while true do
   begin
   helpmesg := hlesson;
   WRITEWIND(level2,'lesson');
   WRITEWIND(text0,'these lessons are available :$');
   WRITELN;
   for i := 1 to segmmax do
     WRITELN('         ',i,' : ',wordarr[i,1].segm);
   case DOPROMPT ('') of
   '1' : CHOOSEMETHOD(1);
   '2' : CHOOSEMETHOD(2);
   '3' : CHOOSEMETHOD(3);
   '4' : CHOOSEMETHOD(4);
   '5' : CHOOSEMETHOD(5);
   'q' : EXITPROGRAM('');
   'm' : begin
        MOVEWIND(level2);
        EXIT(LESSON);
        end;
     end; (* case *)
   end; (* while *)
end;   (* LESSON *)
```

LESSON – Displays the available lessons, then prompts for the lesson wanted. Calls *CHOOSEMETHOD* to prompt for the method to be used.

CHOOSEM.TEXT

```
procedure CHOOSEMETHOD(segm:integer);
var st    : longstring;

(*$I checkque.text*)
(*$I tests.text*)
(*$I meanings.text*)
(*$I practice.text*)

begin
  if segm > segmmax then
    EXIT(CHOOSEMETHOD);
  while true do
  begin
  helpmesg := hchoosemethod;
  st := 'the words in this lesson are:$$';
  for i := 1 to wordmax[segm] do
    st := CONCAT(st,wordarr[segm,i].word,' ');
  WRITEWIND(text1,st);
  WRITEWIND(text2,' 1 - test$ 2 - meanings$ 3 - practice$');
  case DOPROMPT ('') of
  't','1' : TESTS(segm);
      '2' : MEANINGS(segm);
  'p','3' : PRACTICE(segm);
  'm' : begin
        MOVEWIND(text1);
        MOVEWIND(text2);
        EXIT(CHOOSEMETHOD);
      end;
    end; (* case *)
  end; (* while true *)
end; (* CHOOSEMETHOD *)
```

CHOOSEMETHOD — Displays the words in the chosen group and prompts the student for the method to be used: *TEST*, *MEANINGS* or *PRACTICE*.

The Elements of CAL *CHECKQUE.TEXT*

```
function CHECKQUESTIONS(var wordnum:integer):boolean;
var   i   : integer;

    function ANYWORDSLEFT:boolean;
    var  i   : integer;
    begin
     for i := 1 to wordmax[segm] do
      if passed[i] = notin then
       begin
        ANYWORDSLEFT := true;
        EXIT(ANYWORDSLEFT);
       end;
     ANYWORDSLEFT := false;
    end; (* ANYWORDSLEFT *)

begin  (* CHECKQUESTIONS *)
  if ANYWORDSLEFT then
   repeat
    CHECKQUESTIONS := true;
    wordnum := RANDOM mod wordmax[segm] + 1;
   until passed[wordnum] = notin
  else CHECKQUESTIONS := false;
end; (* CHECKQUESTIONS *)
```

CHECKQUESTIONS — Uses the random number generator *RANDOM* to find the next word in the dictionary. Used by *TESTS*, *MEANINGS*, and *PRACTICE*. If all the words have been asked for and no match found, then *false* is returned. If a word is available, then the index into the **array** *wordarr* is returned in the **var** *wordnum*.

ANYWORDSLEFT — Is called by *CHECKQUESTIONS*. Checks the **array** *passed* to see if there are any words left.

TESTS.TEXT

```
procedure TESTS(segm:integer);
var   score, wordnum, numans : integer;
    i, templength : integer;
    st    : longstring;

(*$l uptests.text*)

begin (* TESTS *)
  helpmesg := htest;
  for i := 1 to wordmax[segm] do passed[i] := notin;
  score := 0;   numans := 0;
  MOVEWIND(text1);
  MOVEWIND(text2);
  WRITEWIND(level3,'test');
  while (CHECKQUESTIONS(wordnum)) and (numans < wordmax[segm]) do
    begin
    WRITEWIND(text1,wordarr[segm,wordnum].def[1]);
    if DOLNPROMPT('what is the word? ',st) then begin
      WRITEWIND(text1,'you did not finish the test$$');
      if READY then;
      MOVEWIND(text0);
      MOVEWIND(level3);
      EXIT(TESTS);
      end;
    if st[1] <> '$' then begin
      numans := numans + 1;
      if (POS(st,wordarr[segm,wordnum].word) = 1) and
       (LENGTH(st) = LENGTH(wordarr[segm,wordnum].word)) then
        begin
        score := score + 1;
        passed[wordnum] := pass;
        end
      else begin
        MOVEWIND(text1);
        passed[wordnum] := failed;
        end;
      WRITEWIND(text1,'thanks : answer recorded');
      if READY then begin
        WRITEWIND(text1,'you did not finish the test$$');
        if READY then;
        MOVEWIND(text0);
        MOVEWIND(level3);
        EXIT(TESTS);
        end;
      end (* then *)
    else passed[wordnum] := notin;
    end; (* while *)
  UPTESTS;
end;   (* TESTS *)
```

TESTS — Displays the first definition of a word, then prompts the learner for the corresponding word. When all the words in a segment have been tested, the score is displayed along with reinforcement. The **array** *passed* is maintained, with the current test state of each word in the current segment. This is required by the **function** *ANYWORDSLEFT* and to calculate the score.

```
procedure UPTESTS;
begin
  st := '  terrific!$you finished the test.$but you do not know the meaning of$$';
  templength := LENGTH(st);
  for i := 1 to wordmax[segm] do
    if passed[i] = failed then
      st := CONCAT(st,wordarr[segm,i].word,'  ');
  if LENGTH(st) > templength then
    WRITEWIND(text1,st)
  else WRITEWIND(text1,'  terrific!$you got them all passed');
  WRITEWIND(text2,'');
  WRITELN('your score is ',score,' out of ',numans);
  if READY then;
  MOVEWIND(text0);
  MOVEWIND(level3);
  EXIT(TESTS);
end; (* UPTESTS *)
```

UPTESTS — Does the reinforcement for TESTS and cleans up the display before exiting. The score is found by checking the **array** passed for the number passed and the number failed.

MEANINGS.TEXT

```
procedure MEANINGS(segm:integer);
var   inword : string;
      i     : integer;
      wordnum : integer;
      st    : longstring;
begin    (* MEANINGS *)
 wordnum := 0;
 MOVEWIND (text2);
 WRITEWIND(level3,'meanings');
 while wordnum <> -1 do
  begin
  helpmesg := hmeaning;
  WRITEWIND(text1,'here are the words$');
  for i := 1 to wordmax[segm] do
    WRITELN('         ',wordarr[segm,i].word);
  if DOLNPROMPT('which word? ',inword) then
     begin
     MOVEWIND(level3);
     MOVEWIND(text0);
     EXIT(MEANINGS);
     end;

  wordnum := SEARCHFORMATCH(inword,segm);
  end;
 MOVEWIND(level3);
 MOVEWIND(text0);
end; (* MEANINGS *)
```

MEANINGS — Calls many of the **procedures** used by *DICTIONARY*, but works within one segment of the dictionary. Uses the **function** *SEARCHFORMATCH* to do all the hard work. Also displays all the words in the current segment.

PRACTICE.TEXT

```
procedure PRACTICE(segm:integer);
var  st       : longstring;
     wordnum  : integer;
     errornum : array[1..maxword] of integer;
     i        : integer;

(*$l upprac.text*)
(*$l errchk.text*)

begin   (* PRACTICE *)
  helpmesg := hprac1;
  WRITEWIND(level3,'practice');
  MOVEWIND(text2);
  for i := 1 to wordmax[segm] do
    begin
    errornum[i] := 0;
    passed[i]   := notin;
    end;
  wordnum := 1;
  while CHECKQUESTIONS(wordnum) do
    begin
    writewin(text1,wordarr[segm,wordnum].def[1]);
    if DOLNPROMPT('what is the word? ',st) then
        begin
        MOVEWIND(text1 );
        MOVEWIND(level3);
        UPPRACTICE;
        end;
    if (POS(st,wordarr[segm,wordnum].word) = 1) and
       (LENGTH(st) = LENGTH(wordarr[segm,wordnum].word)) then
        begin
        WRITEWIND(text1,'that is right!');
        passed[wordnum] := pass;
        if READY then UPPRACTICE;
        end
      else DOERRORCHECK;
    end; (* while *)
  WRITEWIND(text0,CONCAT(
      'good, you know the meanings for ',
      wordarr[segm,1].segm));
  if READY then UPPRACTICE;
  MOVEWIND(level3);
end;   (* PRACTICE *)
```

PRACTICE — Displays the first definition of a word from the current segment, prompting for the correct word. When the response is an exact match to the word (spelling must be correct) then the student is reinforced. If the answer to the prompt is incorrect, then *DOERRORCHECK* is called to give some help to the learner. On exit, the words that were not answered correctly are displayed.

UPPRAC.TEXT

```
procedure UPPRACTICE;
var    st    : longstring;
begin
  WRITEWIND(choice2,choice);
  st := 'good practicing!$$but you do not know the meaning of$$';
  for i := 1 to wordmax[segm] do
    if passed[i] = notin then
      st := CONCAT(st,wordarr[segm,i].word,' ');
  WRITEWIND(text0,st);
  if READY then
  EXIT(PRACTICE);
end; (* UPPRACTICE *)
```

UPPRACTICE — Displays reinforcement with a list of the words which were not answered correctly, then cleans up the display before exiting.

The Elements of CAL   ERRCHK.TEXT

```
procedure DOERRORCHECK;
var  t1,t2  : longstring;
begin
  errornum[wordnum] := errornum[wordnum] + 1;
  with wordarr[segm,wordnum] do case errornum[wordnum] of
    1 : begin
          WRITEWIND(text1,CONCAT('sorry the right word is : ',
                    word,'$'));
          WRITEWIND(text2,def[1]);
          if READY then UPPRACTICE;
          MOVEWIND(text0);
        end; (* 1 *)
    2 : begin
          helpmesg := hprac2;
          WRITEWIND(choice2,' m)enu  q)uit');
          MOVEWIND(text2);
          WRITEWIND(text1,CONCAT('sorry$the right answer is : ',
                    word,'$',def[1],'$$ 1 - yes$ 2 - no$$'));
          case DOPROMPT('do you understand now? ') of
            'm' : UPPRACTICE;
      ' ','n','2' : begin
              t1 := CONCAT(
                'I will try to help$$',
                'e - will show you an example$  of ',
                word,
                '$$d - will show you the definitions$   for ',
                word);
              t2 := CONCAT(
                '$a - will tell you how to answer$',
                '  the questions in practice',
                '$$x  - will give you the next question$$');
              if DISPLAY(segm,wordnum,true,t1,t2) then
                UPPRACTICE;
              end;
          end; (* case *)
          MOVEWIND(text2);
          WRITEWIND(choice2,choice);
          helpmesg := hprac1;
        end; (* 2 *)
    3 : begin
          MOVEWIND(text2);
          WRITEWIND(text1,CONCAT
              ('Read carefully!$$',
               word,' : ',def[1]));
          if READY then UPPRACTICE;
          MOVEWIND(text1);
          errornum[wordnum] := 1;
        end; (* 3 *)
  end; (* case *)
end; (* DOERRORCHECK *)
```

DOERRORCHECK — Keeps track of the number of times that a question has been answered incorrectly. If it is the first incorrect answer, then the word and its first definition are displayed. If the second is incorrect, then again the first definition and the correct word are displayed, but then the learner is prompted "Do you understand now?". If the response is "no", DISPLAY is called to provide more extensive help. If this is the third incorrect response, then the learner is reminded to read the word and definition carefully. The correct word and its first definition are displayed.

WORDSDATA.TEXT

g:plants
w:seed
d:a small grain or nut from a plant
d:flowers, plants and trees all grow from seeds.
e:when peter shook the plant, a seed fell out.
e:two weeks after brian planted the seed, a flower
 started to grow.
w:shrub
d:a bush with many separated branches starting from
 or near the ground
d:shrubs often look like small trees.
e:julie hid behind the shrub, but paul could see her foot.
e:they planted one shrub beside the front door.
w:stem
d:the long, thin part of a plant that holds up a leaf,
 flower or fruit
d:the stem joins the flower, leaf or fruit to the
 rest of the plant. you may have seen a stem on the
 top of an apple or a cherry tree.
e:the baby pulled the flower off the stem.
e:it was a red tulip with a thin green stem.
w:thorn
d:a sharp point on a stem or branch
d:many plants have thorns. if you pick a rose,
 the thorns on the stem may hurt you fingers.
e:"ouch!" he cried, "that thorn stuck right in my thumb!"
e:the thorn was small, but sharp.
w:turf
d:soil with grass growing on it
d:turf means the grass, all its roots, and the dirt
 it is growing in. it is used to describe the special
 grass fields used for sports.
e:sandy kicked her soccer ball across the turf.
e:the toes of his shoes dug into the turf
g:animals
w:caterpillar
d:the larva or wormlike form in which insects such
 as the butterfly and the moth hatch from the egg.
d:caterpillars have long bodies and many legs. when a
 caterpillar grows up, it becomes a moth or a butterfly.
e:the caterpillar turned into a butterfly and flew away.
e:we see many caterpillars in spring.
w:hornet
d:a large wasp that stings
d:a hornet is a flying insect that looks and sounds like a bee.
e:the hornet buzzed around the honey.
e:hornets built a nest in our apple tree.
w:jellyfish
d:a small sea animal that has a jelly-like appearance
d:a jellyfish has no bones. it has a body like an octopus,
 but the legs are thinner. you can see through a jelly fish.
e:the jellyfish was a shiny blob floating in the water.

The Elements of CAL WORDSDATA.TEXT

e:after a storm, several jellyfish were left on the sand.
w:rattlesnake
d:a poisonous snake that makes a rattling sound with its tail
d:rattlesnakes are often actors in movies about the old west.
e:out of the sand slithered a poisonous rattlesnake.
e:there are no rattlesnakes where i live.
w:unicorn
d:a legendary animal like a horse, but having a
single long horn in the middle of its forehead
d:unicorns are not real animals. you may have seen
 a picture of one in a book of fairytales.
e:the unicorn was white, with a beautiful flowing mane.
e:the children rode through the sky on the
 back of the unicorn.
g:sports
w:lacrosse
d:a game in which players use netted sticks for
 passing a rubber ball into the other goal
d:north american indians played lacrosse many years ago.
e:debbie and sam played on the lacrosse team.
e:lacrosse is an old sport.
w:recreation
d:play or amusement
d:recreation includes: playing games, reading books,
 swimming, painting-- anything you do for fun.
e:hiking is my favorite form of recreation.
e:do you call hiking recreation? i think it is work.
w:athlete
d:a person trained in exercises of strength,
 speed and skill
d:athletes spend a lot of time becoming good at sports.
e:wayne gretzky is an excellent athlete.
e:i sometimes play games, but i am not an athlete.
w:judo
d:a japanese method of wrestling or fighting
d:judo uses no weapons. one person must be clever
 enough to make the other person fall.
e:tim wears a special white costume for his judo classes.
e:alice has learned to defend herself with judo.
g:weather
w:fog
d:a cloud of fine drops of water that forms just
 above the surface of the earth
d:when it is foggy, the air is grey and you connot
 see things which are far away.
e:the fog was so thick leslie had trouble finding
 her house.
e:the grey fog rolled in off the ocean.
w:storm
d:bad weather with heavy rain or snow, strong winds
 and sometimes thunder
d:a snow storm can leave the ground covered in

WORDSDATA.TEXT   15 Curriculum Four: WORDS

many feet of snow.
e:the storm only lasted three hours, but the roads
 were flooded with rain water.
e:the storm broke three branches off the maple tree.
w:lightning
d:a flash of electricity in a thunderstorm
d:lightning shows up as a bright streak of light
 across the sky.
e:a streak of lightning lit the sky.
e:when i was young, i was afraid of lightning.
w:rainbow
d:an arch of colored light that is seen in the sky when
 the rays of the sun are seen through rain, mist or spray
d:rainbows occur when the sun shines and it rains
 at the same time.
e:a rainbow contains as many colors as a box of crayons.
e:after the rain, a beautiful rainbow appeared in the sky.
w:hail
d:frozen rain
d:hail is small drops of ice falling from the sky.
e:the hail stung her cheeks as she ran across the field.
e:the hail was so thick, it looked like snow.
g:occupations
w:acrobat
d:a person who can dance on a rope or wire, swing on
 trapezes, turn handsprings or do other such feats
 of bodily skill and strength
d:acrobats often perform in circuses.
e:look at that acrobat swing from the trapeze!
e:acrobats must practice every day.
w:actor
d:a man or boy who acts on a stage, in motion pictures,
 or on television or radio
d:a man or boy who acts is an actor. a woman or
 girl who acts is an actress.
e:who is your favorite television actor?
e:sam is an actor in our school play.
w:cashier
d:a person in charge of money in a bank or any business
d:a cashier is the person you give the money to in a store.
e:susan paid the cashier at the supermarket.
e:a cashier in a bank must count hundreds of
 dollars each day.
w:chef
d:a head cook
d:anyone who is a good cook can be called a chef.
e:the chef cooked many delicious deserts
 and mouth-watering meals.
e:there was one chef in the kitchen,
 and three people to make salads.
w:detective
d:a person who investigates crime

257

d:a detective may be a police officer,
 or a person with a private business.
e:the detective searched for clues to help
 find the thief.
e:pete the private eye was a famous
 detective in toronto.

File Format

The data for **WORDS** is stored in a file named CAL: WORDSDATA.TEXT and has the following format.

G: indicates a segment.
W: indicates a word.

Both of these must occupy one line and contain a maximum of 12 characters with no blanks.

D: indicates a definition.
E: indicates an example.

Both of these may contain a maximum of 200 characters which may include blanks. They normally occupy one line but may be continued over several lines by leaving a blank as the first character in each of the continuing lines.

There is a maximum of 2 definitions, 2 examples, 5 segments and 5 words per segment.

This format is obviously specific to the implementation, and may easily be expanded or modified for different implementations.

is — as it always was —" began Trurl, but just then the machine made a faint, barely audible croaking noise and said, for the last time, *"SEVEN."*

Then something snapped inside, a few stones dribbled down from overhead, and now before them lay nothing but a lifeless mass of scrap. The two constructors exchanged a look and silently, without any further comment or conversation, walked back the way they came.

From, "Trurl's Machine", in *The Cyberiad* by Stanislaw Lem.

16 Bibliography

The following bibliography was created with the assistance of Greg Kearsley, Senior Scientist with the Human Resources Research Organization, Alexandria, Virginia and Jack Brahan, Head of Information Science Section, Division of Electrical Engineering, National Research Council, Canada. It is not meant to include all the materials on the subject, but rather those believed to be the most valid and important.

GENERAL PUBLICATIONS

Baker, Frank. *Computer Managed Instruction, Theory and Practice.* Englewood Cliffs, NJ: Educational Technology Publications, 1975.

Brahan, J.W., ed. *CIPS Review Special Issue on Computers and Education.* November/December, 1981.

Burson, Jeanne L. *The Author's Guide to CAI* (4th Edition). Ohio State University, 1976.

Cakir, A., Hart, D., and Stewart, T. *Visual Display Terminals.* [Workplace design and ergonomics.] Toronto: John Wiley & Sons, 1980.

Crawford, Stuart. *A Standard's Guide for the Authoring of Instructional Software.* Reference Manual vol. 3. JEM Reseach: Victoria B.C., nd.

Dennis, J. Richard, ed. Urbana: College of Education, Department of Secondary Education, University of Illinois, 1979.

Hallworth, H.J., and Brebner, Ann. *Computer Assisted Instruction in Schools.* Athabasca: Planning and Research, Alberta Education, 1980.

Hicks, B.L., and Hunka, S. *The Teacher and the Computer.* W.B. Saunders Company, 1972.

Japanese Information Processing Development Center. *Preliminary Report on Study and Research on Fifth Generation Computers 1979-1989.* Fall, 1981.

The Elements of CAL

Kearsley, G.P. "Some Facts About CAI: Trends 1970-1976." *Journal of Educational Data Processing* 1976 13(3):1-11.

National Development Program in Computer Assisted Learning. *The Cost of Learning with Computers*. Edited by J. Fielden and P.K. Pearson. London: Council for Educational Technology, 1978.

Papert, S. *Mindstorms: Children, Computers and Powerful Ideas*. New York: Basic Books, 1980.

Ragsdale, Ronald G. *Computers in the Schools: A Guide for Planning*. Toronto: OISE, 1982.

Sleeman, D.H., and Brown, J.S., eds. *International Journal of Man Machine Studies: Special Issue on Intelligent Tutoring Systems*. (1979)11(1).

Taylor, Robert P., ed. *The Computer in the School: Tutor, Tool, Tutee*. New York: Teachers College Press, 1980.

On The Effectiveness of CAL

Bell, F. "Why is Computer-Related Learning so Successful?" *Educational Technology* (1974)14:15-18.

Fletcher, J., et al. *A Note on the Effectiveness of Computer-Aided Instruction*. Stanford, CA: 1972. ERIC Document Reproduction Service No. ED 071 450.

Los Nietos School District. *Computer Assisted Instruction: How it Raises Children's Achievement Scores*. Edited by N.D. Crandall. California, 1977.

Tsai, San-Yun, and Pohl, Norval F. "Student Achievement in Computer Programming: Lecture vs Computer-aided Instruction". *Journal of Experimental Education* Winter 77:66

CONFERENCE REPORTS

Association for Computing Machinery. *Siggraph 82 Conference Proceedings*. Edited by R. Daniel Bergeron. New York: ACM, 1982.

Council for Educational Technology. *Computer Assisted Learning: Selected Papers from the CAL 81 Symposium*. Edited by P.R. Smith. Toronto: Pergamon Press, 1981.

IFIP. *Computers in Education: Proceedings of the IFIP Third World Conference on Computers in Education*. Edited by R. Lewis and E.D. Tagg. North Holland Publishing Company, 1981.

16 Bibliography

NEWSLETTERS

Your school district, state or province may have an association of computer-using educators. Contact with such a group, even if just to receive newsletters, can be a valuable source of information.

Communications of the ACM. The publication of the Association for Computing Machinery. P.O. Box 12114 Church Street Station, New York, NY 10249 U.S.

Computer Graphics. The publication of the ACM special interest group on computer graphics. 11 West 42nd St., New York, N.Y. 10036 U.S.

Newsletter. The newsletter of the Associate Committee on Instructional Technology. National Research Council, Montreal Rd., Ottawa, Ontario, Canada.

Sigcue Bulletin. The newsletter for the ACM Special Interest Group on Computer Uses in Education. Association for Computing Machinery, 11 West 42nd St., New York, NY 10036, U.S.

MAGAZINES

BYTE. Box 590, Martinsville, N.J., 08836, U.S.

Classroom Computer News. Box 266, Cambridge MA 02138, U.S.

Computer Graphics World. Box 122, Tulsa OK 74101, U.S.

Computerworld. Box 880, 375 Cochituate Rd., Framingham, Mass. 01701, U.S.

The Computing Teacher. Computing Center, Eastern Oregon State College, La Grande, Oregon, 9785 U.S.

Courseware Magazine. 4919N Millbrook #222, Fresno, CA 93726, U.S.

EDN. Computer Center, Box 5563, Denver, Colorado, U.S.

Electronic Learning Magazine. Scholastic Inc., 50 West 44th St., New York, NY, 10036, U.S.

Games. Des Moines, Iowa.

EVALUATION THEORY

Ansfield, Paul J. "A User Oriented Computing Procedure for Compiling and Generating Examinations". *Educational Technology* vol. 8, no. 3: 12-13

Bloom, B.S.; Hastings, J.I.; and Madaus, G.F. *Handbook on Formative and Summative Evaluation of Student Learning.* New York: McGraw-Hill, 1971.

Cooper, C.R., and Purves, A.D. *A Guide to Evaluation*. New York: Ginn, 1974.

Fray, Robert B.; Cross, Laurence H.; and Loury, Stephen R. "Random Guessing, Correction for Guessing and Reliability of Multiple-Choice Test Scores". *Journal of Experimental Education* Fall 77:11.

Gronlund, Norman E. *Measurement and Evaluation in Teaching* (3rd Edition). Macmillan, 1976.

Lippey, ed. *Computer Assisted Test Construction*. Educational Technology Publications, 1974.

Popham, W.J. *An Evaluation Guidebook*. Los Angeles: Instructional Objective Exchange, 1972.

Venezky, R.L. *Testing in Reading*. Champaign Ill: National Council of Teachers of English, 1974. Available through Educational Resources Information Centre (ERIC), National Research Council, Ottawa.

INSTRUCTIONAL DESIGN THEORY

Bloom, B.S., et al. *Taxonomy of Educational Objectives: Cognitive Domain*. New York: Longman, 1956.

Gagne, R.M., and Briggs, L.J. *Principles of Instructional Design*. New York: Holt, Rinehart & Winston, 1974.

Kulhavy, W.K. "Feedback and Response Confidence". *Journal of Education Psychology* (1976) 68(5):522-528.

Mager, R.F. *Preparing Instructional Objectives*. Belmont, CA: Fearon Publishers, 1962.

Rankin, R.J., and Trepper, T. "Retention and Delay of Feedback in a Computer-Assisted Instruction Task". *Journal of Experimental Education* 1978, 46(4):67-70.

Roblyer, M.D. "Instructional Design vs. Authoring of Courseware: Some Crucial Differences". In *Association for Educational Data Systems 1981 Convention Proceedings*. pp. 243-247.

Smith, William L., and Swan, Beverly. "Adjusting Syntactic Structures to Various Levels of Audience". *Journal of Experimental Education* Summer 78:29.

AUTHORING SYSTEMS AND LANGUAGES

Brahan, J.W., Henneker, W.H., and Hlady, A.M. "NATAL-74. Concept to Reality". In *Proceedings of the Third Canadian Symposium on Instructional Technology*. 1980.

16 Bibliography

BYTE. Special issue on LOGO. August 1982.

BYTE. Special issue on SMALLTALK. August 1981.

Clocksin, W.F., and Mellish, C.S. *Programming in Prolog*. New York: Springer-Verlag, 1981.

Gauthier, Richard. *Using the UNIX System*. Reston, Virginia: Reston, 1981.

Jeldon, D.L. "A CAI Coursewriter System for the Microcomputer". *Association for Educational Data Systems Journal* (1981) 14(3):159-168.

Jensen, Kathleen, and Wirth, Niklaus. *Pascal User Manual and Report*. New York: Springer-Verlag, 1978.

Jones, M.C. "TICCIT Applications in Higher Education: Evaluation Results". In *ADCIS Proceedings 1978* pp.398-419.

Kearsley, Greg. "Authoring Systems in Computer Based Education". *Communications of the ACM* (1982) 25(7):429.

Kernighan, Brian, and Ritchie, Dennis M. *The C Programming Language*. Englewood Cliffs, NJ: Prentice-Hall, 1978.

Knuth, Donald. *TEX and METAFONT: New Directions in Typesetting*. Bedford Mass.: Digital Press, 1979.

Ledgard, et al. *Pascal with Style: Programming Proverbs*. Rochelle Park, N.J.: Hayden, 1979.

Ledgard, Henry. *ADA: An Introduction and Reference Manual (July 1980)*. New York: Springer-Verlag, 1981.

Lewis, T.G. *Pascal Programming for the Apple*. Reston, Virginia: Reston, 1981.

Lien, David A. *The BASIC Handbook*. Compusoft Publishing.

Luehrmann, Arthur, and Peckham, Herbert. *APPLE PASCAL: A Hands-On Approach*. McGraw-Hill.

Stewart, Charles, ed. *APPLE PASCAL: A Hands-On Approach*. McGraw-Hill, 1981.

Wasserman, Anthony I. "USE: a Methodology for the Design and Development of Interactive Information Systems". In *Proceedings of the IFIG WG 8.1*. England: Oxford, 1979.

Yates, Jean, and Thomas, Rebecca. *User Guide to Unix System*. Osborne, McGraw-Hill, 1982.

The Elements of CAL

PROGRAMMING THEORY

Aho, Alfred, and Ullman, Jeffrey. *Principles of Compiler Design*. Don Mills, Ontario: Addison-Wesley, 1979.

Dijkstra, E. *A Discipline of Programming*. Englewood Cliffs, NJ: Prentice-Hall, 1976.

Kernighan, Brian, and Plauger, P.J. *The Elements of Programming Style*. McGraw-Hill.

Kernighan, Brian, and Plauger, P.J. *Software Tools*. Reading, Mass.: Addison-Wesley.

Ramamoorthy, C.V., and Yeh, Raymond T. *Tutorial: Software Methodology*. Long Beach, CA.: IEE Computer Society, 1978.

Riddle, W.E., and Fairley, R.E. *Software Development Tools*. New York: Springer-Verlag, 1980.

Shneiderman, Ben. *Software Psychology*. Cambridge, Mass.: Winthrop, 1980.

Wirth, Niklaus. *Algorithms + Data Structures = Programs*. Englewood Cliffs, NJ: Prentice-Hall, 1976.

Wirth, Niklaus. *Systematic Programming: An Introduction*. Englewood Cliffs, NJ: Prentice-Hall, 1973.

COMPUTER BASED TRAINING

Kearsley, Greg; Hunter, Beverly; and Hillelsohn, Michael. "Computer Literacy in Business and Industry: Three Examples Using Microcomputers". *Educational Technology* (1982)9.

Kearsley, Greg; Hillelsohn, Michael; and Seidel, Robert J. "Microcomputer-Based Training in Business and Industry: Present Status and Future Prospects". *Journal of Educational Technology Systems* 10(2):101.

DATABASE THEORY

Date, C.J. *An Introduction to Database Systems* (2nd Edition). Don Mills, Ontario: Addison-Wesley, 1977.

Wasserman, Anthony I. "The Data Management Facilities of PLAIN". Unpublished. San Francisco CA.: University of California.

GRAPHICS

Buxton, William. "Sources for Information on Computer Graphics and Related Subjects". Unpublished. Toronto: University of Toronto, nd.

16 Bibliography

Foley, J.D., and Van Dam, A. *Fundamentals of Interactive Graphics*. Addison Wesley, 1982.

Moore, M.V., and Nawrocki, L.H. *The Educational Effectiveness of Graphic Displays for Computer Assisted Instruction*. Alexandria, Virginia: U.S. Army Research Institute for the Behavioral Sciences, 1976.

Newman, W., and Sproull, R. *Principles of Interactive Computer Graphics* (2nd Edition). New York: McGraw-Hill, 1979.

GAMES

Boocock, S.S., and Schild E.E L., eds. *Simulation Games in Learning*. Beverley Hills:Sage Publications, 1968.

Fletcher, J.L. "The Effectiveness of Simulation Games as Learning Environments". *Simulation and Games* 2(4):425-454.

Harry, L. *Using Simulation Games in the Classroom*. John Hopkins University Center for the Study of Social Organization of Schools, 1969.

Kohl, Herbert R. "Math, Writing and Games". *The New York Review* New York, 1974.

SPECIAL EDUCATION

Augsburger, W., and Lampl, G.R. "The Computer and the Disabled". In *Proceedings of the Third Canadian Symposium on Instructional Technology*. 1980.

BYTE. Special issue on computers and the disabled. September 1982.

Cronin, B. "The DAVID System: The Development of an Interactive Video System at the National Technical Institute for the Deaf". *American Annals of the Deaf* 1979, vol 124 616-623.

Fricke, J. *CAI in a School for the Deaf: Expected Results and a Serendipity or Two*. ERIC Document Reproduction Service No. ED 129 270.

Hallworth, H.J., and Brebner, Ann. "CAI for the Developmentally Handicapped: Nine Years of Progress". In *Proceedings of the 1980 Conference of the Association for the Development of Computer-Based Instructional Systems*. 1980.

Howe, J.A.M. "A New Deal? Using Computers to Teach Children with Learning Difficulties". *McGill Journal of Education* Fall 1979, vol14 343-352.

Sandals, L.H. *Computer Assisted Leaning with the Developmentally Handicapped*. Unpublished doctoral dissertation, University of Calgary, 1973.

COMPUTER LITERACY

Hunter, Beverly. "Computer Literacy in Grades K-8". *Journal of Educational Technology Systems* 10(1):59.

Hunter, Beverly. *My Students Use Computers*. Reston, Virginia: Reston, Forthcoming..

LOCAL NETWORKS

BYTE. Special issue on local networks. October 1981.

VIDEODISC

BYTE. Special issue on interactive videodiscs. June 1982.

Human Resources Reseach Organization Videodisc Group. "Instructional Applications of Spatial Data Management". *Videodisc/Videotex* (1982) 2:3.

Kearsley, Greg. "Videodiscs in Education and Training: The Idea Becomes Reality". *Videodisc/Videotex* (Fall 1981):208.

Woolley, R.D. "Microcomputers and Videodiscs: New Dimension for Computer-Based Education". *Interface Age* (December 1979):78-82.

TELIDON

Godfrey, D., and Chang, E., eds. *The Telidon Book*. Victoria: Press Porcepic, 1981.

Mill, M. *A Study of Human Response to Pictorial Representation on Telidon*. Telidon Behavioral Research Report 3. Ottawa: Department of Communications.

SPECIFIC SUBJECTS
Math

Ableson, Harold, and diSessa, Andrea A. *Turtle Geometry: The Computer as a Medium for Exploring Mathematics*. Cambridge, Mass.: M.I.T. Press, 1981.

National Council of Teachers of Mathematics. *An Agenda for Action: Recommendations for School Mathematics for the 1980's*. Reston, Virginia: NCTM, 1980.

Post, Dudley L.S, ed. *The Use of Computers in Secondary School Mathematics*. Massachusett: Entelek Corp., 1970.

16 Bibliography

English Skills

Brebner, Ann, *et al*. "Teaching Elementary Reading by CMI and CAI". In *Proceedings of the 18th Annual Convention of the Association for Educational Data Systems* (1980):21-25.

Fremer, John and Anastasio, J. "Computer-Assisted Item Writing-1 (Spelling Items)". *Journal of Educatonal Measurement* vol 6, no. 1 69-74.

Sciences

Dunkin, W. *Computer-Simulated Experiments in Physics Teaching*. Alexandria VA: 1977. ERIC Document Reproduction Service No. ED066 876.

McKenzie, J.; Elton, L.; and Lewis, R., eds. *Interactive Computer Graphics in Science Teaching*. Toronto: John Wiley & Sons, 1978.

Languages

Kidd, M. and Holmes, G. "Realizing the Potential of the Computer in the Learning of Modern Languages". *Proceedings of the Third Canadian Symposium on Instructional Technology*. 1980.

SOFTWARE CATALOGUES

Clearing House for Educational Software. Faculty of Education, University of British Columbia, Vancouver, B.C., Canada.

J.L. Hammett Microcomputer Catalogue. Hammett Place, Braintree, MA 02184, U.S.

K-12 Micromedia. Box 17, Valley Cottage NY 10989, U.S.

Ontario Software Catalogue. Haileybury School of Mines & the Ontario Ministry of Education, Haileybury, Ontario, Canada.

Opportunities for Learning Catalogue. 8950 Lurline Ave., Chatsworth, CA 91311, U.S.

Scholastic Microcomputer Instructional Materials. Scholastic, Inc., 904 Sylvan Ave., Englewood Cliffs, NJ 07632, U.S.

17 Glossary

access:
The ability to obtain information from, or place information into storage.

algorithm:
An orderly procedure (akin to a recipe) for obtaining a particular result or solving a problem. Algorithms are often expressed in mathematical terms.

alphanumeric:
Alphabetic and numeric characters.

ANSI
(American National Standards Institute).

analog:
One of the two main types of computer (the other is the digital). Quantities are represented and processed without the use of a language. The representation and measurement of the performance or behavior of the system under investigation takes the form of continuously variable physical conditions (analogies) such as voltages, currents, temperatures or pressure.

argument:
A value (an independent variable) passed to a subroutine or function.

ASCII
(American Standard Code for Information Interchange): Computers use a numerical representation for all characters (i.e., the uppercase and lowercase English alphabet, numbers and special symbols). This standard, consisting of all the above characters and 32 control codes, specifies which number will stand for each character. Since each character is represented by a unique 7-bit binary number, one ASCII-encoded character can be stored in one byte of computer memory. All personal computers use this standard.

assembler:
A systems program that translates assembly-language programs into executable machine-level code (that is, into the computer's native language).

assembly language:
A low-level programming aid that permits the programmer to use mnemonics instead of numerical op codes and alphanumeric labels instead of absolute memory addresses. It is similar in structure to the computer's native language, but is more convenient to use.

automaton:
A machine or control mechanism that follows automatically a pre-determined sequence of operations or responds to encoded instructions.

backplane:
The circuitry and mechanical elements

The Elements of CAL

used to connect the boards of a system.

BASIC
(Beginner's All-purpose Symbolic Instruction Code): A compiler or interpreter language that is easy to learn. Used with most time-sharing and minicomputer systems. Oriented toward beginners rather than experienced programmers. Numerous incompatible versions exist, often called dialects: CBASIC, MBASIC, XYBASIC.

baud:
A measure of the speed with which information can be communicated between two devices. If the information is, for example, in the form of alphabetic characters, then 300 baud usually corresponds to about 30 characters per second. The number of bits transmitted or received per second.

benchmark:
A test that compares the performance characteristics of several devices, programs or systems.

binary:
The base-two number system. It uses only the digits 0 and 1. The number 10 in the decimal system, which has ten different digits and a base or radix of ten, is represented as 1010 in the binary system.

bit:
A single binary digit. A unit of information content corresponding to the decision between one of the two possible states. Also, the smallest unit of measurement of capacity in a memory storage device.

board:
A card that contains circuitry for one or more specific functions, such as memory or interfacing.

bootstrap:
A short loader program that loads a more sophisticated loader into memory. That loader, in turn, loads the desired program. The term bootstrap arises from the idea that the computer is picking itself up by its bootstraps. In other words, it progresses from the bootstrap to the loader to the main program itself.

break:
A key which is used to interrupt a computation and return the computer to a user-input mode.

breakpoint:
A debugging aid. When a breakpoint is encountered in a program, execution of the program temporarily halts.

buffer:
Memory area in a computer or peripheral used for temporary storage of information that has just been received. The information is held in the buffer until the computer or device is ready to process it. Hence, a computer or device with memory designated as a buffer area can process one set of data while more sets are arriving.

bug:
A programming error. Also refers to the cause of any hardware or software malfunction.

byte:
In data processing, a sequence of adjacent binary digits (usually eight) operated on as a word, but usually shorter than a word. The values of the bits can be varied to form as many as 2(8) or 256 permutations. So, one byte of memory can represent an integer from 0 to 255 or from -127 to plus 128.

CAI
(Computer-Assisted Instruction).

call:
An instruction that invokes a subroutine.

17 Glossary

Cathode Ray Tube:
See CRT.

Central Processing Unit:
See CPU

character set:
The repertoire of characters that an output device can display or print. Two common character sets are 96-character ASCII, which includes all ASCII.

chip:
An integrated circuit.

code:
To write instructions for a computer system; to classify data according to arbitrary tables; to use a machine language; to program; to convert analog signals to digital.

coded program:
Instructions, usually in the form of a list coded in the computer's native or machine language, for solving a problem. Often shortened to code.

coder:
A person who prepares instructions sequences from detailed flow- charts and other algorithmic procedures prepared by others, as contrasted with a programmer, who prepares the procedures and flow charts. Also, a device that is capable of translating one type of data representation into another type.

coding:
The design and application of a coded program. The process of writing the detailed step-by-step instructions for the computer to follow. This is done by a coder.

command:
A request to the computer that is executed as soon as it has been received. Sometimes this word is used inter-changeably with the terms "instruction" and "statement". Those terms properly refer to portions of programs and not to commands, which are carried out immediately.

computer:
A device which can accept and supply information and in which the information supplied is derived from information accepted by logical processes. The two main types are digital computers and analog computers, and they make extensive use of electronic devices and circuits.

concentrator:
A device used in data communications to multiplex numerous low- speed communications lines onto a single high-speed communications line.

continuous processing:
The constant handling of disparate input items without grouping them.

control character:
A character or command obtained by holding down the key marked "CTRL" while pressing another key on a keyboard. Any of the 32 ASCII control codes. Their functions range from generating a carriage return to controlling remote devices.

CPU (Central Processing Unit):
The primary component of all computer systems. It is responsible for controlling system operation as directed by the program it is executing.

crash:
A system shutdown caused by a hardware or software malfunction.

CRT (Cathode Ray Tube) terminal:
A type of communications terminal that displays its output on a television-like screen. Synonym of video terminal.

cursor:
A symbol on the display of a video terminal that indicates where the next character is to be located.

The Elements of CAL

databank:
A collection of data organized for rapid search and retrieval. This collection of data, stored in the form of a complex set of tables, describes some aspect of the world outside of the computer (i.e., a library catalogue, a student record file or a budget).

database:
A collection of information in a form that can be manipulated by a computer.

data vs. information:
Data are the basic elements of information which can be processed or produced by a computer. Sometimes data are considered to be expressible only in numerical form, but information is not so limited.

dedicated device:
A device that is used exclusively for one function.

device:
A computer peripheral or an electronic component.

diagnostic:
A systems program used as a hardware trouble-shooting aid.

digital:
Information that can be represented by a collection of bits. Most modern computers store information in digital form. The digital (as opposed to analog) computer can represent information only as separate, discontinuous numbers and works on data mathematically (that is, it does calculations by adding binary numbers), rather than physically.

disc:
A circular piece of material which has a magnetic coating similar to that found on ordinary recording tape. Digital information can be stored magnetically on a disc much as musical information is stored on a magnetic tape. This term is often (and confusingly) used also to refer to a disc drive.

disc drive:
A peripheral which can store information on and retrieve information from a disc. A floppy disc drive can store information from a floppy disc and can retrieve that information.

diskette:
A small floppy disc in a square plastic envelope commonly either about 13 or 20 cm on a side. See Floppy disc.

disc storage:
A type of mass memory in which information is stored on a magnetically sensitive rotating disc. Disc drives are generally both faster and more expensive than paper tape or magnetic tape devices.

driver:
A program that controls (or drives) a device.

editor:
A program that facilitates the editing of textual material or computer software.

electronic mail:
The transmission of messages normally transmitted via the postal system, using electronic communications systems in lieu of the physical transportaton and delivery of paper messages.

execute:
To perform a computer instruction or run a program.

file:
A group of related information records that are treated as a unit. The records may consist of data or program instructions.

firmware:
Software stored in read-only memory. Also a synonym for microcode.

17 Glossary

flag:
A bit whose state signifies whether a certain condition has occurred.

floating-point BASIC:
A type of BASIC language that allows the use of decimal numbers. The name comes from the fact that the decimal point "floats" to a new position in a number, as required, following a calculation.

floppy disc:
A slow-speed inexpensive type of memory storage that uses flexible, or "floppy," discs (or diskettes), made of a material similar to magnetic tape, as opposed to "hard" discs made from rigid materials. It is a convenient method for the "bulk storage" of data, but slower than main computer memory (by 10,000 times) since data is stored in serial form.

flowchart:
A diagram representing the logic of a computer program.

graphics terminal:
A video terminal capable of displaying user-programmed graphics.

hacker:
A computer enthusiast, prone to sleeping near the computer.

hard copy:
Information printed on paper or other durable surface. This term is used to distinguish printed information from the temporary image presented on the computer's CRT screen.

hard disc:
Disc storage that uses rigid discs rather than flexible discs as the storage medium. Hard-disc devices can generally store more information and access it faster. Cost considerations, however, currently restrict their usage to medium and large-scale applications. Smaller, cheaper units are now coming to market.

hardware:
A popular expression used to distinguish the physical parts making up any electronic equipment from the software.

high-level language:
Computer language that allows the programmer to write programs using verbs, symbols and commands rather than machine code. Some common high-level languages are: ALGOL, APL, BASIC, COBOL, FORTRAN, NATAL, PL/1, PL/M and SNOBOL.

impact printer:
A printer that prints characters by mechanical means, such as a type ball (as opposed to thermal or ink jet methods).

initialize:
To set up the starting conditions necessary for the execution of the remainder of a program. For example, in a program that draws a circle, the initialization might include specifying the radius of the circle. To prepare a diskette so that the computer can later store data on it.

input:
Information arriving at a device. The very same data moving around in a computer system will be output one instant (from one part of the computer) and input the next instant (to some other part of the computer). You must be careful when using the terms input and output to specify what they are input to or output from. The word "input" is sometimes used as a verb, even though it feels a bit strange to do so. For example: You must input the data before doing the calculations.

interactive:
Said of a computer system which responds to the user quickly - usually less than a second for a typical action. All personal computer systems are interactive.

intelligent device:
A device that contains its own processor.

The Elements of CAL

interface:
An electronic device that allows two other devices to communicate with one another by converting signals from one into a format that can be processed by the other.

I/O (input and/or output):
A keyboard, a floppy disc and a printer are all I/O devices.

joystick:
A type of input device. It has a stick that is manipulated by the user to produce different inputs. Joysticks are often used in conjunction with graphics terminals.

keyword or key word:
A word that has meaning in a computer language. See Reserved word.

kludge:
Makeshift, as in this program is a real kludge.

label:
A name comprised of letters, numbers or symbols used to identify a statement or instruction or segment in a program.

language:
A set of conventions specifying how to tell a computer what to do.

light pen:
An input device used in conjunction with a video display. When the user touches the display screen with the light pen, the electronics associated with the pen will determine the coordinates of the point that the user touched. These coordinates will then be transmitted to the computer.

loop:
A program segment that is executed several times in a row.

machine language:
Binary code that can be directly executed by the processor, as opposed to assembly or high-level language.

macro instruction:
An instruction that combines several operations as an overall instruction. The extent to which a number of operations can be performed for each macro instruction.

mainframe:
The computer itself, including the processor, main memory, I/O interfaces and backplane.

memory:
The portion of a computer which stores information. See ROM and RAM.

menu:
A list of options from which to choose.

microcomputer:
A computer based on a microprocessor.

microprocessor:
A one-chip Central Processing Unit developed in 1971. An integrated circuit that performs the task of executing instructions.

modem
(MODulator-DEModulator): A device that allows a computer to communicate over the telephone lines (and other communications media). It does this by changing the digital information into musical tones (modulating) and from musical tones to digital information (demodulating). It is used with frequency-shift-keying (FSK) data transmission.

monitor:
A television set. Often one that is specially manufactured to be connected to a computer. Also a program supplied by the manufacturer that allows the user to control the operation of a computer. With computers that operate directly in a higher level language, such as BASIC, the monitor may often be built into the language.

17 Glossary

NABU (Natural Access to Bidirectional Utilities):
An electronic communication computer system for the home.

native language:
The language that a computer was built to understand. It is different for each brand of computer. Synonymous with machine language.

node:
In electronics, a point of zero current or zero voltage on a conductor. A point in a radio wave where the amplitude is zero. A junction point in a network. In computer programming, the dots used in decision trees to represent the situations that can occur in the course of solving a problem.

noise:
An unwanted signal.

on-line:
A device that is connected directly to the CPU.

OS (Operating System):
A collection of programs to aid a person in controlling a computer. This term is usually used in reference to large computers. A small computer operating system is often called a monitor. See monitor.

output:
Information leaving a device or process. For example, the output from a computer can be displayed by a printer or CRT. This term can also be used as a verb, even if it does sound a bit awkward, as in: Watch the computer output a graph. See input.

peripheral:
A unit, such as a communications terminal, that is external to the system processor. Some typical peripherals are floppy disc drives, printers, MODEM's and television sets.

processor:
Synonym for CPU.

program:
A sequence of instructions that permit a computer to perform a task. A program must be in a language that the computer can understand.

programmable memory:
Content changeable memory, as opposed to read-only memory (the contents of which are fixed during manufacture). Programmable memory can be both read from and written into by the processor, and is where most programs and data are stored. Sometimes called RAM, but this is a slight misnomer.

prompt:
A symbol that appears on your computer's display to let you know that it is ready to pay attention to your commands.

RAM(Random-Access Memory):
The main memory of any computer. Information and programs are stored in RAM, and they may be retrieved or changed by a program. For some computers, the information in RAM is lost whenever the power is turned off.

Random-Access Memory:
See RAM.

Read-Only Memory:
See ROM.

real time:
A system function that is controlled by external events. For example, a system that reacts to inputs from a temperature sensor would be considered a real-time system.

reserved word:
A word that you cannot use as a variable name, since it has been pre-empted for use in the computer's language. You also may be restricted from using reserved

277

The Elements of CAL

words in other ways as well. Key words are often reserved words. See key word.

resolution:
The density and overall quality of a video display. Also refers to the number of distinct points that can be plotted by a graphics terminal. Hi Res. A comparative term.

response time:
The amount of time required for a computer to respond to an input from one of its terminals.

roll-over:
A property of some key-boards. Keys may be depressed in more rapid succession on a key-board with roll-over.

ROM (Read-Only Memory):
Memory in which the information is stored once, usually by the manufacturer, and cannot be changed. Programs such as BASIC interpreter (used by most owners of personal computers) are often stored in ROM.

run time:
The time at which the program is executed. Also, the amount of time required to execute the program.

save:
To store a program anywhere other than in the computer's memory, for example on a diskette or cassette tape.

scrolling:
A property of some video terminals. If the screen of such a video terminal is filled, it will move the entire display image upwards; the top line of text will be lost; and a blank line will appear at the bottom.

simulation:
A computer program that mathematically models a process.

software:
A general term for all programs and routines used to implement and extend the capabilities of the computer: e.g., assemblers, compilers and subroutines. "Software" sometimes means data as well as programs.

speech synthesization:
The generation of human speech by electronic means. This is done by "synthesizing" or combining the appropriate electrical waveforms to reproduce the phonemes, which are the basic sounds of which all words can be composed.

structured programming:
An attempt has been made to formalize the elements of good programming. These practices have influenced the development of structured languages like Pascal which stress modularity, clear pathways and simplicity.

subroutine:
A portion of a program that can be executed by a special statement. In BASIC, that statement is "GO-SUB". This effectively gives a single statement the strength of a whole program. A subroutine call differs from a simple jump instruction in that after completion of the subroutine, execution of the program will return to the program section that invoked it.

systems program:
A program that does not perform actual problem solving but rather is used to control system operations or act as a programming aid.

teletext:
An inexpensive, one-way information delivery system designed for mass market home and business use. It makes use of the spare signal carrying capacity in existing television broadcasting channels. It can present from 100 to 300 "pages" or "TV screens of information." See also videotex and vertical blanking interval.

17 Glossary

terminal:
A device for communication with a computer. A typical terminal consists of a key-board and a printer or video display.

time-sharing:
See multiprogramming.

turnkey:
A computer whose format panel is blank or contains few controls. Also refers to a product delivered ready to run.

users' group:
An association of people who all have an interest in a particular computer or group of computers. They usually meet to exchange information, share programs, trade equipment and show off their accomplishments.

utility:
A frequently used program or subroutine. Utility routines are most often associated with systems programs rather than applications programs.

videodisc:
A method for storing large quantities of information in tracks, each of which has an address; the information is read by a laser or other light source. The technology is still in flux and few standards have been established.

videotex:
An information delivery system that makes use of the telephone for two-way communications. It may also be linked into two-way cable TV or hybrid cable TV/telephone systems. Electronic mail is made possible by this system.

window:
A portion of the computer's display that is dedicated to some special purpose.

18 Index

A

ADA, 84, 110, 113, 117
APL programming language, 110, 113
Abstract data types, 120
Acronyms, 4
Adaptive teaching strategy, defined, 33
Analysis of content, 79
Analysis of progress, 79
Apple, 7, 11
Application software
    and facilitative software, differences
        between, 95
    defined, 95
Architect
    defined, 128
    languages, 128-130
    portability, 130
    role in mapping, 87
    role in network implementation, 128-137
    view of facilitative tools, 133
    view of IMPS, 132
    view of language factors, 128-129
    view of mapping, 134
    view of tracking, 133
Artificial intelligence, 27
Author support structures, 13
Automatic code generation, 129

B

BASIC, 7, 84, 96, 109, 110, 111, 118, 128
Branching structure, 45
Bullet proofing, *See* debugging

C

C programming language, 84, 110, 112, 118, 128
CAI, defined, 4
CAL
    and CBT, differences between, 8
    defined, 4
    the course, code and documentation, 189
CBT, 128
    and CAL, differences between, 8
    defined, 4
CMI, defined, 4
CP/M, 96, 114
CRT, 60
Cathode ray tube, *See* CRT
Character set, alternate, 60
Cheating, 42
Choice bar, 64, 93
Chomsky, 28, 29
Closed map structure, 87
COBOL, 109
Comment, 91, 93
    in tracking, 79
Commodore 64, 85
Computer aided instruction, *See* CAI
Computer assisted learning, *See* CAL
Computer based training, *See* CBT
Computer games, *See* games
Computer managed instruction, *See* CMI
Concurrent processes, 117-123
Content analysis, 79
Core memory, 106
Cost-benefit of CAL and CBT, 135-137
Course

281

COURSEWRITER, 119
  defined, 10
  evaluation of CAL courseware, 4
Creating a game, 55
Curriculum Four, 139-166
  an implementation of, described, 169-181
  implementation of, creating the data, 170
  process of implementation, 169-170, 175-181
Curriculum, defined, 10
Cursor positioning, 68, 70

D

DBMS, *See* data base management system
Database, 14, 23
Database machines, 20
Database management system, 96, 99, 100, 119
Databases, 10, 27
Debuggers, 98
Debugging, 121
Dedicated machines, disadvantages of, 107-108
Definitional Layer, defined, 10
Designing pages, 61-65
Diagnosis, 92
Diagnostic sequence, 48, 92
Diagnostic support structure, 91
Disciplines (academic), 26
Drill, 11, 34-38
  basic pattern, 35
  evaluation of, 37-38
  feedback, 37
  questions, 36
  remediation, 35
  rules and examples, 36
  sequence, 36
  sequence, defined, 34
  weighted response to, 35

E

ELF, 119
Engineered approach to courseware development, 86
Essay questions, 40
Evaluation, 122
  in drill, 37-38
  of games, 55
  in inquiry, 44
  in simulations, 47

in tests, 41-42
in tutorial, 52
Example, 29, 30
  defined, 21

F

Facilitative software, 95-101, 110, 133
  and applications software, differences between, 95
  automatic code generation, 129
  CP/M, 96
  data base management systems, 99
  debuggers, 98
  defined, 95
  file systems, 116-118
  graphics editors, 98
  languages, 96
  mail, 98
  operating systems, 96
  PERT, 99
  program editors, 97
  relational data base management systems, 96
  report generators, 99
  SMALLTALK operating system, 115
  software development cycle tools, 100
  source code control system, 99
  terminal handlers, 116
  text editors, 96, 97
  UNIX, 96, 97, 112, 115
  See also Database management systems, Graphics systems, Languages, Open systems architecture, Operating systems
Feedback, 56
  defined, 32
  drill, 37
  general guidelines, 58
  inquiry, 42
  local structures, 58
  simulation, 47
  test, 41
  tutorial, 51
File systems, 116-118
FRACTIONS
  an implementation of, described, 179-181
  code, documentation and data, 190-221
  the course, implementation defined, 153-165
Function keys, 60
Functions, 117

G

Games
- as a learning tool, 53, 55
- basic definition, 53-55
- creation of, 55
- defined, 53-55
- evaluation of, 55
- graphics, 67
- rules, 54
- sophisticated forms of, 54

Glossary, 93
Goals, 18, 25
- defined, 10, 20

Grading, 78
Graphic display devices, 107
Graphics, 65-68, 66, 85, 118
- as a teaching tool, 66
- CORE, 118
- defined, 65
- design, 67
- games, 67
- guidelines, 67
- portability of, 68
- terminals, 65
- TELIDON, 118
- when to use, 57

Graphics editors, 98
Graphics primitives, 70
Graphics tablet, 70
Graphics versus text, 65

H

Hard copy, 72
Help, 91, 93
High resolution, 66
High-range machines, 9, 13
- defined, 5
- versus low-range machines, 85
- *See also* Mainframe

I

IMPS, 4, 5, 17, 22, 23, 25, 30, 104
- defined, 10
- premises of, 9
- rationale, 7-9

Incorrect responses, 58
- in drill, 34
- tutorial, 48

Input devices, 70
- described, 70-71
- graphic, 107
- keyboards, 60, 107

Input variations, 68-71
Inquiry, 42-45
- local structure, comment, a variation on, 91
- defined, 42-44
- evaluation of, 44
- feedback, 42
- keywords, 42
- menus, 45
- question, the, 42
- rules and examples, 42
- sequence, 42

Instructor, defined, 94
Interaction, defined, 32
Interaction speeds, 106

J

Joystick, 70

K

Keyboard, 59, 60
- limitations, 107

Keypad, 71
Keyword, 51
- defined, 32

L

Languages, 96, 105, 108-113, 123
- from the architect's perspective, 128-130
- how to choose, 111-113
- portability, 130
- compiled versus interpreted, 117
- translators, 119
- *See also* ADA, APL Programming Language, BASIC, C programming language, COBOL, LISP, LOGO, PASCAL, PLAIN, PROLOG, SMALLTALK

LANS, *See* Network, local area
Lattice, 126
Libraries, 118
Light pen, 71
LISP, 110, 113, 121
Local structures, 30, 31-58
- defined, 11
- feedback, 58

The Elements of CAL

general guidelines, 57
questions, 57
rules and examples, 57
the sequence, 58
LOGO, 68, 110, 113
Low resolution, 66
Low-range machines, 9, 12, 13, 14, 19, 24, 94, 130, 131
 defined, 5
 versus high-range machines, 85
 See also Microcomputer

M

Mail, 98
Mainframe, 5, 9
 and microcomputer, differences between, 77
 See also High-range machine
Maintenance, 122
Mapping, 59, 83-87
 defined, 83
 closed structure, 87
 in networks, 134
 in site implementations, 85
 layer of, 12-13
 variable structure, 87
Matching questions, 40
Memory
 core, 106
 storage, 106
Menu, 42, 93
Microcomputer, 5, 9, 27, 131
 and mainframe, differences between, 77
 and voice recognition, 72
 as terminals, 127
 See also Low-range machine
Mid-range machine, 94
Mouse, 70
Multiple choice questions, 40

N

NATAL, 84, 112, 119, 128
Network, 13, 14,
 architect's role in, 128-137
 defined, 103, 125
 implementation of, 14, 125-137
 local area networks (LANS), 127
 mapping, 134
 support structures, 134
 tracking, 133-134

O

OSI, *See* Open system interconnection protocol
Objectives, 18, 27
 and local structure, 31
 defined, 10, 20, 22
Open system interconnection protocols (OSI), 126
Open systems architecture, 126
Operating systems, 96, 114
 CP/M, 114
 PLATO, 96
 SMALLTALK, 115
 TICCIT, 96
 UNIX, 115
 See also facilitative software
Output device, 59
 printer, 72

P

Paddle, 70
Pages, design and layout, 61
PASCAL, 84, 110, 112, 128
Pathways, 13, 84, 93
 tracking, 80
PERT, 99
PET, 11, 85
 See also Commodore
PLAIN, 113
PLATO, 7, 11, 96, 119, 129
Piaget, 3
Portability, 87
 courseware, 105
 from the architect's perspective, 130
 graphics, 107-108, 118
 language, costs of, 131
 of courseware, 9
 of data and design specifications, 12
 translators, 119
Presentation, 59
Presentation layer, defined, 11-12
Pre-structured teaching strategy, 33
Printer, 72
Procedures, 117
PROLOG, 110, 121
Program editor, 97
Progress analysis, 79
Progress tracking, 78
Prompt, defined, 32
Prototypes, 121
Pseudo graphics, 68

284

Q

Questions, 22, 32, 46
   defined, 22
   in drill, 36
   in essay, 40
   general guidelines, 57
   in inquiry, 42
   local structure, 57
   matching, 40
   multiple choice, 40
   short answer, 40
   in test, 38
   true or false, 40
   in tutorial, 51

R

Reference, support structures, 90
Registration, 78
Reinforcement, 58
   continuous, 56
   defined, 32, 56
   patterns, 56-57
   random or variable, 57
Relational data base management systems, 96
Remedial support structure, 91
Remediation, 35, 93
   defined, 93
Report generators, 99
Resolution, 65
Response
   defined, 10, 32
   incorrect, 58
   unanticipated, 58
Rule, 11, 21, 27, 30, 54
   and examples, 42, 57
   defined, 10, 21
   in drill, 36
   in games, 54
   in inquiry, 42
   in simulation, 45
   in tutorial, 48

S

Scenario, 45, 46
Scoring tests, 41
Screen, 59, 60-65
Screen display
   flashing, 65
   inverse video, 65
Screen layout, 61
   good, defined, 63
Segment, 83
Sequence
   defined, 32, 58
   diagnostic, 92
   inquiry, 42
   local structure, 58
   simulation, 45
   test, 38
   tutorial, 48
Short answer questions, 40
SIGGRAPH, 107, 118
Simulation, 45-47
   defined, 45
   evaluation of, 47
   feedback, 47
   questions, 46
   rules and examples, 45
   sequence, 45
   tutorial, 50
Site, 14
Site implementation, 103-123
   defined, 14, 104
Skinner, 3
SMALLTALK, 110, 113, 115, 128
SME, *See* Subject matter expert
Software development cycle tools, 100
Software engineering, 120
Source code control system (SCCS), 99
Specification, in mapping, 87
State of knowledge, 36, 48, 51
Storage memory, 106
Strategies, 23-26, *See also* teaching strategies
Structured programming, 120
Student support structures, 13
Subject, 25
Subject matter expert, 8-9, 25
Support structures, 89-94
   accessing, 93
   author and instructor, in networks, 134
   defined, 13-14, 90-94
   diagnostic, 91-92
   help, 91
   reference, 90
   remediation, 91, 93
   student, in networks, 134
   types of, 90
System documentation, 100
Sytem software, 114

The Elements of CAL

T

Teaching strategies, 31, 57
   adaptive vs pre-structured, 33
   graphics, 66
   reinforcement, 56
   the basic five, 32
   the basic five, defined, 33-58
Terminal handlers, 116
Termnet, 126
Tests, 11, 38-42
   cheating, 42
   defined, 38
   evaluation of, 41-42
   feedback, 41
   local structures, 41
   questions, 38
   scoring, 41
   sequence, the, 38
TELIDON, 11, 107, 118
Text format, variations, 64
Text editors, 96, 97
Text versus graphics, 65
TICCIT, 78, 96, 129
Touch screen, 71
Track ball, 70
Tracking, 77-82
   defined, 77
   in networks, 133-134
   pathways, 80
Tracking layer, defined, 12
Tracking records, in mapping, 86
Translation for COURSEWRITER, 119
Translators, 119
   ELF, 119
True or false questions, 40
Tutorial, 48
   defined, 48, 51-52
   evaluation of, 52
   feedback, 51
   incorrect responses, 48
   question, 51
   sequence, the, 48
   simulation, 50
   weighted response, 51
Typesetting, 97

U

Unanticipated responses, 58
UNIX, 96, 97, 112, 115

V

Variable map structure, 87
Video game, *See* games
Voice recognition, 72

W

Weighted response
   drill, 35
   tutorial, 51
Window, 61
WORDS, 140
   an implementation of, described, 176-179
   code, documentation, and data, 223-258
   defining the course, 140-153
Work-station, defined